Gateways to the Soul

"In this wise and compassionate distillation of his life journey, Serge has given us an invaluable handbook for spiritual and psychological health and development in our complex era of unparalleled challenges and opportunities. He provides a series of gateways and key insights into essential aspects of life, such as courage, forgiveness, joy, and work, along with extensive practical reflections and exercises to do at the end of each chapter. A hugely enriching and rewarding read."

— DAVID LORIMER, program director of the Scientific and Medical Network, UK, and author of *Resonant Mind* and *Science, Consciousness and Ultimate Reality*

"This book is a vast compendium of ideas and exercises that can help us take the next steps in our own soul awakening in ways that also make them a contribution to the further evolution of the human species."

— THOMAS YEOMANS, Ph.D., founder of the Concord Institute and co-founder of the International School for Psychotherapy, Counseling, and Group Leadership in St. Petersburg, Russia

"In a time of unparalleled crises, *Gateways to the Soul* uncovers with laser-like precision the soulless, amoral, ruthless dynamic that drives our so-called civilization. Knowing that nothing will change in the outer world unless changes are made in our inner one, it then leads us gently but firmly into the neglected chambers of the soul, bringing clarity, insight, and the possibility of transformation to entrenched unconscious patterns of belief and behavior. This book heals, informs, and enlightens, releasing us from the corroding power of old wounds and old habits, some of which may have festered inside us for centuries. A brilliant manual that teaches us how to live life in a different way, engaging with its abundant energy, discover its secret intention for us, which is to consciously embrace the freedom to be who we are meant to be."

— ANNE BARING, Ph.D., Jungian analyst and author of *The Dream of the Cosmos*

"In this book about wisdom and compassion, Serge introduces us to practical gateways to walk through into our shared future. A spiritual classic."

— DALE MATHERS, Ph.D., Jungian analyst and author of *Alchemy and Psychotherapy*

"Serge Beddington-Behrens is a wise and inspiring soul. His new book is full of insights and provocations that will stir you and help open up your heart and mind."

— WILLIAM BLOOM, Ph.D., founder and co-director of the Foundation for Holistic Spirituality and author of *The Power of the New Spirituality* and *The Endorphin Effect*

"Serge is absolutely right in saying that we cannot retrieve our individual or our collective souls without also retrieving the soul of our beloved earth, with its every molecule as alive as we are. In the harm we have done to our world and in this great storm of crises we have currently unleashed upon ourselves, we can only successfully navigate our way forward and start melting our blockages by realizing our unity with all life."

— ELISABET SAHTOURIS, Ph.D., evolutionary biologist, futurist, professor in residence at Chaminade University, Honolulu, Hawaii, and author of *EarthDance*

"An excellent guide for breaking out of the stories we tell ourselves about who we are and how the world is that will help us become more alive and awake to the untapped potential we all have to create a better world."

— PETER RUSSELL, futurist, eco-philosopher, author of *The Awakening Earth, Finding Your Own Happiness,* and *The Global Brain,* and co-author of *The Consciousness Revolution*

"If you savor this book by Serge Beddington-Behrens, your life will be enriched. You will hear and feel one of the kindest and most beautiful voices of personal and spiritual wisdom from a man who has dedicated his life to serving and uplifting his fellow human beings and this planet that we all share."

— STUART SOVATSKY, Ph.D., author of *Advanced Spiritual Intimacy* and former president of the Association of Transpersonal Psychology

GATEWAYS
TO THE SOUL
Inner Work for the Outer World

Serge Beddington-Behrens, Ph.D.

FINDHORN PRESS

Findhorn Press
One Park Street
Rochester, Vermont 05767
www.findhornpress.com

Text stock is SFI certified

Findhorn Press is a division of Inner Traditions International

Disclaimer

The information in this book is given in good faith and intended for information
only. Neither author nor publisher can be held liable by any person for any loss
or damage whatsoever which may arise from the use of this book or any of the
information therein.

Cataloging-in-Publication data for this title is available from the Library of Congress

ISBN 978-1-64411-045-4 (print)
ISBN 978-1-64411-046-1 (ebook)

Printed and bound in the United States by Lake Book Manufacturing, Inc.
The text stock is SFI certified. The Sustainable Forestry Initiative® program
promotes sustainable forest management.

10 9 8 7 6 5 4 3 2 1

Edited by Jacqui Lewis
Text design and layout by Damian Keenan
This book was typeset in Adobe Garamond Pro and Calluna Sans
with Fontin used as a display typeface.

To send correspondence to the author of this book, mail a first-class letter to the
author c/o Inner Traditions • Bear & Company, One Park Street, Rochester,
VT 05767, USA and we will forward the communication, or contact the author
directly at **www.spiritual-activism.com**

For my darling Irena and Martina

Contents

*What is needed is a correction of our civilization
and a new vision for inhabiting our planet.
If there is the vision it can be realized.*
— DIETER DUHM

*A change of meaning is necessary to change this world
politically, economically and socially. But that change
must begin with the individual...*
— DAVID BOHM

*Without a global revolution in the sphere of human
consciousness, nothing will change for the better in our
being as humans, and the catastrophe towards which our
world is headed...will be unavoidable.*
— VÁCLAV HAVEL

*Love is necessary for the transformation of the world. It is
the only force that can bring peace between the nations.*
— PETER DEUNOV

*Salvaging our society requires nothing less than a
wholesale transformation of dominant cultural patterns,
a dramatic shift in the very design of human societies.*
— ERIK ASSADOURIAN

Serge Forward

A Foreword by Steve Taylor, Ph.D.

SOME PEOPLE BELIEVE that, in order to evolve as human beings, we have to disconnect ourselves from the world's problems, and even forget about the world altogether. You can go to a monastery, a hermitage or a desert retreat, far away from worldly concerns and ambitions. Or you can just stay in your room meditating, and pretend that the world out there is an illusion. Then you can give yourself wholeheartedly to your spiritual development in peace, without being disturbed by the complexities of politics, social problems and family life.

In this book, my friend Serge takes exactly the opposite approach. We are not separate from our fellow human beings or from the world around us, and to believe that we are separate is a sure way to feel unhappy. We must not disconnect from the world, for the simple reason that we are an integral part of it. Since we have caused many of our problems, we are also called to try to heal them. It is our responsibility to respond with compassion and altruism to the suffering of others, to help the human race recover its lost soul. As Serge suggests, it is impossible to separate the current state of the world – in social, economic and political terms – from the inner state of human beings. If the world is insane, it is because we are insane. This is because we have become alienated from our own souls, the souls of others and the soul of the world itself.

The aim of this book is to show us how we can once more reconnect with soul. To this end, Serge offers us a wide variety of gateways, which he has used with clients throughout his many years spent as a transpersonal psychotherapist, life coach, healer and teacher of spiritual retreats. He shows us that every aspect of our daily lives can serve as a portal to spiritual awakening. These gateways are so important that, in my view, unless we enter them, it is impossible for us to find happiness or fulfilment as individuals, and impossible for us to live in harmony with the Earth, or even to survive as a species.

What Serge shows us is that on the other side of these gateways lies a new sacred and ensouled world, where we will feel connected instead of separate, inspired with meaning and purpose rather than listless and confused. The healing of all our psychological, social, economic, ecological and political problems lies in learning to recover our lost soul.

Serge puts a great deal of emphasis on stories, because our insanity is partly due to the stories we have been told about the world and about ourselves. The essential story of our culture is that human beings are selfish and individualistic biological machines, and the world is an inanimate mechanical place, which is there to provide us with resources. Life is essentially meaningless (apart from survival and reproduction), and there is no purpose to our lives apart from passing the time and trying to seek as much gratification and pleasure as we can. This cultural story has had a disastrous effect, creating a nihilism that pervades the air around us, and is at the root of the hedonism and consumerism of our culture. Materialism as a philosophy has led to materialism as a lifestyle. We need new stories, and this book is a treasure trove of them, together with plenty of practical exercises and guidance to point us towards a new view of ourselves and a new vision of the world around us.

One of the joys of this book is that reading it feels like being in Serge's company. As I read, I feel like I am sitting across the table from him in a restaurant – perhaps in the village square in Pollença or Campanet in Mallorca, where we have shared many meals – listening as he talks (often very humorously) about the wisdom he has gained from his many years as a spiritual explorer and psychotherapist. The book has the same gentle and benign quality that he brings to all his friendships.

But the gentleness of Serge's tone does not detract from the urgency of his message. It is essential that you listen to the stories contained in this book – which are so much more convincing and inspiring than the standard cultural narrative of materialism – and allow them to inform your life. We need to transform ourselves inwardly so that we can transform the world. Serge has done us a great service in sharing so many of the gateways of transformation that he has developed over the years. In this book, you can feel his loving soul connecting with yours. This book is itself an example of the "ensoulment" that our world so desperately requires.

Steve Taylor, Ph.D.

Invitation

The Challenge

We human beings are a storytelling species. The world we live in is built on stories or myths telling us what is real, who we are, what we should do, what we can expect from life, how we ought to behave and what we need to believe.

We tell ourselves stories to create meaning for ourselves, to define the values we hold. They determine the way we think and feel and operate. And why our world is so imbalanced, crisis-filled and topsy-turvy – why so many of us treat ourselves, each other and our planet so disrespectfully – is very much connected to the kinds of stories that far too many of us live by today, whereby soulful qualities such as compassion, respect, wisdom, kindness and love are much too distant from the narrative. As the great mythologist Joseph Campbell put it:

> The story that we have in the West…is based on a view of the universe that belongs to the first millennium BC. It does not accord with our concept either of the universe or of the dignity of man…We have to get back into accord with the wisdom of nature and realize our brotherhood with the animals and with the water and the sea.[1]

Yes, my dear friend, the problem we all face today is that we live in a world that has become increasingly desacralized, that limits our ability to expand into our humanity and that tries to shrink and diminish us, to enchain our hearts and scrub away our soulfulness.

My aim in writing this book, therefore, is to invite you to come on a journey with me where you can work at unchaining yourself and begin exploring new, more human and soulful ways to come alive, whereby instead of being part of the problems all around us – which we all are to the extent that we collude with these stories – you can become part of their solution.

I will therefore be asking you to work at bringing a new kind of "sacred space" into the way you live your everyday life, which need have nothing whatsoever to do with old associations relating to sacrifice, churchiness, incense-burning, head-bowing and piety. On the contrary, as you will be seeing, a truly sacred life or a life lived with soul is one with great freedom, harmony, open-heartedness, playfulness and joy.

Living in a "hyper-complex" world

I admit that initially starting to live such a life can be challenging as it involves a lot of changes, but it is also immensely rewarding as not only will you feel much happier and more abundant – yes, life may start being much more fun! – but you will also be better equipped to become an effective change agent in a society that in many respects is getting crazier by the moment. In fact, my friend Jim Garrison beautifully describes our world today as a "hyper-complex one", where "things are getting better and better and worse and worse, faster and faster!"

Certainly, many pundits believe that if we don't seriously turn things around by 2030, our planet will simply have spun out of control, which is why it is imperative, if we wish to avoid catastrophe, that we find new and more meaningful myths to live by that can help us "up" our game and become more fully human. My hope is that this book will help point you in that direction.

Yes, you and I might have a roof over our heads and enough food in our bellies. If so, we are the lucky ones. Millions don't. Indeed, the world is a very sad and scary place for far too many of us. As I write, hundreds of thousands of people are fleeing their countries, having to risk their lives to escape ethnic cleansing, famine or civil war, while the rise of a protectionist and nationalistic spirit in many of the wealthier countries is resulting in these people being cruelly turned away.

OK, our fighting of traditional wars may have declined – more of these kinds of wars today are ending than beginning – but the warring mindset is as strong as ever. It's just that the battlegrounds have shifted into new arenas. Today, many countries are involved in cyber-warfare, in trade wars, in financial warfare to exact sanctions, while a kind of ongoing global civil war continues to rage between different tribes, drug cartels and religious sects. And of course the whole nuclear issue never goes away.

At the same time, climate change continues to worsen, with many parts of the world experiencing huge droughts, while other areas are being continually ravaged by storms and rainfall. The result is that a huge amount of fear, despair and alienation abounds, and particularly in the most financially prosperous countries, drug addiction, drug deaths and depression are ever on the rise.

The result is that today a climate of anger and nihilism exists and it affects many people who are not only aware of the incompetence and dishonesty of many of their political leaders, but also feel that the opportunities they believed were promised them have not been forthcoming. This has given rise to toxic, demagogic and authoritarian leaders being elected in many countries.

Other realities are possible

This is not a pretty picture and I apologize for starting out by hurling it at you so blatantly, but I really want to drive home the idea right at the start that so much of our pain and suffering occurs because of how we believe, and consequently create, the world to be, coupled with the notion that things cannot be changed. Far too many of us subscribe to the popular myth that war, hunger, suffering, separation and scarcity are unavoidable and that nothing else is possible. Luckily, as you'll be seeing, it is not the whole picture by any means, and things can shift.

Yes, many other ways are eminently possible and this book is intended to introduce you to them, to help you come to realize that we may live in much greater harmony with ourselves and with each other and in the process become a true "friend of the Earth". And the more there are of us who believe this and so achieve this, the more we change the consciousness of our planet, which in turn will change the way our society operates, as our outer reality always expresses the state of our inner one.

Inner work

The important thing for you to get is that if you wish for change, you must work for it. I expect you are familiar with that definition of evil as being what transpires when good people do nothing? Thus, this book is written both to encourage and to assist you to "work on yourself" in order to "out" your deeper humanity and with it your capacity for difference-making. To enhance this process, at the end of each chapter you will find a series of exercises and particular questions to ask yourself, so I suggest that you have pen and paper available so you can make plenty of notes.

At one level, you might regard this book as a kind of training manual to help you become more fully human. It might be helpful to set a pace that works for you, and please – and this is very important – be patient with yourself. The truth is that old myths and beliefs often take time fully to die off inside us, and by the same token, new ways of seeing and being may also take their time fully to be born! As my old Oxford professor Theodore Zeldin puts it in his brilliant book *The Hidden Pleasures of Life*:

> Most people are wrapped up in a patchwork of philosophies, inherited from different centuries, which each has put together in a slightly different pattern. The mindset they adopt may change a little in response to the hard knocks of existence, but fragments of old attitudes almost always survive beneath the surface. Nothing limits a person more than these inherited convictions about what is possible and what is not.[2]

One of the big problems we face today is that we live in a culture that does not encourage us to open to new, more expanded possibilities, any more than it legitimizes or encourages us to work at becoming more whole as human beings. In actuality, it frowns upon the idea of our "looking inside ourselves". As a result, our own deeper truths are often not given sufficient permission to surface, and so over the years they get covered over by shallower stories that we've had stamped into us so effectively that it literally seems as if they've penetrated into our DNA and there's no escape!

But fear not, my friend, there *is* a way out. Indeed, there are many exits. Or to use the analogy I like: many gateways!

The significance of gateways

I have used the metaphor of gateways because for many years I have been teaching week-long spiritual retreats in Mallorca with titles like "Dancing through New Gateways". I own a tiny *finca* there with a beautifully shaped gateway and I always use that picture on my brochures.

I think the analogy is appropriate because if we are to seek changes in our lives, we need to find the appropriate gateways that will lead us into them. We then need to discover how to open them, and then have the courage to step through!

And if we succeed in our ventures, we may well discover that our lives start expanding and working for us in ways we would never have believed. We may also begin realizing that much of our pain and dissatisfaction is not only because we are continually asking the wrong questions about our lives, but also because we have spent much too much time looking for answers in all the wrong places. As you will be seeing, I myself have been very expert in this in the earlier part of my life! However, once we've opened a gate, we will need to continue operating in ways to ensure it remains open, as gates can, and they do, close down on us!

Our great challenge today is to learn to uncover new soulful stories inside us, stories filled with positive and life-affirming agendas. The more we manage this, the easier it becomes to resist stories that feed us false news such as the idea that there is no such thing as "soul", that we are all "separate islands unto ourselves" or that the reality we are fed by our media is the only one that exists. These kinds of stories underlie why hateful mindsets exist, such as homophobia, Islamophobia and anti-Semitism.

In your journey, you will also be learning that it is a terrible lie that we inhabit a planet of scarcity where there is never enough of anything, be it water, love, food, inspiration or creativity, which in turn encourages a spirit of destitution and helplessness. This is simply not the case and as you go through this book, you will increasingly come to see that for much of your life you've been fed a whole load of lies – I certainly was – and the tragedy has been that you've believed them.

Working at being human

What I will also be asking you to grasp here is that simply being born a human being is not enough and that of itself it does not guarantee our humanity. If we are to become *effectively human*, we will have to graduate into it, and this doesn't come naturally in the way that acorns naturally evolve into oak trees without needing to do any work on themselves.

No. If you and I are to become properly human, we are challenged to work at it, and if we can fix ourselves, then we can fix our planet. Not before, for we cannot give out anything that we are not ourselves. The great Indian sage Sri Aurobindo understood this: "To hope for a change in human life without a change in human nature is an irrational proposition. It is to ask for something unnatural and unreal, an impossible miracle."

Contents of this Book

This book may be seen as an extension of my last one, entitled *Awakening the Universal Heart: A Guide for Spiritual Activists*. There, I looked primarily at our inner heart and how we can awaken it. In particular, I explored different ways that we can bring heart energy into the causes that we believe in. This book goes into much greater depth about what is "wrong" with the world, based on the premise that we can't fix things unless we *really* know what needs fixing. I hope the chapters on what is wrong with the world will make you feel sufficiently angry and consequently re-energized in your quest to be a force for change.

Part One lays down the context, exploring some of the differences between what I call the "old" and the "new" stories, while Part Two shows us different ways that we can work at making the shift, bearing in mind that simply holding an idea of a new way of being, in our heads, is of itself not enough. As Gandhi said: "We have to be [that is, embody] the change that we want to see happen."

In every chapter, therefore, I discuss how we can concretely bring the qualities of this mysterious "thing" called *soul* into all aspects of our daily lives and thus enable ourselves to start making them into a sacred practice.

Ensouling

Yes, my friend, as you gradually start liberating your notions of sacredness from their old associations with altars, head-bowing and incense-burning, you will learn that there are many ways of accessing our soul life and that it is eminently possible to be spiritual but not religious and that in actuality what I simply call "soul work" is one of the most important and natural things that we can be doing with our lives. In certain instances, the fact of our being part of a particular religion can sometimes serve to damp down our soulfulness.

This book also explores issues around power – we look a lot at how we can induce "the Force" to be with us – how we might tune in to a deeper kind of love, work with our Shadow side, learn to forgive and embrace joy, as well as confront our death courageously, and generally relate more authentically with everyone and everything around us.

So see this as a book instructing you how to bring your true soul life or your genuineness increasingly out of the closet so you can then bring it more fully into everything you are and into everything you do. I call this process "ensouling". En route, you may discover that certain attitudes you have held up to now, and certain things you may have accorded great importance, begin diminishing in significance, while other attitudes and things you previously gave short shrift to suddenly become important.

I hope this will encourage you to broaden your horizons, deepen your sensitivity, let go some of your rigid boundaries and make a shift away from egocentric (me only) or ethnocentric (me and my family or tribe only) viewpoints, to world-centric or holistic (we are all part of one whole) ones. Only from that broader perspective can we begin effectively to heal many of the problems that we face.

My personal connection to this theme

As I will be interspersing aspects of my own journey – of my own search for my own soul – I need to explain briefly where I have "come from".

Basically, my personal story is this. From very early on, I was well indoctrinated in the art of elitism. I was trained to be sexist, snobby, patriarchal and homophobic, and to only be moved to hobnob with people who carried similar prejudices and who saw the world through a similarly superior and narrowed lens. My dear mama, bless her, had been part of the Russian royal family – her parents had fled at the Revolution when she was a tiny baby and this had been very traumatic for her – and my father had been a wealthy industrialist who was awarded titles and had butlers and chauffeurs and all that pizazz, and all this conspired to give me certain rather absurd airs and graces.

I went to a posh public school and afterwards a posh university, and the idea took root that I was part of a superior species raised to rule the world and to whom special rules should apply. In short, in my early life, I embodied many of the patterns that this book suggests require changing, and I think this has conspired to make me so enthusiastic today about the need to work for a transformed world, as the whole elitist theatre, which indirectly is responsible for so many of our world's injustices, never made me happy. In fact, it often made me feel miserable and isolated, sensing somehow that my whole life was based on a colossal lie.

Which it was!

But as the American poet Claudia Rankine put it: "You can't put the past behind you. It's buried into you; it's turned your flesh into its own cupboard." It sure did that to me. For many years. It locked up my unhappiness inside me with a heavy clasp…It took a considerable amount of inner work to begin liberating myself.

The myth of myths

The point about myths is that they tend not to get rammed down our throats. My parents never pulled me aside and said: "Look here, you are our son, so know you are superior, and these are the mindsets and values we want you to believe in and live by…" Conditioning doesn't work like that. Stories enter us much more insidiously and we don't know the distortions and false truths that are ever so subtly implanted into us and which have the power to grow the more we affirm them. While my part in the old story in those days was to believe in the myth of my entitlement, other "old story-ites" operating at the other end of the spectrum are led to believe in the counter-lie of their marginalization.

As I entered my early twenties and began to finish my time at university, the gloom I often felt led me to ask all sorts of questions. I began to see more clearly that the idea of this actually very ordinary person called "me" existing "above others" solely because of his education or who his parents were was both absurd and an outright lie, and it actually had the opposite effect: it made me feel inferior to others.

I went through a phase of not quite knowing where I belonged and consequently thinking that there must be something very wrong with me. Some of this torment ended when a friend turned me on to books by an Indian spiritual teacher called Krishnamurti. I loved it when he suggested that "it is no measure of health to be well adjusted to a profoundly sick society". Did this mean that there might be method in my maladjustment? Might it be that, while I was fitting in less and less to the stories I had been told about how life ought to be, Krishnamurti was implying that the fault might not wholly be mine? It also greatly encouraged me when I came across Erich Fromm's book *The Art of Being*, where he says:

> A person who has not been completely alienated, who has remained sensitive and able to feel…who can still suffer over the suffering of others – briefly a person who has remained a person and not become a thing – cannot help feeling lonely, powerless and isolated in present-day society…He cannot help suffering, even though he can experience moments of joy and clarity that are absent in the life of his "normal" contemporaries. Not rarely will he suffer from a neurosis that results from the situation of a sane man living in an insane society, rather than that of the more conventional neurosis of a sick man trying to adapt himself to a sick society.[3]

That made a lot of sense to me as in my last year at university, I was increasingly questioning the whole way the world worked. Why, I used to ask myself, were we human beings constantly involved in acting out great dramas that had nothing whatsoever to do with what was really important in life – which, curiously enough, we were continually being encouraged to ignore?

Daring to be different

Krishnamurti was damn right. There was something insane about all this, and I recognized that I was also embedded in this insanity and was playing my part in helping keep it all alive. I needed to extricate myself somehow. But how?

It became increasingly clear to me that something needed desperately to change *inside* me and that essentially what was wrong with the world was that too many of us had become too well adjusted to a society brought into being on the back of joyless and soulless myths that not only failed to affirm and celebrate who we human beings really were and what life was really all about, but also ensured that life did not work for most of the people on the planet.

But where was I to go from here? I discovered the writings of Martin Luther King and these couple of sentences said it all: "Many people fear nothing more terribly than to take a position which stands out sharply and clearly from the prevailing opinion. Not a few people who cherish lofty and noble ideals hide them under a bushel for fear of being called different." Yes, I was very much continuing to keep my head under the parapet and I decided I would do so no more. I would commit to "outing" my true self (whoever that Serge was).

So I will finish by saying that that was the best decision I ever made, and that while this process has taken time (none of us can "out" ourselves all at once and it is still going on with me), it has been eminently worth it in terms of the improved quality of my life. Thus, another central intention behind this book is to invite you also to begin "outing" the truth of who you really are and to stop being who you are not, as the truer we are to ourselves and the more we choose to live from that place, the more we benefit the world around us.

In our society, we tend only to use the idea of coming out of the closet if we are gay, but please believe me when I say that we don't have to be gay to live in a closet! I am heterosexual but also lived the entire part of my early life in an elitist closet and, in the process of gradually "coming out", I realized how closed and circumscribed my closet had been.

I ask you, therefore, to dare to embrace lofty and noble ideals, to dare to be different from the crowd and to give up following other people's ideas and believing everything you are told on social media or read in the newspapers. And as many of the gateways into soulfulness are to be found under bushels, please also do a lot of bushel-hunting in the knowledge that you are not alone in your quest and that more and more people today all around the world are, just like you, breaking out of their closets and becoming increasingly engaged in similar enterprises.

Remember too, that stories, just like newspapers, only survive if we continue to subscribe to them. The more we choose to cancel our subscriptions to old, soulless ways of living and seeing the world, the more these old stories – which now are anyway well past their sell-by date and are growing increasingly rancid – will evaporate and dissolve back into the mists of time.

I ask you to read this book in the spirit of choosing to *Go for It*...

PART ONE

Understanding the Challenge

CHAPTER 1

The Gateway of Findhorn

The planet does not need more successful people.
The planet needs more storytellers,
peacemakers and lovers of all kinds.
— THE DALAI LAMA

All you need is love.
— THE BEATLES

Magical Gateway

I was extremely fortunate in that very soon after leaving university, a gateway came stalking me. (Yes, we need to know that what we are looking for is also seeking us out.)

It took the form of my bumping into a friend who happened to tell me about a mysterious spiritual community in Scotland called Findhorn, which he suggested I visit. I was then in my early twenties and the idea felt very right. I knew nothing about communities or what I might expect. He added: "They are a group of people who all live in caravans on a small caravan site. What is best known about them is that they grow huge vegetables there and I am informed that they are so enormous because they are tended with love!"

Huge vegetables. A spiritual community! Love. The idea was intriguing to say the least, and the very next morning, I was on the train up to Scotland. I took a taxi from the station to Findhorn, and – I remember this moment so vividly – *the exact moment the taxi went through the gateway into the community, I had, quite literally, the experience of having entered another world. It was as if I was hit by a blast – yes, it felt exactly like that, it was so intense and so immediate – of huge happiness and peace.*

Experiencing a new story

In those days, the community was not the enormous entity it has subsequently morphed into, but consisted of a small group of people living, as my friend had said, in caravans. I arrived at Findhorn about the same time as the Beatles brought out their hit song "All You Need Is Love". My friend was right. Love really *was* the cornerstone of this extraordinary place.

I remember being greeted very warmly by the couple who ran the community, Peter and Eileen Caddy – who subsequently became lifelong friends – and I immediately felt at home. I sensed they were genuinely pleased to see me, not because I was particularly "special" (the myth my parents had always rammed into me for no other reason but that I was their son) or because of any ridiculous "social connections" (again so important to my parents" myth) but because I was a fellow human being, and for the Caddys, *all human beings are special and precious and so need to be honoured and respected as such.*

In fact, the way they treated me was the way they treated everyone, and I observed that after a few days of being enveloped by what I can only describe as a warm love field, I felt a deeper kinship with my new little "family" than I had ever experienced with my own family.

Dropping the pretences

Love, I learned, brings up everything that it isn't, and it certainly did that for me. My first few days at Findhorn were actually tinged with sadness, as the warmth and camaraderie around me served to highlight how cold and cut off and stiff-upper-lipped so much of my life up until then had been, with all the emphasis being on "show" and "doing what was right by society" as opposed to what was real.

In no way were my parents bad people or neglectful of me, and I never want to make out that they were wrong. They were good human beings and they did their very best for me, but it was a best according to myths they believed in, which were limited, devoted almost entirely to the outer world and to life's surfaces, and consequently devoid of real depth.

I realized, too, that none of us can ever give out something that we ourselves have not discovered inside ourselves. What had been lacking in my childhood, I saw, were the ingredients of genuineness and soft love. I had not been related to in a way that encouraged who I truly was as a human being to be "outed" or celebrated. On the contrary. I had been trained to be a reflector of my parents" values, with the intention that my presence should somehow enhance them in some way, and reflect back positively on them.

Being here at Findhorn, I felt able for the first time to see that I had on a mask that I had worn all my life – a special face that was not really me and that I put on to present myself to the world – and that it was possible to drop it, especially if one was interacting with others engaged in a similar mission. I realized that Findhorn was a kind of training course to help you to be yourself!

Yes, I had gone through a gateway and entered a world where people lived with heart and soul, based on the idea that we are not in actuality separate from one another but all deeply interlinked despite – indeed, because of – our many differences. I began to experience with my heart (as opposed to just knowing with my head) that in truth, we are *all* abundant human beings with a deep right to be, and that our true way is to honour and support and share ourselves openly and honestly with everyone around us. If conflicts came up, which they did, I found people dealt with them with integrity, without always having to be right, which was exactly the opposite to what occurred in the world that I had come from.

Revelation

Here, for the first time in my life, I had the direct experience that it didn't matter what social class you belonged to or what colour your skin was, how rich or "cultured" you were, or how you looked or what job you had. All those considerations that were so central to the world I had come from were here no longer of consequence. And it felt so liberating. Here, we were all human beings together, some of us white-skinned, some of us not, some well educated, others not, some old, some young. But none of this mattered.

We were all human beings together participating in our shared humanity. Above all, I observed that the wisdom both of the children and of the elderly was respected. Again, how different this was from the world where I had come from, where children were seen as not worth listening to, while old people got shut away in care homes as a ghastly embarrassment!

I had the profound experience that everyone in this little caravan site was my brother or sister in spirit. We all belonged to the larger family of humanity. I had stumbled into the direct experience that something much greater than our differences linked us all up together. And it felt so profoundly nourishing.

I decided then and there that I had touched into what life really needed to be about and that if we all learned to operate at this level, our world would be mightily different. It could work. I realized that I simply could not go on doing many of the things I had been doing and living the way I had been living, and that I was not only going to dedicate my life to finding out more about this new world, but, most importantly, that I had to try to "take it home" with me.

I stayed for ten weeks in that community. No more. But it was enough to establish a toehold in a new way of being that I have sought ever after to build upon. When I left, I felt rather lonely; I found that many of my old friends started distancing themselves when they discovered that I no longer shared their values and so was no longer a part of their tribe. It was not until some years later when I decided to go and live in California that I felt I was beginning to come home!

Gateways in Sacred Places

So if you want to make some radical changes in your life – if you also find there is something inherently toxic about the values of the culture surrounding you – then I recommend you start off by visiting Findhorn, or certainly somewhere like Findhorn. Today, there are many such communities scattered all over the globe.

If we position ourselves in the environment of people who have already begun making some of the shifts we are also trying to make – that is, who are further along the path than ourselves – we will find, just as I did, that we can get carried along in their slipstream. In other words, when people around us are genuine, it reflects our own lack of genuineness back to us, as well as begging it to come out of hiding. The key thing is that we begin exposing ourselves to new models of what it means to be human. Yes, we can read books like this one, and they are certainly helpful, but they are no substitute for being in the actual *felt presence* of soulfulness.

Also, as I'll be explaining in more detail later, just because we may have had some uplifting experiences, this is no guarantee of them remaining with us. If I pretended to you that on returning to my flat in London I was totally changed, now loved the whole human race unconditionally and all my snobbery and prejudices had vanished for ever and I was now completely immune from the world of glamour and show, I am afraid I would be lying! But what was important was that I had had, as it were, a "sneak preview" into another world – into another way to be. I had been directly shown that all of life does not have to have the artifice and soullessness of the old story, and that other, more tender and more beautiful and compassionate worlds exist and are there to be embraced.

What Findhorn did for me was give me something new to aspire to and work towards, and I think all of us need similar kinds of experiences when starting out.

Change, however, tends to be gradual. Old stories take time to fade away inside us. Gaining access to a new way of seeing the world and actually having it take root inside us are two very different things. In the second part of this book, you will be discovering that much of what keeps us all wired into our old mindsets and why we often find it so hard to let them go, even if we realize that they don't make us happy, is our own particular wounding. And this needs confronting, as what unites all of us is that we are all emotionally wounded in some form or another, some of us much worse than others.

We therefore may need something more than just living in soulful environments. I found, for example, that there were all sorts of parts to me – stubborn, sad, angry, resistant, hurt and immature parts – that kept me locked into my old mindsets and that these wounded parts would often kick back if things got too good, as the old story, being about separation, scarcity and suffering, has a strong charge to it and doesn't want to die.

My own personal journey, therefore, has involved me having to confront parts of me that feared real intimacy, that had difficulty in truly opening my heart, and I found later that a large part of me resisted all the new abundance of being that I was starting to draw to myself. Yes, underneath all those pretensions and posturings dwelt a sad and insecure little boy who actually didn't feel good enough and was rather afraid of the big bad world and what it might demand of him! It has taken a lot of inner work over the years to allow myself to begin embracing the soulful wellbeing that, I will be arguing in these pages, is the birthright of all of us.

Challenges

Today, we face many new challenges. We now live, as I said in my Invitation, in a hyper-complex and a post-truth – and I would also add, post-shame – world. Our planet is in great trouble as a result of the ways we have been treating her and certainly her immune system is infinitely more compromised than it was in the days of my early Findhorn revelations.

Yet by the same token, there is a far greater urgency for change and, not unexpectedly, there are many more "soulful activists" emerging out of the woodwork in every country. Many millennials are showing huge spiritual maturity and I know that something profound is guiding my 20-year-old daughter, who is currently doing a degree in human rights, psychology and global politics.

However, if we really wish to make deep changes both in our own lives and also in the life of our society, we cannot be Pollyanna-ish. We need to be very clear just what it is that we are dealing with. What I have discovered over and over again, both in terms of my own life and in my experience of practising as a psychotherapist for many years, is that the way to improvement – the way to make things better – is to have the courage to confront what is worst. So in the next three chapters we will be doing exactly that. And please try to absorb what I say not only with your head as mere intellectual information but also to experience it with your heart.

▌ EXERCISES

If you want to do the exercises at the end of each chapter and respond to the questions which I ask, I suggest you buy yourself a big notebook. The longer and more comprehensive your responses are, the more they will serve you. You might also want to copy down my questions and then write your responses afterwards.

- What was your childhood like? Was there soulfulness around? What were the stories about yourself that were "given" you and that you took on? How much were you encouraged to be yourself? A lot or very little?
- How did you feel reading about my experiences at Findhorn?
- Having read this chapter, what thoughts or feelings does it evoke inside you?
- How mired do you think you are in your past? Make notes of those areas where you think your life is least soulful.
- How do you feel about the prospect of continuing to read this book? Do you feel indifferent, bored, excited, anything else?

CHAPTER 2

What's Wrong with the World?

When soul is neglected, it doesn't just go away,
it appears symptomatically in obsessions,
addictions, violence and loss of meaning...
Without soul, whatever we find will be unsatisfying.
— THOMAS MOORE

People were created to be loved. Things were created to
be used. The reason why the world is in chaos is because
things are being loved and people are being used.
— THE DALAI LAMA

A Chaotic World

As I have tried to show you, what is wrong with our world is us – that is, you and me and our immature humanity, held in place by the various outdated myths that have been implanted into us. It is not the trees, animals, insects and fishes that are responsible for creating a planet with crises in so many areas, it is us human beings, in particular those of us who have the effrontery to believe we are civilized. Gandhi, when asked about what he thought about Western civilization, remarked that it would certainly be a good idea.

If I look around me, what most impresses itself is the way we give huge significance to issues of very little importance – such as how we look, what people think about us, what clothes we wear, who wins football matches – while we completely ignore really significant issues such as poverty, war, inequality, the destruction of our environment and world hunger. Is this because we don't want to take responsibility for what we have done to our planet, preferring to blame others? Or is it because we are too small-minded to take in the bigger picture? Perhaps we are simply too scared to face certain facts and prefer to continually distract ourselves with trivia so that, ostrich-like, we can bury our heads in the sand and pretend certain things don't exist? It may be a mixture of all three. Certainly, I feel that we are not only a race of *extractivists* (a recently invented word used to describe those who aggressively extract limited resources from our Earth) but also *distractivists* and certainly *destructivists*!

I say this as far too many of us delight in behaving murderously towards those of our fellow humans who are different from us – who have different skin colours, belong to different cultures, see God differently or have different sexual orientations – while being quite content to allow our governments to spend many billions each year to "defend ourselves" and en route, put ourselves in ever greater financial debt – world debt now being in the trillions – by creating increasingly deadly weapons of mass destruction.

Isn't it rather insane that wars are very financially profitable and so for a long time we've arranged our economies around them? In other words, we need to go on making weapons of mass destruction and create all that pain and suffering that comes with war, just to survive! When world leaders are in crisis at home, they often like to start a war. (For example, the Falklands War "saved" Margaret Thatcher!)

We do this when we could be spending the money on feeding all the hungry people on our planet or seeing that education reaches more people or improving healthcare. So why don't we?

The reason is that feeding and educating the poor doesn't make us materially rich, whereas war games do. And the name of one of the main games being primarily "played" on our planet is for the very rich to become even richer. Many wealthy people like war as it ups the price of oil, which is what all the fossil fuel brigade desire as it means their shares increase in value, and anything the already wealthy, who currently control much of what goes on in the world, and have the power to rig the system to work in their favour, can do to increase their wealth is always *numero uno* on the agenda.

This is why there is so much inequality in the world.

Man's insanity and dishonesty

A further example of our insanity lies in the fact that while on the one hand, we always want to be happy and avoid being sad, we seem to be obsessed with – nay, addicted to – what is destined to make us most unhappy: that is, trivia, gossip and tragedy.

As drama is their lifeblood, our news programmes and newspapers constantly go to great efforts to feed our addictions by always giving us the most minute and up-to-date details about everything terrible that is going on. One plane that crashes is given front-page news for days on end, while the three million planes that land safely every month are forgotten.

The great psychologist Abraham Maslow put it much too mildly when he described what he called "normal man", that is, conformist or in my terms "old-story" man, as "living in a state of mild and chronic psychopathology and crippling immaturity". Unfortunately, there is nothing mild but something deeply psychopathic in the dramas that conspire to hold our societies together and in the kinds of stories that underpin them.

Things are better than they used to be

This all said, we need to put things in a proper perspective. Yes, things are bad and there is still much we need to do in many different areas. But in many areas, many things are better than they were, and so we can say that our world is getting both worse and better at the same time. Here are five examples of the latter.

- Inequality, while still a huge issue, has declined.
- Far fewer people live in poverty than they did 50 years ago.
- The child mortality rate has gone down since the 1990s.
- Women's rights and gay rights are improving and today in many countries gay people can marry.
- Increasing numbers of cures for AIDS now exist.

Insufficient consciousness

One of the biggest problems of our times – and it lies behind why our world doesn't work for so many people, why we remain so attached to old myths and why so many of us put up with operating under such a dysfunctional and unsustainable system – is that *too many of us operate at too low a level of consciousness*. This is an evolutionary problem, the result being that we are insufficiently aware of the totality of who we are, and our worldview is too narrow. We move through our lives wearing severe blinkers around our eyes, not letting ourselves see things we don't want to see, and if we do perchance catch a glimpse of something we would prefer did not exist, we either use some strategy to snuff it out or we pretend it isn't there.

Too many of us, therefore, operate either at egocentric levels, where all we are concerned about is ourselves, or at ethnocentric levels, where our concerns may reach out to include our family, tribe or clan – those who are "like us" and see the world like us – but no further. No one "outside the box" is considered.

So where does this limited consciousness or narrow thinking leave us? It inclines us towards prejudice, bigotry, fanaticism, xenophobia and fear. The right-wing, nationalist mindset, which is rapidly gaining momentum in many countries, is inordinately narrow, rooted in fear and terror of the unknown, preferring to look backward to the past, not forward to the future.

A lot of what is wrong with the world is embodied in what is wrong with America, where, statistics tell us, 50 percent of the people could not care less about what goes on beyond the small radius of their own personal concerns. They are wholly uninterested in the fact that millions of children starve and die in war, and that huge injustice reigns – unless of course the injustice happens to engulf them. This is not because they are "bad people", as many believe, but because a higher world-centric stage of development has not yet opened up inside them. I will elaborate on this later on.

Climate change denial

Evidence of this "lack of evolutionary development" is particularly noticeable in the case of climate change deniers, who, despite the increasing evidence of our planet facing ever more frequent and destructive typhoons, tsunamis, droughts and earthquakes, adopt that stance because acceptance would mean being compelled to question the values they live by. This in turn would mean they would be forced to acknowledge the consequence of an unregulated capitalistic system fuelled by huge corporate greed on the part of the large gas and oil companies: unless something radical shifts, we are on track for a 4-degree-Celsius rise in warmth by the end of this century, which in turn could mean the end of clean water, the rising of sea levels (caused by melting glaciers) and the resultant submerging of many large cities; and the possible extinction of human life on the planet.

The deniers say that it hasn't happened yet, so why should it ever happen? If it does, they presume (since many of them are wealthy) that they will be able to live in areas of the planet where they will be unaffected.

Poverty consciousness

Not only is the old story in denial of the well-being of the planet but it is in denial of well-being in general, leading to a state of mind that I will simply call "poverty consciousness", a condition of feeling poor in spirit or inwardly impoverished. People caught in this affliction also often feel victimized and trapped in the "blame game" and consequently lack the ability to experience life's richness or nature's magic. When beset by this condition, life always gets dumbed down and seen through a glass rather darkly.

What enormously contributes to our feelings of impoverishment is the story of believing we are a separate entity – an isolated ego, an "island, entire of ourself" – disconnected not only from ourselves and from our deeper feelings, but also from other people and from the world around us. This enables us to create environments around us that are conducive to hate and allow for abusive activities to occur. For example, in war it is much easier to kill others if you first dehumanize them, as then you are free to demonize them. Thus, we use propaganda to turn those we choose to be our enemies into spiders, worms, Gooks or Huns. So what if we trample on a few of these worms or spiders!

Emptiness and consumption

Because our deepest urge is to feel unified, to fuse with others, to feel linked with nature and our world as a whole, our inability to do this secretly causes us great pain. Deep down, we feel empty. It is the price we pay for keeping out the experience of life's richness or subtler meanings, and today, sadly, far too many of us feel this way. To try to offset or suppress it, we may find ourselves creating all sorts of artificial "wholenesses" for ourselves, whereby we obtain a kind of pseudo-well-being in various ersatz ways.

So, for example, if we cannot properly flow with or allow ourselves to get close to someone we supposedly love, we may try to possess or control them. Even buy them! Similarly, if we cannot experience the happiness of being out in nature, if we have money, we may try to purchase land so we can own it. Or if we can't feel natural joy, we may take drugs to give us this feeling artificially.

Employing these various "substitute strategies" may help temporarily to ward off the feelings of emptiness. Sadly, in the long run, it only increases them. Indeed, for those of us well embedded in Krishnamurti's "sick society", these behaviours are seen as normal and are even to be encouraged. But normal is not the same thing as natural, and trying to fill up the empty hole inside our psyches with ever-more distracting "stuff" – stuff like needing to own lots of things so we can feel "substantial", having an overly "busy" social life, needing to always be in control, and above all consuming, consuming, consuming – in my eyes, these are distinctly *abnormal* activities.

I think one of the biggest paradoxes we face today is that while our consumer habits may keep our emptiness temporarily at bay, they also conspire to make it grow, so we are always on a treadmill of needing to engage in even more consuming, which is just as well for our old-story economy, as it can only survive if this habit is encouraged. In his excellent book *The More Beautiful World Our Hearts Know Is Possible*, Charles Eisenstein describes our consumerist plight very graphically:

> We cannot feel the beautiful world because we are lost in consuming all the time…There is a scarcity of play, awareness, listening and quiet. How much of the ugly does it take to substitute for a lack of the beautiful? How many adventure films do we need to compensate for our lack of adventure, how many superhero movies must we watch to compensate for not living in our greatness, how much pornography do we need to substitute for intimacy, or entertainment to compensate for missing play.[4]

Addiction

Another symptom of what is amiss with our world is the ever-escalating rise of addiction, be it to drugs, alcohol, sex, gambling, whatever. Here, it is not only society's poor who are susceptible – who are in need of some kind of substitute or "filler" to give their deprived lives some meaning – but many who are very well off. Indeed, monetary wealth is no real protection against emotional and spiritual poverty and the depression and anxiety that we may feel if we are unable to live a life with genuine depth and meaning to it. In both the UK and America at this moment, the opiate epidemic is claiming thousands of lives.

Having worked in addiction rehabilitation clinics, I have come to see that getting someone off their addiction is only step one. Unless the addict can also be guided to surrender their attachment to the consumerist mindset and be assisted to make the transition from normality to living a more natural life – that is, a life more in tune with their true nature and with nature around them – there is always the danger of relapsing.

Demonization and vulnerability

In our old story, we also love to demonize, that is, to make others wrong or project our own Shadow side onto them (I will explore this in more detail later on), and here the addict is especially vulnerable and often bears the brunt of a lot of hostility.

The truth is that most addicts are neither weak nor bad. They are simply ill. They embody a particular set of symptoms that reflect those of our fragmented society and are at the mercy of certain compulsions. Thus, more than anything, they need our support, understanding and compassion, just like anybody who is suffering or has fallen on bad times.

Sadly but unsurprisingly, old-story-oriented human beings – who, are also not famed for being able to accept or love themselves – tend not to behave too generously towards those who suffer or who are lost or down and out. If we can push people away who remind us of the mote in our own eye, then we are spared from needing to look too closely at those vulnerable areas in our own lives.

The point is that when our consciousness is undeveloped, our self-awareness is also limited. This leads us to believe that who we are is simply composed of the images that we – or in many instances others – have of ourselves, which inevitably makes for huge vulnerability, as often these images are far from the truth.

Scarcity

Everything I have been describing inevitably gives rise to the experience of scarcity, whereby we are creating a world for ourselves where there is "never enough" – never enough money, never enough food, water, friendship, love, opportunity, inspiration, resources, protection and so on – to go around.

Again, it is not only financially deprived people who experience scarcity. Many wealthy people also do, and one reason they may devote their lives to accumulating a lot materially may often be in order to try to keep this demon at bay.

This experience of "poverty consciousness" can be internal or external. With *some* people it is both, and is especially connected to a lack of self-esteem or self-worth, which again is held in place as a result of our not yet being connected to the truth of who we really are – or put another way, not having the experience of living from our *soul self*. Money, we remember, can only buy us *things*. Love, friendship, kindness, soulfulness, joy, inspiration – the truly important qualities of life that allow us to feel whole and full as human beings – these cannot be purchased.

Abundance

For the truth, as you will soon be discovering, is that *there is not lack in the world.* On the contrary, *there is huge abundance; there is enough love and money and water and resources for everyone. If, that is, we shift our perceptions and live in ways where we don't squander it.* For example, we in Britain don't need to spend £3 trillion on a new Trident missile system. In Charles Eisenstein's words, again from the same book: "What if there is a world with a lot more pleasure, more touch, more lovemaking, intimacy, singing, dancing, fresh water and walks in the countryside. These pleasures are not far away yet our society denies them."[4]

That is the whole point. This is what is so wrong with our world: denial or fear of wholeness, joy and abundance. Many of us live as if we don't deserve these things, as if we *should* suffer!

And the result is that we set up our lives to experience deprivation. Scarcity consciousness, separation consciousness, poverty consciousness and its dark face, greed consciousness – all these exist wherever we look, symbolized by the fact that many of us are more invested in creating problems for ourselves than creating happiness and wholeness.

▨ EXERCISES

- ▪ What feelings has reading this chapter brought up for you?
- ▪ Is any of what I have said news to you or did you know it already?
- ▪ Have you learned anything from this chapter and do you agree or disagree with any of the things I have said?
- ▪ Do you feel yourself in any way connected to or part of any of the sad stories that I have depicted? Where do you feel you stand personally around issues concerning poverty consciousness, separation and insufficiency?
- ▪ Do you feel your life is abundant?

CHAPTER 3

Inequality, Neoliberalism, and the Rise of Populism

*The great problem in the world is not that more be given
to the poor but that we take less from them!*
— SATISH KUMAR

No culture can rest on a crooked relationship to truth.
— ROBERT MUSIL

Inequality

Perhaps what is *most* wrong with the world is the huge differences between the world's richest and the world's poorest countries. Yes, large economic gains are being made, but only to those at the top of the income distribution, as the rich have used their privileges to shape policies that further increase the concentration of wealth, often against the interests of the middle and lower classes.

This inequality is due mainly to aggressive wage restraint, tax dodging and the squeezing of producers by companies, while businesses are too focused on delivering ever-higher returns to wealthy owners and top executives. According to a recent Oxfam report, the world's eight richest individuals control the same wealth as the poorer half of the world's population and the gap continues to widen. I recently came across statistics telling me that the 300 richest people in the world have more money than the 3 billion poorest; and that the 600 richest, and the income they have made alone, could eradicate world poverty three times over. Stunning statistics.

Possibly, the wheels may now be beginning slowly to turn, not least because these statistics are much more out in the open; for what has radically changed in the last half-century is that the injustices in the world are becoming increasingly exposed for what they are. The global interconnectedness that the internet affords certainly contributes to this development.

Globalization as exploitation

What is deeply wrong with the world today is the amount of exploitation that exists. Too many people have grown wealthy on the backs of others being kept poor and deprived and the world for millions is genuinely a very miserable and scary place, ridden with poverty and debt. Imagine for a moment being a refugee fleeing war-torn Egypt, or a child living in the Gaza Strip, or that you are desperately trying to eke out an existence in a failed state like, say, Somalia or Zimbabwe.

Or imagine you live in Syria and you have just escaped being barrel-bombed by your president and have also survived (just) the chemicals also being used against you, but unfortunately, your home has been reduced to rubble and both your parents have been killed. This is real news, not shock-drama news. Can we let that into our hearts? Many people exist like this, deeply traumatized and suffering from massive psychological problems.

Globalization, while in principle a beautiful idea as its true ethos is about working for the good of the whole with nations cooperating together and sharing resources, has blatantly not worked because the story underpinning it has been a wholly exploitative and materialistic one. In an article entitled "Globalization and the American Dream', Helena Norberg-Hodge and Steven Gorelick point out that

> [i]n reality…globalization is a continuation of a broad process
> that started with the age of conquest and colonialism…From then
> on a single economic system has relentlessly expanded, taking
> over other cultures, other peoples" resources and labour. Far from
> elevating people from poverty, the globalizing economic system has
> systematically impoverished them.
>
> If there is to be any hope of a better world, it is vital that we connect
> the dots between "progress" and poverty. Erasing other cultures –
> replacing them with an artificial culture created by corporations and the
> media they control – can only lead to an increase in social breakdown
> and poverty…systematically widen[ing] the gap between the rich and the
> poor…[G]lobal economic activity has already outstripped the planet's
> ability to provide resources and absorb wastes.[5]

The idea was that by seeking to maximize wealth, social, cultural and ecological health would follow. However, this never occurred. In actuality, the very opposite often took place, as the story behind this impulse was, as I said, purely materialistic.

Instead of respecting local cultures and local economies by recognizing that they too are part of the larger, global whole and from a "small is beautiful" perspective have much to contribute to that whole, globalization instead pulverized them with a "big is the only way forward" mindset. The result was increased material well-being for the already well-off.

Earth crisis

We human beings are destroying our planet. We have poisoned our oceans with mercury, blanketed the land with radiation. We've filled our oceans with plastic waste that comes back to haunt us in the fish we eat; we've devastated genetic diversity with monoculture farming, strip-mined the hills for industrial metals, sprayed deadly chemicals on crops that have nearly wiped out our honeybee pollinators, so vital for the health of our land, and bulldozed acres of rainforest – our trees being the "lungs" of our planet, essential for maintaining her homeostasis. *And too many governments turn a blind eye to these crimes against our future.*

Understandably, our planet is reacting to the way we plunder her limited resources for financial gain, and is fighting back. Global warming, extreme droughts and floods, earthquakes and sinkholes are symptomatic of our having pushed our global ecosystem way beyond its natural limits.

Unsustainability

Our world is becoming increasingly unsustainable – politically, socially, economically and ecologically – as it is governed by a whole host of obsolete stories, such as, for example, the idea that our resources are inexhaustible, that nature is a mechanism and we can engineer it like building a bridge, that growth in trade benefits ordinary people or that free, unregulated markets efficiently allocate a society's resources. These stories are untrue in all instances.

The paradoxical nature of the issues we face is summed up by three interesting facts: firstly, that large numbers of children die of starvation while in other parts of the world, there is an epidemic of obesity; secondly, that, while our survival as a species is at stake, many of us are more interested in holding on to our privileges and making more money; and lastly, that, despite knowing that destruction lies ahead if we continue to rely on fossil fuels, rather like the smoker who keeps puffing away despite his doctor telling him that he is then susceptible to lung cancer, we still persist in our addictions.

Many of these insanities may be laid at the feet of an ideological project called neoliberalism, which I will spend a little time explaining as it encapsulates much of what is most inhumane about the old story.

The "Story" of Neoliberalism

The largely anonymous ideology of neoliberalism basically holds that the market is always right, regulation is always wrong, privatization is good and public ownership is bad. Essentially, it is an extreme form of capitalism.

Naomi Klein, in her book *No Is Not Enough*, writes that under this doctrine, governments exist primarily to create the optimum conditions for private interests to maximize their profit, based on the theory that the profits and economic growth that follow will benefit everyone in the trickle-down from the top. If this doesn't work and inequality worsens, as it invariably will, then this entirely loveless and inhumane ideology states that it must be the result of the personal failings of the individuals and communities who suffer from it. They must have a "culture of crime" or be work-shy druggies. Alternatively, some other excuse – generally racially tinged – may be given.

George Monbiot sees lying behind it the idea that competition, not cooperation, is the defining characteristic of human relationships and that one needs to view other nations not as friends to explore partnerships with, but rather as "enemies" competing for the spoils of power.

For the neoliberal, tax and regulation should be minimized, inequality is virtuous and no effort should be made to create a more just society. (The rich who grow richer persuade themselves they got that way through their merit – ignoring the advantages of inheritance, education and class – while, as I said, the poor must pin their failures upon their own personal inadequacies.) So, if you don't have a job, it is not because there are fault lines in society making employment difficult; it is because you are not sufficiently enterprising. If you're not a financial "winner" – if you don't know how to use your brains to get one over on your competitor so he can be squashed – you are a loser!

Can you see how much this story is permeated by beliefs around scarcity, poverty consciousness, emptiness and separation and how it exists as a rationale to justify greed? Of course, to accept, for instance, that climate change exists and is real is to admit the limitations of this particular story, a story that also likes to use crises as opportunities to "distract" people so that unpopular policies like cutting taxes, deregulating corporations and decimating the regulations in place designed to defend the poor, all of which of course favours the wealthy, can be sneaked through.

Right-Wing Populism

The powerful emergence of right-wing populism and nationalism the world over may be seen on one level as a reaction to this creed. People across the globe are trusting their governments less and less. They feel they've been sold short. In fact, it is much easier today to define what people are against than what they are for.

I view populism as a symptom of the world existing in that insecure place that I see as being "between stories". It takes the form of a suspicion of and a hostility towards all elites and mainstream institutions, whereby people feel (not unjustly) that these institutions and elites are corrupt and have "let them down". This anger is coupled with an inability to move with the forces of change, as not only has its pace greatly speeded up and is continuing to do so, but the more one comes from a mindset predicated on scarcity and separation, the more leaden-footed one is and so the harder it is to keep up. The problem is that populism is a self-limiting ideology providing simple solutions to complex issues. George Monbiot defined it once as "the art of agitating disaffected voters to vote against their best interests [e.g., Brexit] by amplifying problems and not offering anything in return...It is the relegation of fact and reason to lies and emotion."

As we have already seen, low-level awareness is generally accompanied by a refusal to take sufficient responsibility for one's life; hence, in unsure times, there has emerged a desire for leaders viewed as demagogic "strongmen" – who, in actuality, turn out to be weak, insecure, greedy, materialistic and narcissistically-inclined despots who think nothing of telling lies and spouting out conspiracy theories, yet who people believe will "fix" things for them and so make them feel less insecure. As I write, more and more of these disreputables seem to be springing up in more and more countries, one particularly well-known one having emerged in the United States, who seems to delight in sowing the seeds of chaos, lies and confusion wherever he goes, not only to the detriment of his country but also to that of the whole planet. What all of them seem to have in common is not only that they are infinitely more corrupt than those elites they are increasingly replacing, but that they somehow manage to get the very poor to vote for and support the interests of the very rich!

Speaking at a conference in South Africa in 2018, marking a hundred years since the birth of Nelson Mandela, Barack Obama had this to say:

> Politics today is rooted in fear, resentment and retrenchment and this politics is on the move at a pace that would have seemed unimaginable a few years ago…
>
> Just look around: strongmen politics are ascendant suddenly and the modern political context is strange and uncertain, with each day's news cycle bringing more head-spinning and disturbing headlines. We see much of the world threatening to return to a more dangerous, more brutal way of doing business. The free press is under attack, the state control of the media is on the rise. Social media, once a mechanism to promote solidarity, has proved just as effective in promoting paranoia, propaganda, hatred and conspiracy theories.

Totalitarianism

The goal of the totalitarian propaganda practised by these "strongmen", then, is to sketch out a consistent system that is simple to grasp and is intended to distort reality. People buy this fiction because, in the words of Hannah Arendt in her book *The Origins of Totalitarianism*, "the masses are obsessed by a desire to escape from reality…because they can no longer bear its incomprehensible aspects".[6] In other words, totalitarian movements conjure up a duplicitous world that is more acceptable to people's needs than the "real reality" itself, so that those who feel uprooted can find a home and don't have to face the huge shocks that real life and real experience can give them.

In this way, totalitarian propaganda is conditioned to shut the masses off from the real world and make them believe in a fictional one. It may well be, however, that the shock of the Coronavirus is so colossal that it serves radically to change the whole nature of the game. Its shock effect could waken the masses from the spells cast upon them, thus enabling them to start seeing reality as it really is, which includes wising up to the many lies their leaders spin them.

The problem with our world leaders

Today we seem to have a system or story that does not enable men and women of true calibre to assume leadership roles (where are our great world leaders today, I ask myself), and furthermore many people in many countries do not want – or, perhaps we can say, are resistant to, for the reasons I have already given – leaders of quality and integrity.

Certainly the world of international relationships operates along very old-story lines, the game seeming to be about which of the biggest countries can best do down their rivals and project most power.

As I write, I'm not sure I can think of any politician in the world today who truly holds the qualities of a soulful consciousness (as, for example, I experienced in Findhorn). Most candidates for statesmanship today, it seems, are attracted to the job on account of the vast status and power that comes with it; as a sceptical friend wryly pointed out: "Many of them are little more than moneylaunderers in the trafficking of policy and power."

The days of a Nelson Mandela, who was able to perform such a miracle for his country as his heart was big enough to embrace all the people of South Africa, or a Gandhi, who embodied the new story in every fibre of his being and who, like Mandela, walked his talk, seem to be over.

The Myth of Continual Growth

Essentially, the big problem today is that our planet is held in the thrall of a deregulated capitalist system predicated on a false story that tells us that there has to be continuous growth taking place all the time!

Who says? *This* is what is destroying us. The truth is that there *can* be progress without artificially forcing growth; there *can* be enough food and water for everyone; we *can* have peace between nations; we *can* stop spending billions on creating more devastating weapons to destroy ourselves and instead take more and more people out of poverty; and as I suggested earlier, countries *can* do a hell of a lot more than many of them are doing to ease the plight of the millions of refugees.

Why I regard this virus as a potential game changer is that it touches every single one of us, whoever we are, rich or poor, and wherever we live on the planet. Yes, it is causing much physical death and this is deeply tragic, but it could also herald the gradual demise of our entire dysfunctional system. It may well be that whole new strategies begin emerging, focused around survival, healing, and assisting the most vulnerable on our planet.

EXERCISES

- What thoughts and feelings has reading this chapter brought up for you?
- Does what I have said resonate with your worldview or does it contradict it? Note any issues this may have brought up for you.
- How does the existence of so much inequality in the world make you feel? Does it make you sad, angry, numb or something else?
- Are you in any way a small part of those forces which engender inequality, perhaps without being initially aware of it? Think hard.
- If so, are you induced to want to do anything about it? If so, what?
- What does the existence of neoliberalism bring up for you?

CHAPTER 4

Wetiko and the Killing Stories

*Believing war will produce peace is equal to believing
butter will be produced by churning sand.*
— SATISH KUMAR

*Desacralization pervades the entire experience
of the non-religious man of modern societies,
and with the rise of patriarchal religions, this sense of
containment within the sacred order began to fade.*
— MIRCEA ELIADE

*We must rapidly begin the shift from a thing-oriented
society to a person-oriented society. When machines and
computers, profit motives and property rights
are considered more important than people,
the giant triplets of racism, materialism and militarism
are incapable of being conquered...*
— MARTIN LUTHER KING

Wetiko

This is our last chapter where I look at what is wrong with the world. The reason why I put so much stress on this is not just to be negative, but simply in order that we don't walk about with the wool pulled over our eyes, which is what the system does its best to do to us.

Fascism won't evaporate by our pretending it is not raising its head. World greed won't disappear unless it is confronted. Populist brands won't wither until we see how truly pernicious they are and then set about trying to jam them – block or cut them off. As you and I are products of the culture around us, if we want personally to "out" the genuine us, this also has to involve our coming to confront – often with great sorrow – some of the worst evils in our world.

I recently came across the word *wetiko*, an Algonquin term to describe a cannibalistic spirit that can possess us, whose symptoms include feeling utterly driven by greed, the need for material success and selfish consumption. Sadly, far too many of us today are influenced by this dark presence or, at worst, completely possessed by it.

Those who feel no compunction about any damage their actions may do to others, or who intentionally cannibalize our Earth's limited resources, are for me human beings deeply tainted. I see *wetiko* as analogous to a virus eating away at our souls, keeping out joy, beauty and birdsong and thus preventing us from knowing ourselves in any depth, connecting in a genuine way with our fellow human beings, or being able to feel the alive and beautiful spirit of nature.

The rajassic way

Another way to understand the differences between old and new myths is to view the world in terms of three different "qualities of life", or, from the perspective and in the language of Indian thought, three *gunas*.

Each *guna* represents a different way of perceiving the world. In his excellent book *Spiritual Compass*, Satish Kumar explains how, in Sanskrit, the terms for these three *gunas* are *sattvic*, which stands for everything embodying soulfulness, *rajassic*, which is the old myth, and *tamassic*, which is what happens to the old myth when it falls increasingly under the spell of *wetiko* and begins degenerating. I'll explain.

The rajassic way is how a great deal of the old story presents itself, namely permeated by a lot of narcissism, glamour and glitter. Why we can get so attached to it and why it can be so compelling – and I can definitely see why, in the past, I personally got so drawn into it – is because it is seductive, fashionable, extravagant and exciting. It wants to achieve big goals and improve everything all the time – engineer realities to make them better. It is basically the neoliberal story that tells us we may use force and cajolement to achieve our ends.

As we have seen, most Western politicians think and act along rajassic lines and this mindset infiltrates all diplomacy. In this domain, it is legitimate to do sleazy deals and tell lies and pally up with dictators with appalling human rights records (e.g., Blair and Gaddafi) if there is money to be made. Everything is seen as a commodity to be bought and sold. For rajassic man, if something goes wrong, you either get rid of it or you denigrate it – recycling not being on its agenda.

This is the world of institutionalized religion and the mindset that pursues economic growth at all costs and espouses globalization. In this mindset, big is beautiful. Huge is even better. Huge businesses, gigantic multinational corporations, vast central government, huge supermarkets, colossal business deals. We saw all this in the last chapter.

The tamassic way

The rajassic way very easily descends into the tamassic when business is only about profit and when people are excluded, or when politics becomes solely about control, power, corruption and self-interest. When this degradation occurs, evil emerges and *wetiko* rears its hideous head. Satish puts it beautifully:

> We then have a world where business is without spirit, trade is without compassion, industry is without ecology, finance without fairness resulting in a breakdown of society and the destruction of the natural world, which is then divided into a battlefield of nations competing with each other for power, influence and control over minds, markets and natural resources.[7]

Basically, then, the tamassic story is a more distorted or corrupted version of the rajassic one.

All wars are tamassic. Extreme religious fundamentalism is tamassic, and it is tamassic politics that led to two world wars, the Cold War, 9/11 and, more recently, Syria and Bashar Assad's torture dungeons. Human-rights groups say that the regime (at time of writing) has tortured to death or executed up to 100,000 men, women and children.

The Killing Story

What is so hugely wrong with the world is the killing story or the story of the seeming inevitability of war. We still subscribe to it as it has been with us for so long and has become so engrained that we have come to see it as the way life has to be, and that butchering one another is one of the main ways we choose to solve problems! In *Awakening the Universal Heart* I wrote:

> What all wars have in common is that they reflect a pathological mindset within man; they are evil, misinformation gets propagated, soldiers and civilians and children die, women and men get raped, people get tortured,

whole cultures get destroyed and a huge amount of trauma and suffering is created, and it takes all parties a long, long time to recover.

What all wars share is that instead of our facing the enemy inside ourselves – instead of confronting the murderousness inside our own hearts – we prefer to project it outside of ourselves…We erroneously believe that good will come about if we can only eradicate what we perceive as being the evil out there. In doing so, we forget that in the very killing process itself, we morph into the very thing we are seeking to eradicate.[8]

Yes, wars happen for many social, economic and political reasons, but I stress once more that a large part of what makes them explode into expression is the violence and propensity for destructiveness that you and I carry inside us. (We will explore this more in the chapter on the Shadow.) What essentially I am saying is that as a species, we will carry on killing until sufficient numbers of us find a story of peace emerging inside our hearts.

I recently asked my wise friend Anne Baring, an eminent Jungian analyst, what she thought Jung would have had to say about ISIS were he alive today. Her reply was that he would have said that it represented "the unrecognized Shadow side of Western civilization coming up to meet us". I like this idea as many European countries, under cover of respectable "outer faces", have engaged in some very dubious activities over the centuries and perhaps the reason why we have created this monster is because for too many years we have used sledgehammers to crush walnuts! And actions always have consequences.

Certainly, I put a large part of the unrest in the Middle East today down to the policies of wealthy nations over the last century, especially their desire to use and abuse this part of the world, to take greatest advantage of both its oil wealth and its vulnerabilities in order to satisfy geopolitical and corporate objectives. We are paying the price today for nations in the colonial era having been occupied and hacked into different segments with little regard for the internal disruption created, simply to suit the convenience of those corporate interests that saw the process of making money and increasing their power as being the hallmark of "wise diplomacy".

If, today, one of the biggest problems the world faces is migration – in the last decade 50 million refugees have been unleashed on the world, mostly children under the age of 18 – then its roots certainly go back to those days. Indeed, one of the greatest tragedies is that those in power never seem to think of the long-term consequences of so many of their policies or recognize that initiatives that might bring short-term gain to certain specific interests are so often achieved at longer-term costs. This is yet another symptom of the limitations of our old thinking.

I believe that many of the wealthier nations have a responsibility today to be more hospitable towards those in need and come to regard the process of taking in and seeking to integrate refugees not only as a challenging service they can perform – yes, of course, it stretches their resources – but also as payment for past wrongs committed. It is disgraceful that so many politicians in countries that could afford to do much more for the refugees as well as allow more in do not do so, a) because of a failure of imagination, and b) because of sheer cowardice – fear that people will not like it and so will not elect them in the future.

A story of disconnection

Instead of being able to see all world problems as somehow interconnected and as being symptoms of a deeper global malaise, the rajassic/tamassic mindset, in its separative thinking, tends to view them as if they are all disconnected and so need to be solved individually.

This is why old-story approaches never seem to work in the long run and always veer towards addressing symptoms, never going to the cause. Or perhaps people are terrified of facing the fact that, as Satish puts it again, "they are the cause of the problems they confront, i.e., that the intended solver of the problem is the very thing needing solving!"

Certainly, I find that most of the problems I encounter with my clients are interrelated. Often, someone will come to me with several issues, complaining, say, of difficulties around money, sex and intimacy, dissatisfaction with their work, and an inability to let go and enjoy themselves. These issues may all seem separate, but they are not. *They are generally all "held in place" by the context in which the person views the world,* and in most instances their problems are not going to be solved by digging into each one individually, but rather by the person learning to change the context of how they live their lives.

In other words, shift the context and the content also changes and becomes other than how it appeared. Often, if this occurs, problems can vanish in their entirety. Einstein's famous remark about problems not being able to be solved at the level they manifest at, then, is as true psychologically as it is politically, economically and socially.

Extractivism

The tamassic spirit or *wetiko* is most visible in the behaviours of many of the large fossil fuel companies, many of which, as we've seen, are so immense and so rich that they can do pretty much exactly what they want. Therefore if, say, they wish to start extracting oil from land occupied by tribal peoples, they will simply use their money to bribe them or win lawsuits against them as they know the people lack the financial clout to fight back. They can also pay politicians to support them, as the latter need their money if they are to win their elections.

As I mentioned earlier, the process of extracting more and more resources from the Earth to become rich (which is the polar opposite to being a steward of our planet) is called extractivism. In her book *This Changes Everything: Capitalism vs. the Climate*, Naomi Klein describes it as follows:

> It is the reduction of life into objects for the use of others, giving them no integrity or value of their own, turning…mountains into "overburden" (as the industry terms rocks and forests in the way of bulldozers). It is also the reduction of humans either into labour…or, alternatively, into social burden, problems to be locked out at borders and locked away in prisons…In an extractivist economy, the interconnections between the various components of life are ignored…Extractivism is connected to the idea of "sacrifice zones", places that, to their extractor, somehow don't count and so can be poisoned, drained or otherwise destroyed, for the supposed greater good of economic progress.[9]

The extractivist story, so utterly permeated by *wetiko*, sees nature not as something to be learned from, respected and delighted in, but rather as an asset to make money out of and consequently as an enemy to be overcome.

Too rigid to shift

What is most problematic, however – and I come across this in my work all the time – is the fact that even though the many crises we face today are causing people identified with soulless worldviews to question their continuing validity, the lack of flexibility associated with living at rajassic or tamassic levels of consciousness makes it hard actually to change tack. Put simply, the very limitations built into being an extractivist – or a reductivist or destructivist; they're essentially all different expressions of the same mindset – means one has a problem in facing the demise of one's particular way of operating, because there is no trust in the process of transformation, or in the idea that abandoning one lens through which we see the world may lead to another more preferable one, or that death may lead to rebirth. The problem of operating at limited levels of consciousness is that we primarily see ourselves in terms of the images we have of ourselves and how we think others view us, which in turn relates to the nature of our work and our wealth, and so we are scared of letting go our old, familiar positions.

Having others see us a certain way, then, is more powerful than any desire to surrender our status or give up our power or honestly confront the fact that what we do threatens the survival of life on Earth. Were we to do so, we might have to face the fact that we may be redundant and with our lack of imagination, we could see no other way of operating.

Understanding Our "Self-serving" System

We have been touching on the inequities of what we have vaguely referred to as "the system"; perhaps it is now time to confront it head on and ask ourselves: "What actually do we mean by 'the system'?" Yes, we can say it's the capitalist system or the economic system, but these are just particular faces or names that it has, depending on your perspective. I see it as being something more all-encompassing, something that intrudes ever so subtly into all areas of our lives, so that we often fail to see it for what it is, because its tentacles lie everywhere.

The first thing to say is that it is "the system" that conspires to keep us entangled in the rajassic and tamassic mindsets, that gives us a proclivity towards waging war and being greedy, materialistic, consumeristic and extractivistic. It also has an investment in distancing us from recognizing who we truly are and thus acknowledging our true embeddedness in nature and in the cosmos. The system is eminently soulless – indeed, soul is its arch-enemy – and if it can have us be possessed by *wetiko*, which will bind us to it more tightly, it will celebrate.

The system's main need is to survive and in order to do so, vampire-like, it requires our lifeblood, since its whole *raison d'être* depends on us. This is why it doesn't want us to evolve and celebrate our soul-hood; it doesn't want us to feel more abundant and experience joy and free will, as then we will need it less – we will come to live more and more outside of its entanglements – and this weakens it. So it needs to get us entangled in it and at best addicted to it. This is why it is such an advocate of things dramatic!

The system, constructed to serve itself and needing our dependence on it to do so, is inherently dishonest and in no way honours those goals that it purports to address, i.e., that it is there to assist us. The result is that *everyone* gets taken for a ride in some form or another, even its most fervent upholders.

To keep us locked into it, the system therefore ties our hands in such subtle ways that we don't even notice. For example, while we may rightly criticize governments for their austerity programmes or for not spending enough money in areas where there is real need – say, in education or the health service – *the system is set up in such a way that nations can't do what is best to solve the global, environmental and social problems, because such policies would cost too much and would therefore have to be scrapped. In this way the system protects itself.*

The big catch-22

In other words, the world is caught up in a giant catch-22. From a rajassic perspective, nations can't "save the planet" without incurring huge costs and so losing out to competition. As Scilla Elworthy puts it in her book *Pioneering the Possible*: "It is not that Starbucks and Amazon lack ethics but the system they are in, that is, a destructive, competitive global economy, makes it hard to do the right thing, for if you do so, you lose out to your competitors."[10] So you are kept in the thrall of doing the "wrong thing" in order that the system thrives! In an article in *The Times* in 2014 we read that HSBC "confesses to having an organizational bias where good people let bad things happen to survive". They admitted to "an increase in policy-driven behaviour at the same time as a decrease in using our moral compass in decision-making".[11]

Contrary to what many believe, I actually don't think most bankers or oil executives are necessarily "bad" people. Rather, they are caught up in a system that legitimizes dishonest behaviours. The more deeply entrenched you are in the system, the more susceptible you are to being entrapped by *wetiko*, which, viewed another way, can be seen as the system's secret weapon! Andrew Harvey hits the nail on the head when, in his book *Radical Passion*, he tells us that "[t]he very systems that rule our religions, corporations and political parties are what keep us radically disempowered, paralysed and depressed. All the cruelty, madness and injustice "out there" is an emanation of a collective false self dangerously out of control."[12] OK. The old story. The false self. The system. All the same thing.

Stepping outside the system

What is most wrong with our world, then, is that it is too deeply embedded in a rajassically/tamassically entwined story or system a) which has a potentially low-level moral compass, b) whose prime agenda is to maintain and serve itself, and c) which does not recognize, and is intrinsically opposed to or threatened by, the existence of "higher" or more imaginative or more integral levels of functioning. In a word, soul is its arch-enemy! Why?

Because the more we expand ourselves and touch into what it truly means to be human, the more we start standing outside the system. And the system doesn't like that, so it does its best to curb us, see that we don't grow and don't go soul searching; and one way it does this is by ensuring we are continually in a state of agitation and conflict. (No wonder it is at war with meditation!) As the vampire needs to suck people's blood to survive, so the system needs to live on our sweat and tears.

It is not that the system doesn't talk of "change" and "doing things in a new way". It does. And it even talks of smashing down the edifice on which it is sustained. But this is all part of the way it dupes us – its "false truths" – as what it calls "new approaches" are simply more extreme versions of the old strategies. For example, the rajassic way tells us that if we only invent more powerful antibiotics, use stronger fertilizers, send better-trained troops to the trouble spots, use weaponry that can pinpoint the targets better, print more money, find new sources of oil, genetically engineer crops with higher yields, our problems will be solved.

My dear friend, this is all nonsense. They won't. At best, problems will be temporarily covered over or moved into some new arena for others to deal with.

I'll give you another example: many of us think we can stop global warming politically, by compelling countries to cut their carbon footprint. Yes, of course that helps, but *the more important question to be asked is the deeper one as to why we remain so dependent upon coal, why we consume so much, and what it is about our lifestyles and attitudes that created global warming in the first place.*

Is this because we are entangled in some way with the system? The answer is yes. Old story equals system in many, many aspects.

We also naively think that world poverty will go away if those at the top of society give more money or if we are more successful in our aid programmes and ensure less money gets stolen by corrupt officials. Again, these things help, *but only up to a point*. Again, the deeper questions needing to be asked – and which soul – (sattva) *does* ask – are: a) why does the system encourage greed and corruption and induce people tainted with these afflictions into positions of power and responsibility within it, and b) what it is about our scarcity/separation/poverty mindset and how the rich view the poor that serves to keep poverty in place?

EXERCISES

- How do you feel having read this chapter? Do you agree? If not, what do you think?
- What most angers you about the system and, in general, about the state of the world?
- Is there any part of you that you think may have rajassic or tamassic inclinations, or which, in some way or ways, is entangled with the system and so personally holds the old story in place in your life? If so, where? Write about it in detail.
- How motivated are you from 1 to 10 to try to disentangle yourself, and what strategies do you think might be needed to help you in this mission? Do you feel you can do it on your own or do you feel you need some kind of assistance? If the latter, what do you feel you need? A coach? A psychotherapist? We will return to this issue in a later chapter.

CHAPTER 5

Gateways into Soul

We must learn to live as souls on Earth.
— ROBERTO ASSAGIOLI

When a civilization loses its meaning of soul, it is coming to an end...I feel our civilization has lost its meaning of soul some time ago. That is the bad news. The good news is that when we can come to new images of soul, we're creating a new civilization.
— MATTHEW FOX

A De-Souled World

I have given you a guided tour into many of the things that are most atrocious and soulless about the way our world operates, and now, at last, we are going to shift the focus. We are going to explore the domain of soul, and I hope that by the end of this chapter you will have considerably more clarity on this topic and will realize that *essentially what is most amiss with our world — most destructive about the system — is that it is utterly lacking in soul, and this is because not enough of us have learned how to activate soul inside ourselves.* In other words, the system *out there* is reflective of us inside ourselves. In his book *Care of the Soul*, Thomas Moore puts it like this: "The great malady of our times, and implicated in all our troubles and affecting us individually and socially, is loss of soul."[13]

When cultures remain essentially soulless, they show little motivation to explore life's deeper meanings or ask profounder questions as to where they might be going, and when this happens, as we have been seeing, they start degenerating. Yes, my friend, the reason why we often treat our fellow human beings who are vulnerable so callously, or why we are so rabidly materialistic and like tearing down our rainforests may essentially be laid at the feet of insufficient soul.

It also follows that the more destructive we are, the more soul gets reduced. The more it is reduced, the further we devolve from our true nature. As a symbol of how far we have deviated, consider that in days past, the tallest and most imposing building in the town square used to be the church. Today, it is the big bank.

Not only do we have few sacred rituals in our mainstream culture, but our churches no longer hold sacred energy. Indeed, the religion many of them offer us today is mostly arid and uninspirational – priests being more preoccupied with debating whether or not homosexuality should be accepted, or whether women should be made bishops, than really helping us find God. In the words of the late Bede Griffiths, a truly holy man whose life embraced both Christianity and Buddhism: "If Christianity cannot recover its mystical traditions and teach it, it should just go out of business as it has nothing to say."

And of course there is nothing remotely sacred in the fundamentalist stances that are so prevalent the world over today, which are all about fear, closed-heartedness and the denial of our dark side, and where followers believe you are justified in killing those who believe in a different God.

So what has happened? Why are so many people so soulless in so many countries today? How has mankind managed to de-soul itself so enormously? Is this sudden or has it gradually crept up on us?

Why the loss of soul?

To answer this question we need to go back a long way in time. Soullessness and all its many discontents have not always prevailed. Thousands of years before the advent of religion, people living in shamanic cultures were naturally conscious of the grandeur of nature and felt very much that they lived within a sacred order where they felt aligned with a higher reality that ensouled all of life. Consequently, there existed a deep reverence for life and man felt himself very connected to the natural world.

However, the rise of patriarchal religions that emphasized our "fallenness" as opposed to our blessedness saw this containment within a sacred order gradually fade away, and in Plato's era, the world witnessed a strong moving away from nature and a shift towards reason and knowledge. As our egos developed, they began to lose their deep, instinctive sense of connection to nature, and consequently humanity became increasingly open and vulnerable to exploitation. The shaman who saw soul in all things and revered the natural world became replaced by the hero or conqueror who didn't, and who instead saw his role as needing to overcome obstacles and "kill evil dragons". This mindset of course is still prevalent in the world and today's "strongmen" politicians, who we have looked at already, see themselves as heroes in this mould.

Thus, the world entered a vale of suffering and a God was born who was feared and seen as cruel, rejecting and judgemental.

In the fourth century, St Augustine's doctrine of "original sin" severed humanity even more from soul, and introduced us to – or even, fixed us into – a consciousness of scarcity and separation by imposing on us the belief that we were somehow contaminated by sin and therefore separate from God. Christianity therefore stopped being a religion of love and became one of punishment, and, I believe, has led directly to the scientific reductionism we see around us now. The more the left brain or reasoning side of us evolved, the more humanity's soulfulness became suppressed. Judaism, Christianity and Islam all now possessed a zeal to conquer and subdue, and they needed to find hate objects to demonize and project their dark side upon.

In the sixteenth and seventeenth centuries we saw the Protestant Reformation, dedicated to eradicating Catholicism. In England this resulted in 95 percent of the artistic heritage of the Middle Ages being obliterated, representing a huge rape of the nation's soul.

Francis Bacon's influence was also very strong at that time. His suggestion that we needed to control nature, as (in his view) in itself it had no purpose and was not part of the wider cosmos, led to an increasing de-soulment and humanity's further shift away from participating in the being of things to desiring power over things. His thinking allowed a space for reductionism and extractivism to grow and flourish.

Science therefore took the view that nature, animals and man had no soul and did not belong to a sacred order – and what has no soul may be tortured and abused. Thus, we moved towards a transcendent ('above the world") and punishing male patriarchal deity completely separate from the forms and structures of life. In other words, God no longer existed within matter or in the concrete world.

Then, in the Industrial Revolution, we saw an even further movement away from soul towards a worshipping of the machine, and towards a position where everything that was non-rational was viewed as nonsense and where consciousness was perceived merely as a product of the physical brain (with any so-called "mystical experience" being regarded solely as an aberration of our brain chemistry!). In his book *Harmony: A New Way of Looking at Our World*, Prince Charles writes: "We have come to function with a one-sided, materialistic approach that is defined not by its inclusiveness but by its dismissal of those things that cannot be measured in practical terms."[14]

Do you see how strong this de-souled mindset still is in our world today? Is it any wonder, for example, that the Western story has allowed for the eradication of tribespeople – people who live close to nature and close to soul, such as Maoris, Aboriginal Australians, Native Americans? I stress once more: soul is eminently threatening to the forces of soulless-ness. On the one hand, this is because it secretly reminds a person of what they have lost or, in many instances, never even gained, and this awareness is painful. On the other hand, it is because there is an instinctive sense of soul's enormous power. So at best, soul needs to be kept at a distance or, failing that, it needs to be eradicated. At one level, the old story or the system is simply a conspiracy against soul.

Projecting soul onto soullessness

However, while soul can be repressed, it cannot be killed, for the simple reason that soul is who you and I essentially are. So what happens in a culture like ours, structured around soullessness, is that while we may trivialize, ignore or demean what is genuinely soulful – psychologists talk about our tendencies to "repress anything remotely sublime" – we none-theless have a need for it, and the result is that we will create spurious gods; we will deify or project soul onto what is intrinsically soulless.

For example, we like to attribute "sacred meaning" to money or football teams, or to deify some well-known pop star or celebrity. This is because we still need our high priests and priestesses to look up to and see as examples upon whom to base our lives; only instead of the "real thing", that is, truly soulful human beings, the rajassic among us will tend to sacralize those who are the most glamorous or famous.

In his book *Knowledge and the Sacred*, Seyyed Hossein Nasr tells us:

> Knowledge, too, has become desacralized…especially among those segments of the human race transformed by the process of modernization, with the result that that bliss which is the fruit of union with the one and an aspect of the perfume of the sacred, has become well-nigh unattainable and beyond the grasp of the vast majority of people today.[15]

This is an important point to understand. I think our failure or our resistance towards reaching up and embracing what I will simply call higher or deeper knowledge, which can be so healing and transformational for us if we can only learn to "bring it down" concretely into our daily lives, is another reason why there is so much stress, anxiety and addiction, and so little joy and wonder, in the world.

Today, the tragedy is that we seek information as opposed to real knowledge.

Social media has great power over us and I see a connection between our incapacity to connect with joy and the kind of inspiration and knowledge that can truly nourish and empower us, and our tendency to be overly obsessed with our iPhones and Instagrams. I recently went to the Louvre in Paris to view Leonardo's great painting of the Mona Lisa, and observed that few people looked at it for more than a couple of seconds as they were much more interested in taking selfies of themselves in front of it. Thus, art that is magnificent and has the power to elevate us is instead merged into our narcissistic glorifications.

Playing substitute soul games

However, because soul is who you and I inherently are, we are, as I said, always instinctively in search of it. But because we can only "get" it at the level we are at – consider that lovely saying that "when the pickpocket meets the saint, all he can see is his pockets"! – we do our soul searching in all the wrong places. Fashion models, pop stars and celebrities may be decent human beings but perhaps not always the best embodiments of soulfulness.

Many alcoholics, for example, deep down, could be described as unrealized mystics, as I believe what the alcoholic *really* craves is not the ersatz spirit from the bottle, but genuine spirituality. However, because they may be still encased in a mindset of scarcity and separation and have not yet created the structure within themselves enabling them to access the "real thing", the best they can do is experience a "dumbed-down" version of it.

Put simply, not only do none of our "dumbed down" or substitute attempts to find soul work, but, sadly, they actually conspire to take us even further away from it.

Defining Soul

So perhaps it is now time to ask ourselves: what really is soul? What exactly is this magical something that I am suggesting is the essence of who we all are and the solution to many of our problems, and yet which so many of us seem to have lost touch with?

I see soul as the animating principle that makes living things alive and links all of life together. It exists not only in all of us, but in all of life, in rocks and trees and bees and animals and plants; indeed in our planet as a whole, and in the entire cosmos. The Platonists spoke of *anima mundi*, the soul of the world, and regarded the entire cosmos as a living being with a body, soul and spirit. Aristotle saw that an acorn grows into an oak tree because it is pulled towards its final destination by its soul. St Teresa of Ávila hints at soul's multidimensionality and luminosity when she suggests that we "consider our soul to be like a castle made entirely out of a diamond or of very clear crystal, in which there are many rooms."

Thus, our souls – yours and mine and everyone's on this planet – are those dimensions of ourselves that not only link us to all aspects of ourselves and to one another and inform us how and where we fit in with the greater scheme of things, but also enable us to know what our true life purpose is and thus potentially guide us towards fulfilling it.

When we discover soul, we find our truth or what gives us bliss. We stumble into what we really need to be doing with our lives. However, in order to make this connection, we need to learn to listen to ourselves much more carefully and, most importantly, *much more deeply* than many of us are accustomed to doing. Soul is always there but we don't experience it, or we miss it because we do too much hovering about on the surface of things. However, whenever we allow something or someone truly to touch us or move us strongly – and it can be in the direction of either pain or joy – soul becomes present. In this context, Thomas Moore also wrote that "[s]oul is not a thing but a quality or a dimension of experiencing life and ourselves. It has to do with depth, value, relatedness, heart and personal substance." This is why our making an effort to live with greater wakefulness or awareness is such a key catalyst for bringing soul into expression. Artists, poets, writers, musicians and creative people in general are naturally more connected to their souls as they tend to be more involved with heart, depths and substance.

The beauty of soul is that we don't have to be part of any particular religion to experience it. Soul transcends all religions, and many people who profess to be religious (and again I particularly think of fundamentalists) can be the most soulless of all, while many of those who profess no religion may be the most soulful.

Soul in all things

It is not only people who have souls. So too do animals and trees and rocks and fleas and rivers. So too do organizations and institutions and nations.

However, if we have not yet managed to connect effectively with our own personal soul life, our ability to recognize soul's existence outside of ourselves will be limited. And a big problem today is that too many of our large corporations, institutions and political parties are peopled by men and women who have little knowledge of nor interest in the world of soul. I cannot sufficiently stress the damage that an individual nation does, both to itself and to the larger world community, by disregarding its deeper soul purposes and only thinking in terms of what will serve its own interests.

All the great world leaders have had a connection with soul. Winston Churchill, at a vital point in British history, stood for its courageous soul, while Nelson Mandela probably embodied South Africa's compassionate soul. Similarly, all great world figures in their particular field stand for some aspect of the soul of the nation that they come from. Thus, a Tolstoy may be seen as embodying the literary genius of the Russian soul, a Johann Strauss as symbolizing the joyous Austrian soul, and Lao Tzu the wise Chinese soul. Whenever I see qualities of love, joy, peace, freedom, courage, truth, justice, wisdom or compassion being embodied, I know that soul is always hovering close by.

So when you or I start connecting to our souls, we start experiencing that there is a "deeper meaning" to everything about our lives and that perhaps we haven't come into the world *just* to "be a success" or make money (as our conventional mindsets like to tell us), but also to learn certain lessons or make a contribution to society, to be a raiser-up or an enhancer of the world around us in some way. And if tragedy happens to befall us, if we have soul, we can perhaps come to recognize that there may be some meaning to it, something we need to learn from it, which in turn can then hopefully give us the strength to deal with it more effectively.

What makes my soul come alive is choosing to do things that make my heart sing, such as spending quality time with very close friends, working with my clients, swimming in the ocean, and yes, even writing this book!

When I do things that feel right for me, that give me joy, that let me know that in the way I am living, I am somehow aligned to the truth of who I am, then I know I am connecting with my soul. I know, too, that the more I consciously try to deepen this connection, the more my soul life will blossom. Indeed, the more soul I choose to put into everything I do in my life, the more this dimension of myself becomes "outed" and the more I become who I truly am.

I always try to do my psychotherapy work in a soulful way, which means that when a client comes to see me, I am always asking myself: what is it that their soul really wants and is asking of me? What is their deeper truth lying concealed beneath that bundle of symptoms they are presenting me with or the words they are speaking, and how, by listening to them carefully – that is, being open to my own soul as I sit in front of them – can I best elicit it?

I know that the more closely I can be in touch with my depths when I work with people, the more this will help coax their hearts and souls into view. I say this as souls can sometimes be a little coy and timid and may at times need a little assistance to come out of hiding.

The mystery of soul

Soul is undoubtedly mysterious, yet I think it signals its existence by a definite presence. When we describe a person as being "soulful", what we are saying is that we experience them to have a certain *je ne sais quoi* about them, a certain authenticity or a wisdom or sometimes a sweetness of being, which goes way beyond mere charisma or chutzpah.

This isn't always obvious. Sometimes we encounter someone who may initially seem quite ordinary, but if we persevere with them or perhaps experience them in the field in which they specialize or have a particular gift, we realize there is truly something quite luminescent about them.

We also talk about a person, regardless of their chronological age, being an "old soul". This is about how naturally connected they are to this dimension of themselves and how strong the linkage seems to be. Some of us link up with this dimension only occasionally; others do so more often and still others connect very deeply and remain connected. But certainly, when we are in the presence of someone who is deeply ensouled or who is a deep and loving and evolved human being, some of their light can be passed on to us as well. With some people, their light seems to shine out of them effortlessly and naturally.

A little soul story

I'll tell you a little story about this. I used to live in Gloucestershire, where I was very privileged to have a world-famous blues guitarist as my next-door neighbour. I am pretty much a pipsqueak guitarist, but I love playing the blues – I actually find it very joyful music – and at my fiftieth birthday party, my neighbour did me the enormous honour of playing some blues songs with me. Simply being included in what I can best describe as his awesome "blues soul field" was so empowering that for the hour we jammed together – or rather, he played and I tried to follow – I had the feeling for the first time in my life that I too was a "real blues musician"!

And this wasn't some pumped-up ego experience. His natural soulfulness in the particular area where he was a genius had rubbed off on me; that is, it had "ensouled" me in a very special way. I was temporarily transformed. This is an example of the power that soul has, and is why, as I explained in *Awakening the Universal Heart*, being in the presence of a genuine, big-souled spiritual master can be so transformational for us.

Where Do the Gateways into the Soul Lie?

If I ask myself how best to connect with my soul, four ways immediately come to me. The first is choosing to experience deeply whatever is going on inside me at any moment. Thus, mindfulness and soulfulness are close buddies. The second is connecting to the core "is-ness" of what is happening in the world around me, that is, when I am existing in present time (I'll say more about this later). The third is consciously doing what is true for me (I am now writing this book and so I feel connected to my soul right now). The fourth is letting myself connect deeply to what I find beautiful and real and allowing it to enter me. This might include listening to soulful music that I love, or reading literature written by soulful writers, or soulful poetry (Keats, Blake and Wordsworth all precipitate me into the world of soul).

Also, being a rather bad bongo player, I resonate strongly with another of Seyyed Hossein Nasr's remarks, also in *Knowledge and the Sacred*, that "there is much more intelligence and in fact food for thought in the drumbeats of a traditional tribe in Africa than in many a book of modern philosophy"! [15] Certainly, when I was at Oxford University, I met many philosophers, all of whom were very clever people; I learned many things from them and found our mental chatter intellectually stimulating.

However, in retrospect, I cannot think that any of them emanated what I now understand as soul.

In actuality, none of these enormously clever men remotely touched me. I felt they lived in their heads and, even then, that there was a huge difference between knowing about ideas and knowing an idea from inside itself, which I guess is what a truly soulful philosopher is able to do. In my life, I have been privileged to have spent time around some truly soulful spiritual teachers. Some of them uttered few words, but because those words were so impregnated with soul, they had a profoundly transforming effect on me.

Why "soul" and not "our soul"?

I prefer to talk about "soul" rather than "our soul", because while I think we each have our own individual or personal connections with it, essentially only one soul exists.

A few months ago, I had a strong experience of this. I had hiked for several hours to a spot in the Mallorcan hillside overlooking the ocean and as I sat there quietly watching the sun go down, I connected to a deep peace inside myself, which I felt was not so much "my peace", but rather belonged to life itself and was sitting there waiting for me to enter its field. And as I began experiencing this peace, I watched as this quality grew inside me and then slowly morphed into joy. While I was experiencing this joy personally, it didn't feel remotely personal.

How was this possible? Nothing had happened externally in my life to bring this about! In fact, I was facing quite a few upsetting hassles at the time. But then I realized that if we allow ourselves to listen to the life that goes on inside us beneath the surface of our ordinary, everyday awareness, we begin connecting to a domain where true abundance always exists and consequently where soul is to be found. And when we link up with this abundance, we start to realize that our external hassles may not be as big as we often make them out to be, and perhaps they only feel that way because we are not feeding ourselves enough soul food, not exposing ourselves enough to areas where soul is sufficiently concentrated. (Often, when we are in pain, we start to shrink our ensouling capabilities when we actually need to be expanding them.)

I tell you this: when we can touch a sacred place inside ourselves where life is OK exactly the way it is and where we don't feel we always have to be struggling to obtain those goodies we've convinced ourselves we need so as not to feel deprived, a gateway into soul will start opening up that has the capacity quietly to dissolve our deprivations without our doing anything!

We must know soul to be soul

While we all have souls, or rather *are* souls, unless this dimension of ourselves is consciously being activated and we gradually build up our own unique relationship with it (which for each of us is different), *it is as if we don't have soul.* In his book *Original Blessing*, the Catholic priest Matthew Fox puts it like this: "We don't have a soul until we become a field where God is working compassion."[16] And if we don't want to think in God terms – remember I said that we don't need religion to have soul – we can instead say "until we connect with the love and goodness residing in our hearts".

However, as I will be stressing, having soul or giving birth to our soulfulness takes work and whether or not you and I ever become soulful human beings, and, if so, how deeply and strongly, is entirely up to us. In his book *The Life Divine*, Sri Aurobindo tells us:

> As the crust of our outer nature cracks, as the walls of separation break down, the inner fire burns in the heart, the substance of the nature and stuff of consciousness refines to a greater subtlety and purity and the deeper psychic experience becomes possible in this subtler, purer, finer substance; the soul begins to unveil itself...manifesting as the central being which upholds mind and life and body...It takes up its greater function as the guide and ruler of our nature. [17]

Sacred places and wilderness spaces as gateways to soul

Certain spaces and places strongly emanate soul and can touch us deeply if we feel a natural affinity with them. When I visit somewhere special like, say, Chartres Cathedral, or when I meditate over a great master-piece of sacred art, I always feel ensouled. I think sacred places and sacred art reflect the perfection and goodness of life, the harmony and order embodied in the cosmos, and thus their soul force helps us also to connect to beautiful parts inside ourselves, which, sadly, we often spend so much time denying or covering up.

Why do we love wildernesses? The reason is that they contain pure soul food – empty of all the consumerist contamination and dross and trivia that our materialistic society inevitably tries to fill us up with every day.

These beautiful places somehow enable us to let go and unwind and *clean ourselves out*. Thus, they enable a certain purification to take place.

I find that when I am in these big empty places, untouched by so-called "civilization", I can allow myself to be "fed" by life at a whole other level. The extraordinary breakthroughs that can occur for us in wildernesses, when we are alone with ourselves, are always revelations of soul. We remember that it was in the wilderness that Yahweh spoke to Moses from the burning bush and where Jacob dreamed of the heavenly ladder whereby he could make his ascent to God.

Indeed, the fewer things there are around us, the fewer distractions we have, the clearer will be our connection to the sacred dimensions of life. Modern man has too much clutter around him.

Tragic evokers of soul

Tragic experiences may also coax our souls out of hiding in the same way that joyful ones do. In *A Sleep of Prisoners*, the playwright Christopher Fry beautifully described this process:

> *The frozen misery*
> *Of centuries breaks, cracks, begins to move,*
> *The thunder is the thunder of the floes,*
> *The thaw the flood, the upstart spring,*
> *Thank God our time is now when wrong*
> *Comes up to face us everywhere,*
> *Never to leave us 'til we take*
> *The strongest stride of soul*
> *Men ever took.*
> *Affairs are now soul size...*[18]

What I see Fry suggesting is that the old order is now crumbling and falling apart and increasing numbers of us are becoming aware of areas of our lives that do not work and that are soulless. And the effect of seeing this is waking us up.

We are realizing that our old ways of viewing the world and dealing with life have to end ("Affairs are now soul size") and that unless we address our problems from a deeper (soul) perspective – and advance further in this arena than we have ever gone before – nothing is going to change.

The Dark Night of the Soul — and a new dawn

Yes, my friend, suffering can also be a profound awakening catalyst, and there exists a particular crisis, aptly named the "Dark Night of the Soul", which, when plunged into, results in the extinguishing of everything happy and positive in our lives. We find ourselves overcome by the darkest despair and feel that everything about our lives is bleak and hopeless as we are brought face to face with all that is worst about us, all the attributes that ordinarily we try to avoid confronting — such as our selfishness, our anger, our resentments, our greed, our manipulations, our destructiveness, our dishonesty and our vanity — basically, everything that keeps us logged into our old stories! All our camouflages, all our false faces rise up to meet us. What becomes brilliantly illumined for us are those parts of ourselves that we try to conceal not only from ourselves but also from others. The cat is now let out of the bag and this process can be very painful. Often, the journey towards "outing" our true self begins by asking us to "out" and confront our false one!

Therefore, this soul crisis can potentially be very healing, for when our soullessness shows its true face, or when light is shed onto what is dark about us, it offers us the opportunity to do something about it. It opens up a potential space for us to see ourselves as we are, to address these now-emerging shadowy and damaged aspects of ourselves, hopefully in the knowledge that for as long as they are not transformed, we will simply continue to remain rooted in all our old identifications, separations and limitations — basically everything connecting us to our old culture and keeping us attached to the system.

In my own life, I have had to go through quite a few Dark Night experiences, and they were certainly all painful. However, in terms of the growth that resulted, these experiences were most important, for what happens in a Dark Night is that we do a lot of shedding of old skins, that is, we rid ourselves of a lot of old patterns. And this is what desperately needs to happen on our planet. As James George put it: "A new order on Earth will not begin…until we all learn to see the pollution in our own hearts. And that will not happen until many of us, a critical mass, experience with remorse a real change of consciousness." And who knows, my friend, the Coronavirus may well be that necessary consciousness changer, that soul-awakening catalytic force that will bring a new order that much closer to us, for, like it or not, all of us — all of humanity — are currently embarked on a collective journey into a very deep Dark Night.

EXERCISES

- What have you learned about soul as a result of having read this chapter?
- Do you often feel connected to your own soul? If so, how, and what are some of your experiences?
- What personal gateways do you have that lead you to your own soul and do you spend enough time evoking them? If not, do you want to start doing so, and if so, what do you need to do?
- Are you willing to put effort into this?
- Have you ever had a crisis of soul, be it big or small? If so, what happened?
- What do you do or not do in your life to keep soul away?

AFFIRMATIONS

I am a soulful human being and I choose to live my life soulfully.

I choose to honour the soulful me in all I think and feel and do.

I choose to bring soul into all my personal relationships, into my work and into all areas of my daily life.

CHAPTER 6

Gateways into a Soulful Society

Today we face a task we don't know how to accomplish.
Only with a new story can we do so.
— CHARLES EISENSTEIN

Don't be satisfied with stories of how things have
gone with others. Unfold your own myth.
— RUMI

Blindly following ancient customs and
traditions doesn't mean that the dead are alive,
but that the living are dead.
— IBN KHALDUN

Failure of the Counterculture

Some of us in the 1960s had a go at trying to change the world, or "open it up" – bring more soul out of the closet – after the repression and fuddy-duddiness of the 40s and 50s. This was the dawning of the hippie movement and what became known as the "counterculture", characterized by the use of the word "alternative", as in "alternative medicine" or "alternative technology", and by ideas of "turning on, tuning in and dropping out" and "making love, not war". It had a lot of innate soulfulness to it and I identified very much with this movement. I also lived for much of the 1970s and 80s in California, where a strong offshoot of the counterculture known as the human potential movement was also being born. In those days, we used to talk about a wonderful "New Age of Aquarius" where we all believed the heavens would open up to us and that a new society of love and peace was just around the corner. Many women began to find their power and decided to bring it out of the closet and own their sexuality, and it certainly heralded the start of a liberation of sorts.

In retrospect, I think there was something inherently ungrounded about what was happening. We all seemed to forget that life had a dark side to it, and that as, Carl Jung put it: "If you want to find enlightenment, you first have to go down into the Shadow." I think it was our failure to acknowledge the dark side of life – perhaps we didn't then know how – coupled with the naive assumption that "all you needed was love", that lay behind our not "making it". Perhaps our soul force then was not sufficient to dissolve the old structures. Perhaps too, the old culture or the system was not yet as ready as it is now to be relinquished.

And maybe also, the crises we faced at that time were not sufficiently severe and the shocks we received were not great enough to galvanize us into real action. At that time, our climate had not gone as berserk as it has today, nor had the Middle East gone as loco. Terrorism existed, but only quite tamely. Conversely, perhaps we simply didn't try hard enough and all the would-be change agents didn't sufficiently address their own narcissism. Certainly, I plead guilty on this front.

I think the counterculture/new story movement in those days had a great naivety to it, which I again own up to. Yes, there was certainly a strong anti-war movement, with many hippies gathering to try to "discredit the suits", but as Charles Eisenstein wisely pointed out in a lecture, there was not enough coordination between those who chose the "drop out of society and go east" spiritual path and those who chose to attack the system, a strategy that today we are aware is unwise (because the more the system feels itself under siege, the more powerfully it asserts itself).

In addition, there was no cohesive plan of what to put in place of the old story, the result being that the "*ancien régime*" in its many manifestations was given a lot of liberty to fight back, which it did. Some believe this may even have served to strengthen it, since struggle and conflict was, and of course still is, its main lifeblood.

Another way of looking at things is to say that in those days the old story was working a lot better than it is today, as it had not yet entered the phase it is in now where – quite literally – *everything* it stands for is being questioned. In the 60s and 70s, we still believed the many lies the old story told us: for example, the idea that continuous growth was necessary for a healthy economy. It took another half-century for many of us properly to realize how truly fraudulent the system was and how few really profited from it, and that policies meant to benefit us actually gave rise to so many of the evils that are so plainly visible around us today.

Going for Newness

Coming back to today, increasing numbers of us are now seeing that the old ways are simply not working in any area of life, and that the need to create a new culture that works for all people instead of just for a few is not simply a "nice idea" but an absolute evolutionary necessity. Increasingly, more people are seeing that the "it's OK, folks, business will go on as usual" approach is a sure way to encourage the ending of all human life on the planet.

In other words, trying to hold on to a mindset that is becoming increasingly obsolete and irrelevant and which opposes where the flow of life is wanting to go, and hoping that it will still magically refresh and inspire us if we just give it a little tweaking, is cuckoo thinking! As Prince Charles expresses it, again in his excellent book on harmony: "We cannot solve the problems of the twenty-first century with the worldview of the twentieth century."

Dame Ellen MacArthur, who single-handedly sailed around the world, also believes this. In an interview in a newspaper, she told us: "Rather than plugging the holes of a sinking ship, shouldn't we be aiming to build a new one that can sail forever?" That was also the great Buckminster Fuller's approach: "You can never change things by fighting the existing reality. To change something, build a new model that makes the existing one obsolete."

That, my friend, is our great challenge today…

And you and I need to be the builders of this new model. It is not up to "them", whoever "they" may be, to do so. It is up to us. And today, a powerful new zeitgeist or "spirit of the times" is in the air and doing its best to inspire us to move in new directions.

Nations in need of more soul

Most countries need more soul. The poor old UK certainly does. As we have seen, the confusion and chaos over Brexit has merely served to highlight the deep, deep divisions in our society and the ever-widening gap between the haves and have-nots. These problems are certainly not going to be resolved with a "politics as usual" approach. Russia, which still seems to be suffering an inferiority complex after the loss of its empire, also desperately needs a new story. Similarly, what has happened to Africa's deep spiritual traditions? How come so many African nations are being ruled and destroyed by *wetiko*-possessed kleptocrats and tinpot dictators?

China also needs to recover those sources of wisdom which a few centuries ago made it a very great nation.

And of course, the Middle East desperately needs a new story. At one time Islam was the centre of world culture. What has happened that has enabled this noble religion to have become so cruelly hijacked for tamassic purposes? OK, colonialism had a big part to play but we can't blame it for everything, and I think that if Islam does not somehow manage to reform itself and find a new story relevant to where the world as a whole is now moving, it will be to the detriment of us all.

A more soulful politics

We have already touched on the limitations of today's political systems, for which, quite understandably, there has grown up a deep distrust, regardless of what party or ideology the politician belongs to or whether they happen to be from the left, right or centre. I would like to see a more soulful approach emerge whereby in order to qualify for entering politics, potential candidates would be required a) to do inner work on themselves along the lines I will soon be showing you, and b) to go through rigorous tests, and if they prove not to have integrity, to be in any way psychopathic, narcissistic or manipulative, and if their motives for going into politics are not wholly to be about wishing to be of service to their country, they should be debarred from entry.

But if that were the case, perhaps we'd have no punters at all!

A more soulful religion

In the last chapter, I touched on the core aridity and soullessness in so much Christianity today, and its connection to being embedded in a lot of guilt, suffering and damnation. This is rife in our collective consciousness and it affects all of us, even if we don't have a Christian faith, or go to church.

In this model, far too much emphasis is put on worshipping the crucified as opposed to the risen Christ and as I suggested, man is seen as a poor, "fallen" creature, chock-full of "original sin", who not only *should* quite rightly suffer for "not being as perfect as our Heavenly Father is perfect" but also *should* redeem himself by "working from the sweat of his brow", that is, joylessly. More on all this hullaballoo later.

In old-story Christianity, there is a strong split between high (good) and low (bad) and on no account should we reverence our "low" and "sin-filled" bodies! This engenders self-hatred and lies behind why we neglect and at times abuse our physical health and eat and drink to excess.

In a truly soulful or new-story Christianity, we are all originally blessed, not cursed. All parts of us are sacred, including our sexuality and our bodies, and the name of the spiritual game is to follow our hearts, make work our joy, celebrate our creativity and view sin as meaning to deny our true sacredness and engage in activities that are inappropriate for us.

A more soulful psychology

A greater soulfulness is very much needed in my field, psychotherapy, and I am happy to say that it is rapidly emerging. Traditional psychotherapy tells us that we are nothing but our ego selves and that the aim must be to "fix" our ego personality disorders so we can become better adjusted to Krishnamurti's distorted society.

My own work operates from a place of recognizing that while of course our personality disorders need addressing, this needs to be the beginning and not the end of the line. If people want to be truly healthy and integrated, they will also need to work at bringing their soulfulness out of the closet so that their ego can learn to be its faithful servant.

And when this higher soul self starts emerging, less and less will people feel moved to adjust themselves to a society they are coming to see is very much out of kilter. Rather, they will feel moved to try to create a new kind of society that works not just for the few but for the many.

Stan Grof, the "father" of transpersonal psychology, expressed the shift as follows:

> While the traditional model of psychiatry and psychoanalysis is strictly personalistic and biographical, modern consciousness research has added new levels, realms and dimensions and shows the human psyche as being essentially commensurate with the whole universe and all of existence.[19]

Re-envisioning heroism and the meaning of leadership

As we begin expanding our soul awareness, and as more dimensions of life come into play, we gradually come to view many things in a very different light. For example, at present, as I have pointed out, we like to deify rich celebrities or glamorous pop or sports stars – see them as our heroes.

Perhaps our new hero will be the spiritual seeker, inwardly rich, a genuine human being, tender, gentle, wise, quiet perhaps, a seeker after truth, an activist for a better world. No glamour. No need to be in the headlines. No longer so engaged in fighting dragons "out in the world", but rather more concerned with confronting one's own internal ones.

So while the old-style hero does things out of the recognition he will get, the new-style one will do things because they are appropriate.

Similarly, praise will no longer be solely directed towards our old-style celebrities and multimillionaires, as in the old story, but towards all people and all aspects of life. We will praise ourselves and praise animals and nature and praise our friends and praise the person we pass in the street. The shift, then, will be from a culture that is exclusive and likes to put certain people or things down, to one that focuses on elevating all dimensions of life.

From this place, leadership will also be seen from a new perspective. The old model is to lead from in front and instruct others what to do, which actually is discouraging of incentive and therefore inherently disempowering. The new model will be to "lead from behind", creating a space to empower others to come up with their own initiatives so they may find what liberates them. This represents a shift from taking power away from people to enabling them increasingly to stand in their own strength, which is a theme we will explore in more detail later on.

In the new story, we will all have the same human rights whoever we are. Thus we will see a shift away from laws favouring certain people above others, and indeed a moving away from them being solely restricted to persons. Today, the animal rights movement is gaining in power and the environment is also starting to have its rights respected, whereby those who intentionally damage nature – the evils of ecocide – will be liable for prosecution. I celebrate this.

While the old mindset likes to use force to resolve conflicts, the new one will prefer to employ dialogue. While in the rajassic world we want to "have", in the new story we'll prefer to "fuse with" or "be". In the old story it is always "me" first. When soul enters, it will be "we" also. In the old, having abundance is seen solely in financial terms; in the new it will be more about possessing health, wisdom and happiness. (A lot more on this theme also coming up.)

Thus, we'll have a new kind of capitalism motivated by heart and soul instead of by fear and greed, international diplomacy moved by a concern for what is in the best interest of our planet as a whole, as opposed to being conducted solely from the point of view of "what's in it for my country".

But our new culture will be built upon the back of the old, albeit with discernment. It will not be a wholesale rejection of it so much as a going back into it and trying to lift it up to a new level. As we move through this book, this point will be clarified.

Honouring the past

It is therefore important that the new world of emerging soul never responds with hostility to those who still operate along soulless lines. One can disapprove of certain mindsets, yes, and make one's views known. One can take stands for new approaches, do one's best to expose attitudes or lampoon behaviours that are regarded as anti-life and therefore no longer palatable, but what is key is that one must never respond aggressively or violently to the persons involved.

A few years ago I attended a conference where people spoke angrily about whether or not they ought to lynch the CEOs of the large pharmaceutical companies who they felt were committing crimes against the planet. Some animal activists were also talking about bombing those establishments where experiments were being made on animals. This aggression always makes me shudder, as it is so inappropriate. To my way of thinking, those who go around self-righteously bashing bankers or making people out as being wrong for being materialistic are simply showing that they are still very much living out reductionist/destructivist conflicts inside themselves, not raising the quality of life.

Yes, by all means be outraged and indignant, but don't dump your negativity. We don't make a person "good" by telling them they are "bad" or behaving in a hostile way towards them. In other words, we need to resist playing *their* games! I don't believe anybody is bad, deep down, but I do believe people have been subjected to certain experiences that have resulted in certain inherently "anti-life" ways of seeing the world becoming firmly consolidated inside them. And the *wetiko* virus runs deep.

I also regard the approach of trying to convert people as smacking of violence. So, for example, if people meet me and realize they like something about the way I see the world (which occasionally happens) and they want to know more about it and what I do, I will be happy to share some thoughts and perhaps draw their attention to some of my lectures or writings. But not otherwise. I will never try to force my point of view on someone and make them feel wrong if they don't share it, as to my mind, people don't shift properly through force. They shift because they grow more open-minded and come to realize that certain things are not working, either in their own lives or out in the world; consequently they recognize that changes are needed, and gradually, as this recognition grows, it becomes stronger than their resistances.

Satyagraha

I appreciate Gandhi's approach. He never invalidated anyone. Rather, he treated everyone he met with great respect, as he always related from a place of recognizing the divinity or the soulfulness inside them. This approach of recognizing the *atman* or "divine presence" in another was known as *satyagraha*.

So when Gandhi met with the British leaders who had done so much damage to his country, he in no way invalidated their humanity. Rather, he told them he respected and honoured and blessed who they were – which he did – but then added that he hated the way they had treated his countrymen. Thus, he made the important distinction between who a person is and what they might have done.

We can learn much from this approach. The biggest insult is to disparage someone as a human being simply because some of their actions may have been offensive. From a soul perspective – as you will be increasingly seeing as we move through this book – we are all sacred and the more this is recognized, the more this dimension of ourselves will be able to come out of the closet.

An anthem of soul

The main shift we will be seeing, then, will be one leading us out of a domain of scarcity, alienation and separation into a world of greater interconnectedness and abundance.

We will stop defining ourselves solely by *how much we have* (the obsession of the separate self) and instead recognize *how much we are*. Our imagined standing in the world will shift to being determined by how much we can experience ourselves as being an integral part of it.

It follows that the more we feel part of our environment, the less we need to try to possess it. The same of course goes for our relationships. I predict that in the not-too-distant future, when we meet someone for the first time we will no longer enquire as to what they do (so that we might the better pigeonhole them), but rather start asking them what they love or what has most meaning for them.

Our new soulful anthem is beautifully encapsulated in Chief Seattle's famous reply to the president of the United States in 1852, when he was asked if he could buy the Indians' tribal lands:

> The President wishes to buy our land. How can you buy or sell the sky? The idea of buying the land is strange to us. If we do not own the freshness of the air and the sparkle of the water, how can you buy them?
>
> Every part of this earth is sacred to my people. Every shining pine needle, every sandy shore, every mist in the dark woods, every meadow, every humming insect. All are holy in the memory and experience of my people... The rivers are our brothers...so you must give to the rivers the kindness you would give to any brother...This we know, the earth does not belong to man; man belongs to the earth.
>
> All things are connected like the blood that unites us all. We love this earth as a newborn loves its mother's heartbeat, so if we sell you our land, love it as we have loved it...

Whereas the rajassic person sees that the more they give, the less they have, the soulful or sattvic person recognizes that the more they give, the more they receive, and so they know that as they choose to share of themselves and be a space to empower and respect and support all of life around them, so the universe will respond in kind and thus they will be inwardly richer. Henry David Thoreau, an Earth activist crusader nearly two centuries ahead of his time, explained it beautifully in *Walden* when he wrote: "I perceive that we...live this mean life that we do because our vision does not penetrate the surface of things...We think that this is which appears to be...We must learn to reawaken and keep ourselves awake, not by mechanical aids, but by an infinite expectation of the dawn."

Bold visionary thinking

This accords with what the Dutch futurist Fred Polak believed: "Bold visionary thinking is the prerequisite for effective social change." What is therefore required is for more of us to hold powerful new images of how we would like our future to unfold, so I will end this chapter by asking you to imagine a world where:

- We remain always mindful of the significance of soul and of the need to bring it more fully into all areas of our lives.

- We work at opening our hearts more so we can relate to all our fellow human beings with greater kindness, love and compassion.
- We realize that being human includes our willingness to serve the well-being of all life on Earth.
- Nations spend more money on social services, health and education than on building weapons of war.
- We invest our energy more in communicating and cooperating together than in fighting one another.
- Men feel moved to empower and respect women more, and more women come into decision-making positions that are equal to those occupied mainly by men.
- Hunger is abolished completely.
- We shift from a position of wanting to take things from the earth and exploit it, to one of wanting to give to the earth and celebrate it.
- A more humane and enlightened form of capitalism emerges that works for the good of all people, especially the very poor.
- Love replaces indifference and abundance replaces scarcity.
- Every human being can live in freedom and dignity.
- All immigrants are welcomed and integrated into local communities.
- The monster of globalization morphs to a position where we "get" that small is not only beautiful but can also be profitable.
- The rich no longer become so on the backs of the poor.
- The air is pure and we can all drink fresh water.
- We move away from a fascination with the love of power to instead start creating a world where we focus on the power of love.
- We start expanding into our soul lives so that we grow increasingly immune to the virus of *wetiko*.

Let us add Mohamed ElBaradei's words from his book *The Age of Deception*: "Imagine a world where we would settle our differences through diplomacy and not through bombs or bullets...Imagine such a world is in our grasp."[20]

I recently bumped into a poet at a conference and asked her what sort of world she would like to see emerge. She replied instantly that she would like one "where the earth won't be sold to the highest bidder and where profits are no more made from others' toil and where every banker will be an artist in fair play".

I thought that was mighty cool.

■ EXERCISES

- What feelings do you have as a result of having read this chapter? What particularly interested you about it and what do you feel you have learned about yourself from it?
- Are you willing to work with or spend time thinking about the suggestions I just gave you of what is required if we are to have a healthier planet?
- Specifically, do you have any comments on what I said about religion and politics and new ways of viewing heroism?
- How do you deal with people whom you encounter who are very rigid in their views? Is what I have suggested any help to you?

PART TWO

Growing Soul

CHAPTER 7

Gateways into Inner Work

*The destiny of everything that lives is that it should
unfold its own nature to its maximum possibility.
Man is no exception. But he cannot – as a tree
or a flower does – fulfil this destiny automatically.
He is only permitted to become what he is intended
to be when he takes himself in hand, works on himself
and practises ceaselessly to reach perfection.*
— KARLFRIED GRAF DÜRCKHEIM

*We who are heirs of a complex civilization are charged
with one major historical task: to aid the world in
achieving true culture. It is up to us to make the light of a
truly humanitarian culture shine throughout the world.*
— ALBERT SCHWEITZER

Requirements for Transitioning Realities

When Krishnamurti, in one of his lectures, suggested that "really to live requires a great deal of love, a great feeling for silence, a great simplicity with an abundance of experience; it requires a mind capable of thinking that is not bound by prejudice or superstition", he was laying down a few key guidelines for how you and I might best live a more genuine and soulful life.

So this I say to you, my dear friend: if you and I *are* to attempt to live such a life, four things are important. Firstly, we will need to have a sense as to what this new life might entail and if we are really prepared to commit ourselves; secondly, we will need to consider how best we can remain immune from the many glamours and seductions that the old rajassic worlds constantly dangle before us; thirdly – and this is very important – we must find a way to heal ourselves of our emotional wounds, as it is so often these wounds that keep us clamped down into the old culture; and lastly, we must ask: how can we best expand and develop our soulhood?

All of these things require a lot of work on our part. None of them are "givens"; that is, they don't happen of their own accord. Extracting ourselves from our old habits and old attachments needs very specific work, and becoming someone of honesty and integrity doesn't occur just because we fancy it. If we wish to evolve to a place of becoming the solution to the many problems on our planet as opposed to still being their cause, a special kind of labour is required.

Taking responsibility for our evolution

One of the big differences between ourselves and other forms of life on earth, then, is that if you and I are to progress our humanity, we need to take a very conscious hold of our development. It doesn't just happen on its own. To many people the idea of *working on oneself* is a somewhat alien concept, especially to those brought up on the belief that work is only something one goes out to, not in to! However, the truth is that most of the gateways that might lead us into living a more soulful existence are not going to open wide enough for us to pass through unless we take the process of earning our inner living more seriously.

Expanding internally

Yes, my friend, we need to realize not only that we may not be quite as "alive" or self-aware as we might imagine, but also that we thrive on many illusions about ourselves. For example, we may believe that we are a "lovely person" and nothing is wrong with us and we don't need to do this silly thing called "working on ourselves". And if we want our planet to change, then riding a bicycle, using solar energy, giving up using plastics and recycling our trash more efficiently are all that is needed.

I wish they were.

Yes, it is great if, say, we are starting to consume less and are curbing our carbon footprint, no longer use plastic and now put our cardboard and our bottles in the right places to be recycled. However, if we really want to make a genuine difference in the world and be a significant force for change, *the state of our inner world also needs radically to shift, as so much of the damage we do comes from our disordered psyches.* We must learn to heal our emotional wounds and discover how to extricate ourselves from where we are still tied into rajassic values, behaviours and beliefs. We must also learn to create new values, behaviours and beliefs – for I remind you once more that the discombobulated outer state of the planet is a reflection of our own inner topsy-turviness.

14 areas to work on

If we are to make the transition from old to new story, there are 14 main areas that need focusing on. All of them have been significant in my own life, and we will be touching into all of them at different times in this book. They are not arranged in any particular order.

We need to:

1. Address our emotional wounds, as our psychological deficiencies or insufficiencies play a key role in keeping us attached to our old-story mindset.
2. Be aware of the various beliefs, values and, most important, hidden agendas that we hold and which keep us embedded in our past, and then do something about them. All too often, we are wholly unaware of those forces inside us that propel us to do some of the strange things that we do.
3. Recognize our resistances to change and be willing to confront and work with them.
4. Develop a friendlier way to relate to people, and choose more conscious or "awake" people – people more *au fait* with the new story – to spend time with.
5. Expand our consciousness and become more self-aware, which requires that we learn more about contemplation, prayer and meditation.
6. Change many of the ways we live so that less and less about our lifestyles perpetuates the old realities.
7. Discover how to be of service in those areas where we feel we can best make a positive difference.
8. Be increasingly aware of the shams and false stories that our rajassic culture continually tries to instil in us and make us believe are true.
9. Live with a more open heart. It is often our lack of heart that keeps us marooned in the patterns of our past.
10. Be more aware of our dark side – our Shadow – so we no longer suppress it, deny it or project it onto others.

11. Build up our power in the right way, so that instead of being moved to try to control and dominate others, we feel moved to allow others to feel empowered in our presence.
12. Live with more joy, positivity and openness to the beauty of life.
13. Relate to the world of work or the business of earning our outer living from a radically new perspective.
14. Generally work at deepening our soul life so that we may shift from being a "desacralizer" to increasingly having our daily life become our sacred practice.

And all these 14 things are interconnected. Essentially, then, our challenge is to learn to be more open to life – to be more sensitive, to see more acutely, to feel more deeply and ask more questions and speak more wisely, to listen more with our hearts and, in many instances, to live a radically different lifestyle from our current one. We will need different goals and objectives, together with an ability to feel much more grateful for what we already have as opposed to being disappointed about what we feel we don't have.

Choosing to earn our inner living

Self-enquiry is terribly important for all this to come about. The problem with old-story man is that he never asks himself the right questions and so he seldom has much of a clue as to who he really is, believing he is just the images that he and others may have of him. But this is not who we are. Plato understood this and knew the importance of having true self knowledge. "Know thyself", he told us, "and thou shalt know the whole universe."

This inner knowing has two distinct levels. At one level, it is about our becoming more aware of the personality or ego self that we have developed over the years, replete with all its conditioning and various inner agendas. Knowing this self is important as it enables us to be more conscious of our various tendencies, strengths and vulnerabilities and therefore be more mindful of some of our main life challenges.

However, we all have another self which, if we wish to be more fully human, we also need to learn about. I call this our higher soul self and one of the best ways to open up gateways into it is through the act of our inquiring into our true nature – asking ourselves all the time: who am I? Indeed, the more we do so, the more this self will inform us about its deeper dimensionality and therefore start telling us who we *really* are!

Many people whose lives evolve entirely around their ego identities have no knowledge that this other self, which is continually in a state of evolution, exists, as it will probably not have seen the light of day. But I stress once more: if we want to start living in a new way, we will need to work at "outing" it with our intention being that it increasingly becomes the "eye" in us determining how we see the world.

Linking our conscious with our unconscious selves

I regard doing inner work, then, as being *as* important as, if not at times *more* so than outer work, for if we don't have a good relationship between our unconscious and our conscious selves, not only will it interfere with our ability to take proper responsibility for our lives, but it will also impede our ability to start growing soul. As Robert Johnson puts it in his book, aptly named *Inner Work*:

> The disaster of the modern world is all about the complete splitting off of the conscious mind from its roots in the unconscious. All the forms of interaction that nourished our ancestors – dreams, visions, rituals and religious experiences – are largely lost to us today, dismissed by the "modern mind" as primitive or superstitious. In our hubris, we cut ourselves off from our origins in the unconscious and therefore from the deepest part of ourselves…So we live as if we had no unconscious, no soul realm, as if we can live full lives by solely fixating on the material, external world – as if making more money, getting more power, accomplishing more things were all that was important…In fact, we turn our "inner world" into an enemy by negating it.[21]

Thus, we see the plight of many people! Carl Jung also saw that most of our pain and neurosis and physical illness stem from the isolation of our ego minds from the life of spirit inside us. He rightly saw that unless our inner life is effectively lived – and for that to occur, it needs first to be *reached*; as I just said, we need to find gateways leading us into it – we cannot really enjoy, savour, appreciate or have a genuine intimate relationship with the world around us, as we are only ever engaging with its surfaces.

Our unconscious is not just that domain where our repressed memories lie, *it is the creative source of everything that evolves into our conscious mind.* In Johnson's words again:

It is the real source for human creativity; it's the primal matrix out of which our species has evolved a conscious mind. It is the place where the gods live, where our divinity dwells and which, if we are to be the full human beings that each of us in essence truly are, we need to learn how to build the right kind of bridges linking us with it. [21]

So if we wish to get out of our current messes, if we wish to create a happier and healthier outer world for ourselves, a great amount of creativity on all our parts is required, regardless of our profession, and I hope you can see that it is very much about our evolving a more intimate relationship with our unconscious.

For that is the way into soul: exploring these deep subterranean dimensions of ourselves.

Living a symbolic life

"Man", Jung once said, "is in need of a symbolic life. We live too banally, superficially. We need to get meaning out of what happens to us. We need to honour the life of our soul."

What living a "symbolic life" implies for me is trying to understand the deeper significance of everything that comes up or happens for me, be it joyful or painful. For example, when a couple of years ago I needed a serious operation, I didn't see this as "damn awful", which I would have done if my sole organ of perception had been my ego. Rather, I saw it – and still see it – as an opportunity to help me develop some bravery and confront my own precariousness (something I have tended not to do!) as well as to understand more about death and, in so doing, open up in myself a deeper understanding of its intricate connection to life. The result was that I have included a chapter in this book about death as a gateway to soul, which I would not otherwise have been moved to do.

As I write today, I am having a problem with one of my eyes. Its vision is dimming. Thus, I am needing to ask myself: what is it that I am not seeing properly? I am very engaged in this question.

At various times in my life in the past, always when I was experiencing stress, my back would "go out" and I would need to see a chiropractor. I have not needed this treatment now for four years because I have come to realize that the issue was about my needing more symbolic "backbone"; as a result of working on this issue, I think I have now acquired it. As a result, my back no longer needs to "go out".

Seeking to live a symbolic life, therefore, is about stopping living in ways in which we are always dividing what occurs for us into "good" or "bad", which is one of our ego's favourite reductive pastimes. (Often, what is "bad" for the ego self may be positive for the higher soul self, and vice versa!) Instead, we seek to derive significant insights from ordinary, everyday occurrences. One of the beauties of this approach is that we then don't have to seek constant stimulation from things exotic or dramatic – our life can have natural as opposed to artificial spice put into it!

Ralph Waldo Emerson expressed it like this: "Only that which we have within, can we see without. If we meet no gods, it is because we harbour none." And too many of us meet no gods because we've never regarded it as important to find out about our unconscious, or deemed it necessary to explore the world of soul. Put another way, if you and I cannot elicit significance from tiny things – experience, say, the exquisiteness of a sunset, the magic of a powerful storm, the beauty of a baby's smile – it is because we have not yet "brought to life" the deeper domains of our human nature. Our soul life, which also exists in the realms where Emerson's gods dwell, has never been properly excavated.

As a result, our sensibilities are still too coarse to enable us to go through the doorways leading into the subtler worlds where we can appreciate life's deeper meanings. Therefore, those seed qualities of joy and beauty and love and wisdom and truth, which all of us carry inside us as potentials, never properly germinate because we've never put the time and effort into conscientiously watering them.

This needs to change, not only because we are in search of a new story but also because we want more joy, fullness and meaning in our day-to-day existences.

Different Ways of Working

Inner work is not one thing or done in one particular way. It is many things and it can be done in many ways depending upon what is going on in our lives at any time, what level we primarily operate from and what approaches work best for us.

Thus, it can be simple or complex. Because all parts of us are interconnected, we can work on different aspects of ourselves all at the same time. For example, we can work at healing our ego wounds while at the same time focusing on developing our capacity to love at a deeper level.

For one person, inner work may include daily meditation and chronicling all their insights in their diary, while for someone else it may imply focusing intensely on their dreams – listening to the messages that their unconscious dream world is trying to get through to them – and/or working with a psychotherapist. Deep study can also be a very integral part of inner work, Indeed, the close exploration of the spiritual writings given us by the great masters may temporarily transport us through gateways into higher states of consciousness.

Listening to music and allowing its magic to work inside us can also at times be very important. For many years, I worked with a teacher who showed me how different kinds of music address the different chakras or energy centres in our body. So if I wanted, say, to work at opening my heart, listening to Pachelbel's Canon in D would be very helpful, while Beethoven's "Ode to Joy" would be instrumental in helping me keep it open! Similarly, dancing to African drumming music can be helpful if we wish to activate more aliveness inside ourselves.

The power of journal writing

The central feature of my own, personal inner work, and one that I heartily recommend to you here, revolves around keeping a journal that *I have with me at all times*. In it, I write down questions I need to be asking myself, conclusions I come to about things and areas of my inner life I feel need exploring, as well as observations of myself and of others and of the world outside that I feel are of relevance. I also observe what things touch me deeply, how I feel I am doing at any time (am I "on top of my life" or is it "running away with me"?), where I feel my gateways lie, together with new insights regarding some of the prominent patterns or habits I have that especially challenge me.

Journals are an excellent way to practise "standing back" – being insightful observers of ourselves. For example, we can write down: "Ah yes, I observe myself being about to be extravagant" or "Ah yes, I can see my emotionally prickly side being activated" or "Ah yes, I am seeing a part of me that is strongly resistant to something I am about to do and I see I need to listen to this part and what it has to tell me."

The beauty is that when we can stand back and observe aspects of ourselves – certain moods or inclinations or desires – we then potentially have mastery over them as opposed to their controlling us. For example, I have a tendency to be rather impulsive and also to be disorganized.

Because I have worked at standing back and observing myself, I am not only more aware of these traits but I can then choose other ways to be when I observe them starting to surface. I will explore this more in the next chapter.

Journals, and writing more generally, are also a wonderful means to get things off our chest that are weighing heavily on us, as by putting our thoughts and feelings down on paper, we can empty ourselves of what may be cluttering us and we will feel much lighter. For example, if we are angry with someone, we can put all our feelings in a letter: we don't have to send it but the catharsis will have occurred nonetheless.

Journals also help us with things that are puzzling us and where we need to have better understandings. I went through a phase in my life where I needed to do a lot of work around my relationship with my father, and writing down my thoughts and feelings tuned me in much more strongly to my unconscious and enabled many truths to surface and many questions to get answered. It follows that the more insights that emerge from inside ourselves – from our own self-perceptions as opposed to from others – the more potentially transformational they will be for us.

Trusting our own inner knowing

It is important in this work that we gradually come to trust our inner knowing. A musician mate of mine wrote a beautiful song that included these words. I've never forgotten them:

> It's in every one of us to be wise.
> Find your heart, open up both your eyes.
> We can all know everything without ever knowing why.
> It's in every one of us,
> By and by.

I still often sing it (in my rather croaky voice) at some of my retreats. The truth is that inner knowing really *is* in every one of us. We've just got to learn to trust those deeper intuitions that we all have, knowing that the more we try to "feel ourselves" into things, the more this part of ourselves will grow.

Journals, then, are one of the best ways not only to enable us to connect with our lower unconscious but also with our higher one – with all those areas of spiritual wisdom that we don't as yet know we possess, but which are always available to us if we only make the effort to uncover the gateways leading us to them.

Therefore not only can our journals be great gateway openers, but they can also be wonderful sources of useful information, as whenever I come across something that interests me or a quotation that stands out, I like to write it down. In this way my journal is my good friend on many levels, both enabling me to connect more deeply with myself and reminding me to be more aware of what I need to be exploring or working on at any time.

Exploring our beliefs and values

As I have said, an integral part of inner work revolves around seeing which of our beliefs and values are healthy and which are not. It is surprising, if we dig deep, how much prejudice and judgementalism can surface that we had no idea existed.

For example, I had thought that I had expunged homophobia from my heart many moons ago, only to find this was not exactly the case when a gay friend of mine came to stay, bringing his new ultra camp boyfriend with him. This brought up a lot of prejudicial "stuff" still lurking inside me.

However, once I could see it, I could then do something about it. We can't deal with things about ourselves that we don't know exist. In this case, it took the form of my confronting my prejudices head on and then visualizing myself taking them into my heart and "asking" my heart to help dissolve and transform them. (I'll say more about this kind of heart work later on.)

I cite this example as all of us will, at different times, be called to confront attitudes and values within ourselves that we didn't know we still had and that we may not like or approve of. We may also encounter parts of us that don't fully respect people different from ourselves, or parts that may be mean, dishonest, aggressive, critical, wimpy, greedy, manipulative, narcissistic and so on. What is key here is that we observe and so "own" these parts of ourselves, see them as "belonging" to us, as in this way we won't project them out onto others. And even if we observe a serious prejudice inside us, we must never attack or make ourselves wrong for it in the illusion that this will transform it. It won't. It will do the opposite, as the more we invalidate ourselves, the more likely it is that the unwanted pattern will remain! I will elaborate on this point later on.

The importance of meditation

However we choose to work, if we want to know ourselves better, be more conscious, have greater insights, find it easier to make all the lifestyle changes required of us, meditation must be the foundation that underpins everything else. By helping to calm us, it gives us more space to operate and thus, importantly, enables us actually to experience that while we all have bodies, feelings and thoughts, they are not who we really are, and a "higher soul self" really does exist.

By quietening what Eastern teachers like to call our restless "monkey" ego mind (because it is always jumping about all over the place), meditation also allows space for our inner hearts to start opening, as well as being a wonderful antidote to many of the old-story distortions and unhealthy habits and worldviews that we have learned to live by and which are strongly held in place by our restlessness. Indeed, if practised regularly, meditation opens up many new gateways for us and helps purify us of many of our negative emotions.

However, it is not – and never should be – a substitute for other forms of work. For example, we can't meditate ourselves out of trauma, abuse, a bad relationship with our mother or a narcissistic personality disorder. But by giving us more space to "be", meditation can help us create a larger and calmer investigative field in which we can make more progress in trying to work through our problems in these areas.

I recommend you start practising it as soon as possible. There are many venues that teach it, and many good online courses. Just make sure you feel good about the person teaching it.

Different perceptions on inner work

We can use several different metaphors to describe our journey of self-discovery. We can talk about moving out of darkness into light or coming from what is hidden into what is revealed. We can also use the analogy of awakening from sleep and say that in our rajassic or old-story states, we are pretty asleep to who we *really* are!

We can also see inner work as a way of learning to open ourselves up to parts of ourselves that we are ordinarily closed off from and, in the process, widening the orbit of our awareness. This enables us, among other things, to experience common ground with people hailing from cultures very foreign to our own, or to comprehend experiences very different from anything we have ever personally savoured.

In concluding this chapter, I remind you that we can't simply "go for" our "higher" layers unless we will first have resolved some of the difficulties in the "lower" ones – that is, in our ego or in our personality lives. In other words, we must not engage in what my old friend John Wellwood called "spiritual bypassing": that is, believing we can successfully skip over or transcend the many negative patterns that may still live inside us and that, by doing so, they will go away.

Sadly, this is never the case. Everything that has not been properly worked through or integrated has the capacity to trip us up, often when least expected. In other words, we can't properly "graduate" into a new consciousness unless we first discover and work through many of the patterns, habits and beliefs that still attach us to our old selves. A large part of the work ahead, therefore, involves us, metaphorically speaking, examining ourselves under a magnifying glass, where we may also start to realize that we are not just "one person" but that we have a cast of many characters or sub-personalities that live inside us, which somehow all need integrating.

Yes, my friend, you may think that you are just "one person", but you are not. How the lover, the child, the adventurer, the joker, the victim, the socializer, the recluse, the conservative, the mystic, the wild person all get along together inside us is very important. I have spent a lot of my life trying to bring my "jock" closer to my "mystic", to make my "joker" get on better with the "serious part" of me, and to get my "male" and "female" sides to dialogue together more harmoniously.

Don't be under any illusion: none of us come into this world without some kind of wounding or vulnerability. It is an integral part of being a human being. If we do not explore our phobias and complexes and neuroses, find out more about what underlies our resentments and rages – why, say, we still continue to project our bullying father onto all our bosses, feel inadequate in the presence of certain people or remain obsessed with having to be rich – however much we want to live a full and happy life and embrace a new way of being and living, we may find our best endeavours being thwarted.

■ EXERCISES

Ask yourself the question. Who am I? Your answers might start with shallow, obvious statements like "I am a person, a man, a father, a human being, a violinist", etc. and may graduate to deeper responses like "I am part of humanity, cosmic dust, an assembly of atoms, a soul", etc. It can be useful to do this with a partner.

Every two minutes you ask them "Who are you" and let them talk and don't interrupt, and after ten minutes, you swap places and the one being questioned now becomes the interrogator. This exercise will open up many gateways and is to be done often.

- What have you realized about inner work from reading this chapter? I suggest you go over it again slowly and make some notes.
- Are you willing to start using a journal?
- What is going on inside you right now? Sit down in a comfortable chair and take a few deep breaths in and out and calm yourself. Close your eyes and start focusing your attention inside yourself and be aware of your process. Make some notes.
- Ask yourself: how is my body feeling? Stiff, light, heavy, lithe? Observing the world of your body is working with an important gateway into a new story and all too often we ignore it or take it for granted; but its wisdom has much to teach us, because our bodies always have a felt, intuitive sense of what is appropriate for us.
- So open yourself to your body's knowing. Say to it: "Body, what do you have to tell me? Am I treating you properly? Do you need more rest, more exercise, a different kind of food, less alcohol, more fruit, more quiet?"
- As you connect to your body, thank it for being a good friend to you and for supporting all your other activities.
- Now open yourself to your feelings. How are you feeling? Daunted, numb, excited, bored? Make notes and establish a relationship with the world of your feelings.
- Now open yourself to the world of your mind. What are you thinking? Make notes.
- Note down what reading this book is bringing up for you thus far – what you feel your challenges are, how and where you may be stuck in the old story or if maybe you are in a no-man's-land in between stories! Ask yourself: what have I learned so far about myself and about the state of the world? Just let yourself write whatever you feel moved to write, bearing in mind that the more you put into these processes, the more you will get out of them.

- Ask yourself: do I have dreams? Am I willing to observe my dreams? Is this an area that interests me?
- Now look at meditation. Do you already meditate? If not, do you want to learn and, as I suggested, maybe find a class or do an online course? There are many.
- Make some notes as to what you think is most important for you to help you embrace the next step of your journey. For example, do you need to take time off from your job to focus more on your inner work? Or do you need to address some big emotional wound inside you that you think is preventing you from moving forward? Do you need more gentleness or more self-discipline? What do you think you most need in your life at this time? Write it down.

CHAPTER 8

Inner Work in Action

Without zealous work,
deeper meanings will never be found.
—JOHN BENNETT

Self-Reflection

We are now going to venture a bit deeper into the "essence" of inner work. In this chapter I am going to give you a few different samples of it in action, and at the end I will again ask you some key questions, which I would like you to try to answer as fully as possible. I am also going to limit inner work primarily to two main areas: self- examination or self-exploration and journal work, where, as you have just seen, we engage in writing down what we are observing and so learning about ourselves.

Please note that this approach will not take into account if you have severe psychiatric disorders; in that case other kinds of support may be required.

Our focus here, then, will primarily be on the following: how can we start to heal our personality wounds that keep us embedded in the rajassic/tamassic stories? How can we gain more self-knowledge, become more whole and so try to live with greater self-awareness and authenticity?

As I mentioned in the last chapter, working at developing the ability to stand back and observe ourselves objectively is an important part of this process. It gives us much more mastery over our lives, as a) it lets us see our patterns from a space of our not being identified with them, and b) it therefore allows us to choose how we feel or respond to whatever is going on outside of ourselves, as opposed to simply being at its mercy. This is very important. Too many of us live by continually reacting to the outside world all the time – always letting externals dictate things for us. So for example, if someone tells us they like us, we feel good; if they tell us they don't, we feel bad.

This means that we never really feel free to allow our inner life to unfurl from within, and we are always having to manipulate our outer world to get it to affirm us, so we will feel OK. (This pattern, I think, lies behind the "pleaser personality"!)

Choosing a stance of what I'll call *intentional objectivity*, where we stand back from ourselves and observe ourselves, therefore not only gives us the freedom not to react to life all the time, but it also enables us to choose how we operate at any time. So, for example, if we observe ourselves about to say something critical to someone, we can intervene, saying to ourselves: "No, I will not say that. I will choose to say something kind." Conversely, if we see fear emerging from within us, then we "have" it as opposed to it "controlling" us, and we are in a much better position to know how to handle it. Or say someone comes into our orbit who brings up some strong Shadow issue for us – say they are fat and we observe that we can't bear being reminded of the fact that we need to lose weight and so we see some aggression start to come up inside us – we can observe what is being activated and thus we can choose to not project out our negativity onto them. (Much more on this later in the chapter on the Shadow.)

Get it? Self-observation, which improves the more we practise it – and at the end of this chapter, you'll see an exercise on this – means we have more freedom to choose how we relate to our world and therefore how we live our lives at any time. What enormously helps this capacity to observe ourselves is the increased self-awareness and mindfulness that we gain through regular meditation.

Asking for assistance

Sometimes we may feel we need outside help to deal with some of the issues that come up for us – as certain pieces of inner work can be difficult to engage with on our own. If that is the case then we can call help in. It can take the form of our finding someone who we feel is sympathetic to our issues, and is well trained, to guide us and is someone whose aim, we feel, is to help us grow our humanity as opposed to assist us adapt better to the system.

But if we cannot find the right person or if this is too expensive, there are so many workshops out there on so many different topics that one of them is bound to be appropriate. There are also many online training courses on offer, and if you find one that appeals to you, then go for it. It can be very supportive doing inner work alongside others engaged in the same undertaking. I also can be contacted as I teach many seminars on subjects around this book.

If, however, you cannot find anyone or anything out there to assist you, and it is "just you", remember this: whatever it is that we need to be working with at any time will, if we really pay close attention to ourselves and stay connected with our process, begin to surface for us. We may not yet be consciously in touch with our soul, but our soul will always be working from inside us to try to surface for us whatever "it" deems we need to be aware of at any time.

The key thing is that we choose to remain awake to what is "coming up" for us and realize that at different times, different issues will surface vying for our attention. I cannot stress this point strongly enough: namely, that being aware of what is emerging at any time does more to bring transformation into our lives than almost anything. So, for example, if we currently have issues around fear and anxiety, and we make the choice to remain conscious of, rather than numbing out from, feeling these emotions, we are engaging in an important piece of inner work. We might also want to note down our experiences in our journal.

Will to wholeness

Having been engaged in inner work for many years, both on myself and with my clients, what I have learned is that there exists what I will call a natural, intelligent "will" at work that always seeks to move us in the direction of greater health and wholeness, and that the more we make the effort to connect with the deeper parts of ourselves – we can call it our soul, our deeper self or our unconscious – the more we naturally start to draw this "intelligent will" closer to us and the more it will operate on our behalf. Later, I describe this as "having the Force being with us."

A vignette of inner work in operation

I will now give you a little made-up vignette of how inner work might unfurl if we give ourselves time to do it and we start off with no agenda other than choosing to be self-aware and to dedicate ourselves to following our process.

We begin by sitting down in a comfortable chair with our journal on our lap and we close our eyes, focusing our awareness inside ourselves, and simply observe what is going on.

To start with, there may be nothing happening, but as we stay with our experience of this nothingness for a bit, we may observe that it starts having little intimations of a "somethingness" to it, which takes the form of our observing that we are feeling rather numb.

So feeling numb is the point where our inner work begins. We stay experiencing it fully, and most importantly, we *don't* try to analyse it or change it but we accept that this is where we are right now. Too many of us are amateur analysts and it doesn't generally help. I don't recommend self-analysis unless you are really connected to how you function and have some experience of how analysis operates.

I repeat again: allowing ourselves to stay fully experiencing whatever it is we are experiencing is, for me, the golden rule of inner work, and in this instance we are simply observing ourselves feeling numb. In staying with these feelings – not trying to fix them or judge them, or change them, or, as I said, analyse them – we then observe another shift slowly start to occur, and a deeper layer of sensation that had been camouflaged by the numbness now starts to surface.

We now observe that anger is coming up. Interesting! We were feeling numb and now we are feeling angry. I wonder where that has emerged from! We stay with these new feelings, just observing them, again not trying to fix or judge or analyse or act them out or in fact do anything at all.

After perhaps another five to fifteen minutes, we may start to observe that our anger is also starting to shift. It is now morphing into sadness. Ah, sadness! We observe that our hearts feel heavy. So we stay experiencing our sadness/heaviness. If tears want to come up, we allow them. In the course of perhaps 20 minutes, then, we've gone on an inner journey from nothing to numbness to anger to sadness.

Then, as we stay with our sadness, just observing it, we also observe some thoughts begin to come up associated with it, and we remember that that meeting we had with that person four days ago really upset us for some reason and that we must have buried our feelings.

Ah, we ask ourselves, what actually was it that upset us? We may at first remember that we felt rather "put down" by them and that they made us feel small. We realize we made ourselves feel numb because feeling small was painful and so this was our ruse to not feel.

We realize this often happens in our lives and that the slightest thing can easily make us feel small and that is why we are often very disconnected from our feelings. We note this down in our journal and other insights come up as we do so and we jot them down as well.

Moving to betrayal and rejection

The more we write, the more we open up a space for further reflections and therefore for further questions to begin to surface. Is this the real reason why we are upset? Or is something deeper going on? If we really stretch our investigative abilities, what comes up is that what *really* upset us is that we felt that person betrayed us. Yes, this may be an over-the-top response, but it is our particular experience.

The game is really starting to deepen.

So we write down the word "Betrayal" in our journal.

Ah, betrayal! But why should this have such a strong charge? I mean, all the person did was renege on a small promise they made. In seeking to answer that question, we come to realize that actually betrayal looms much larger in our lives than we ever thought. And it always has.

A light pings on inside us. A breakthrough! We remember our father betrayed our mother in having affairs and our mother would always say she would do things for us and then not do them. Goodness, our childhood reeked of betrayal! And then there are also memories of partners betraying us and friends breaking their promises…

Yikes! We jot all this down. No wonder the slightest whiff of betrayal brings up pain. It is about our past, not our present. So *that's* why we "numbed out". When we feel betrayed, we feel rejected and to stop those horrible feelings coming up, we observe that we opt out of feeling altogether. We see we have suddenly unearthed a huge issue for ourselves and we go on writing. As this pattern emerges more and more out of hiding, we observe that we now begin feeling very tired and heavy, which we know is often a sign of our resisting going deeper. Remember what I said earlier about rajassic man's fear of depths and why we devote so much energy to keeping busy and consuming – filling up all those empty spaces inside us so we don't have to feel!

But back to this particular process. We realize that there is a huge "charge" here. We see that that perhaps underlies why we don't trust those at work, why we hang back from being intimate with our friends, why we also don't trust ourselves. Boy oh boy. We've just opened a veritable Pandora's box and it all started out with our just choosing to "stay with" not feeling anything!

Perhaps we can ask for an important dream that night to give us further information. Perhaps we can go to a shaman or a psychotherapist and get further help. Perhaps we just remain with our process. Perhaps we need to write down more of our insights. Here, we need to know that our truly deep issues never get resolved overnight, but always in stages and in different ways. It is therefore really important that we "stay connected to" our inner process and allow it to guide us, as this maintains a sense of continuity. Remember what I said in the last chapter about trusting our inner knowing.

How do we heal?

Often clients ask me: "Serge, OK, I now understand that I have x and y issues but what do I do to heal them? How do my wounds heal?"

My reply is that there is not one thing we do or need to do. It is different for each of us, and as I said, we each have different issues and operate at different levels. Certainly I see this process as always being a great mystery. Some wounds seem to heal quite quickly; some take longer and are much more complex; some we seem to "grow out of" quite organically as we shift to new levels in our lives. Some, on the other hand, never seem to budge. Certainly, I have one particular issue in my life that has never shifted and I have come to see that perhaps I need this particular wound always to remain with me as it keeps me on my toes and thus over the years, I have come to look upon it more as a blessing!

In general, my sense is that if we stay connected to our wounded pattern or patterns and keep asking the right questions and choose to be courageous – that is, be willing to go where our pattern indicates it wants us to go – we will find ourselves gradually beginning to live into our healing. Let me give you an analogy. Imagine we cut ourselves and dirt gets into the wound. Well, the blood will naturally flow and in so doing will wash out certain toxins. At the same time, a "call" will also be made to other areas of our body to summon the appropriate healing antibodies to come to the wounded spot. After a few days, new skin will magically start growing over the wound.

Pretty mysterious, eh? We ourselves "do" nothing. It just happens. Well, we can say the same thing about the healing of wounds to our psyche, only here we perhaps need consciously to really *want* to heal, to really *want* to grow and transform, to choose to connect as strongly as we can to our experiences, and then the "will of life to engage in deeper levels of wholeness" will continue.

Certainly, the healing process is speeded up once our unconscious will have brought to the surface that pattern or those patterns inside us that for a long time had been blocking us and that previously we had had no knowledge of. In other words, once we start seeing an issue for what it is and we then take it into our hearts (this is important and I will explain what I mean in the chapter on the heart), the game begins quite radically to change, as our unconscious is now able to "get to work" in ways it could not do before. Basically, what I am saying, then, is that so long as our "dragons" (our deep wounds) remain in their lair – that is, stay unknown to us and undetected – they can control us. Once we have unearthed or "outed" them, then we can begin having power over them.

Opening to the synchronistic healing power of life

We need to trust, then, in what I like to call *the healing or helping power of life,* or *the inherent magic of life!* The more we do so, the more we start observing that our lives are full of what Carl Jung called synchronicities, otherwise defined as the simultaneous occurrence of events that appear significantly related but have no discernible causal connection.

So relating this to our imaginary inner journey I just chronicled, it might be that after our experience of betrayal, we then have an important dream that we manage to remember and write down, and the next day we happen to bump into a friend in a café who in turn "just happens" to specialize in dream analyses and interprets our dream for us, and so our journey continues and deepens. This so excites us that we go and buy a book on dream analysis and read it avidly so that now we are able to work with our dreams, which, by the way, always speak to us in symbols.

At a certain time in my life, I had a big problem that held me back enormously and I just didn't know what to do about it. At a conference, I "just happened" to find myself sitting next to a woman who was a specialist in exactly my issue. After five sessions of working with her, I was fully released of my pattern. My encountering her, I felt, was not by chance.

Similarly, when eight years ago I met the woman who I am now very happily married to and who I experience as a profound healing presence in my life – a true soul mate – I realized I did not connect with her by chance, but rather because I was at last "ready" to meet a person of her calibre. In other words, certain blockages inside me that, up until then, had prevented me encountering such a person, had now been overcome or sufficiently "worked through" and so the gateway was open! Put simply, when we may not receive things we feel we need, it is often because we have blockages standing in the way. For example, we may not get the job that earns us more money not because we are insufficiently qualified, but because we hold an unconscious belief that tells us we don't deserve to. Work through the belief, see the blockage for what it is, and the gateway will start to open.

What I am suggesting, then, is that the more we draw away from the mundanity of our primarily lived-on-the-surface rajassic mindsets and start intentionally opening ourselves up to our deeper patterns or the deeper mysteries of life, the more we are likely to encounter gateways leading us into dimensions of ourselves that have great healing possibilities.

Asking the universe for help

If we feel we need help, we can also ask for it from the "intelligent universe", for it is always on our side and it can hear our pleas. I certainly regard prayer as being a key part of inner work and often things don't work for us because we miss out on this. In my last book, I devoted a whole chapter to the power of prayer.

So we can say "Dear universe, I am stuck. This big pain pattern has just surfaced for me and I don't know where to go or what to do. Please help me. Please give me the healing I need or the insights I require to heal myself."

The universe *will* respond so long as we really make the effort and our asking is genuine, sincere and done in earnest, even if the response does not always come at once or in the way we might expect. In fact, the more we work at coming to view the universe as being alive and intelligent and our friend and therefore "on our side," and we realize that we are always connected to it, the more we start trusting that whatever we may need from it we will attract towards ourselves.

Outing our hidden agendas

Working at becoming increasingly acquainted with the many agendas operating inside us that determine how we see and function in the world, but which are as yet unknown to us, is therefore very important. It is surprising how many of our actions emerge from beliefs or values inside ourselves that we never knew we held, be they negative or positive.

At one of my retreats where I was teaching people to do journal work, a man announced to me that he had discovered through his writing that the reason why he was a workaholic was because he had a story going on in his head that he could only feel secure if he had £20 million in the bank. "Now I can see this pattern for what it is," he told me, "I realize how absurd it is and I really want to change it, the advantage being that I will then give myself time to do other things in my life but work!"

Never judge yourself

I remind you again never to judge yourself when you discover negative beliefs or bizarre inner agendas existing inside you. The problem is that if we punish ourselves for being the way we are, it will just close us down again and prevent us from doing the necessary transformational work as we'll feel "I am punishing myself enough – there's nothing else I need to do".

OK. Write down three headings in your journal:

- What are my life aims or what do I want from my life?
- What do I believe in or what is really important to me?
- What values are most important to me?

If you answer these questions as honestly and as concretely as you can, you may not only uncover agendas inside you that will leave you pleasantly surprised – "Wow, I never knew I had such an altruistic streak" – but also some that may upset you – "Yes, I have to confess, I see that I *do* take more trouble with people if they are rich and socially well connected than if they are poor and dark-skinned. Oh Gawd!"

Just write down your answers and make objective – but not critical – comments beside them.

Working with stress

Let us now look at how we might work with stress, as it is a big killer today. It may well need working with beyond just going to the doctor and getting tranquillizers to quieten the symptoms.

Often, we can be so out of touch with ourselves that we don't realize we are stressed unless it gets so bad that it can't be ignored. But if we do let ourselves experience it, we can recognize it as a message from our souls informing us that something, somewhere is off-kilter in our lives.

As would-be Sherlock Holmeses of our inner worlds, we can start using our journal as a magnifying glass to focus on ourselves in order to ask ourselves why we are stressed. Here, it is important that we look at various responses. Is it because of the way we are living? Is it because we are not listening to our hearts? Are we trying to do too much? Do we perhaps have a tyrant "sub-personality" inside ourselves who pushes us too hard?

Or are we stressed because we are working in a soulless environment that doesn't give us permission to be ourselves? Or is it that our lives are loveless and our resultant loneliness is making us anxious?

What changes are needed? If we ask ourselves the right question, our psyches will know the answer; and part of the work is connecting to the place where that answer exists.

▨ EXERCISE to let go of regrets

Many of us have regrets in life and hanging on to them can often block us and be a source of stress, so here's a simple exercise we can work at to let our regrets go.

Close your eyes and relax. Select something that you greatly regret. What is it? Is it something you did or did not do, or something that just happened to you through no fault of your own? When did it occur?

How do you feel about it? Connect strongly to your feelings. Feel the regret fully and ask yourself: what does my regret do to me? In other words, what is the price I pay for holding on to it?

Now think: what would it mean if I could begin to let it go? Begin readying yourself to let the regret pass out of your system. Lie down and visualize yourself surrendering the regret. If it is located in your heart, just imagine that with each breath out you are letting go more of it. Say to yourself: "With each exhalation, more of my regret about situation x is flowing out of my system and with each in-breath I am filling myself with good energy to fill the old empty space."

You can also use the four elements of fire, water, earth and air to help you release your regret. You can either use one element that you feel more drawn to, or if you wish, all four. With **fire**, write down your regret on a piece of paper and then throw it on the fire. As you watch it burn, imagine the regret burning up inside you. With **water**, stand under a shower and imagine the water is flowing through you, flushing out your regret; see it going into the drain and being washed away for good. With

earth, lie down on the grass and imagine giving your regret to Mother Earth and it passing out of you into the soil. With **air**, stand outside on a windy day and say: "Please, wind, blow my regret out of me."

Another technique is to dance the regret out. In my groups I like to use African drumming music for this, where I get people to dance vigorously and chaotically scream out their regret with the thought that "I am releasing this regret from anywhere in my body where it might have got trapped." Afterwards, I light some candles and ask people to lie down and I may play some gentle flute music and ask people to say to themselves: "I am freeing myself of my regret. It is moving out of my system and I am feeling more and more liberated."

It is also surprising how much we can accomplish simply by talking to ourselves, saying things like "I see it does me no good to carry this regret. I choose to banish it from my system right this moment."

That said, it is also important that we have patience. Many old patterns keeping us fixated in some of the "rajassic glamours" that we explored earlier, and which may have "lived" with us for much of our lives, may take time to exit from our systems. This is why, as you will be seeing in later chapters, it is so important that we learn to cultivate the soil of our inner being and choose to plant seeds inside us composed of qualities like love, truth, joy and beauty, for when these seeds begin sprouting, we will have inside us a soil that is increasingly non-conducive to having negative patterns living there.

Working on our relationships

If we wish our intimate relationships to remain fresh and flowing and if we wish them to evolve and be more soulful, we may also need to work on them with our partner, which means always taking the time to discuss things openly, especially if issues come up that may cause conflict.

Sadly, in many old-story relationships, where depth and honesty tend not to be high priorities, this doesn't happen enough. There is the mistaken belief that if we talk honestly about difficult things, it will be "too much" for the other to bear, and so the relationship will break up. In truth, relationships break up because important things *don't* get talked about and get brushed under the carpet.

If both partners can come from that "symbolic life stance" I spoke of earlier, problems and difficulties can be viewed not as obstacles but as potential gateways for transformations to occur. I think the deeper purpose of intimacy is to be there to help our partner with their evolutionary challenges and to allow them to assist us with ours.

My experience is that through close relationships, we not only confront what is worst about ourselves, but also what is best. Having had many extremely dramatic relationships earlier in my life – with women who would bring up many of my unresolved emotional issues – I now look back with a certain fondness, as I learned so much about my many negative patterns at that time and the insights I got could not have been obtained in any other way.

Yes, my dear friend, many relationships go awry because we think that if we love someone, that in itself is enough. This is an illusion. Here are five of the more challenging issues that can come up between couples and which tend to not get resolved unless specifically worked on.

1. We try to "do" our relationship along old-story lines; that is, too unconsciously, which in today's climate probably won't work, for "the times they are a-changin"! We need to work at finding how to bring more consciousness into what we have together.
2. Both partners, even if they have similar aims, may operate at different levels and move at different tempos. Again, these differences need voicing and both partners may need to work at discovering how to flow better together, how to find common ground, which again can only happen through honest, open discussion.
3. One can lose one's own sense of self in a relationship (an experience more common in women) and so may need help to reclaim it. This is especially a liability if one partner is very controlling and tries to possess the other. Again, honest, open discussion is required, with each partner saying what they feel they need of the other.
4. Couples can get caught up in "blame games": "If only you would change, all would be fine." Each partner needs to realize that *they* may be the one who needs to change, and *then* all will be fine!
5. Couples often don't experience enough joy together, as both partners bring too many of their own issues around scarcity, suffering and separation to the relationship table. This serves powerfully to extinguish passion. Both sides need to acknowledge this and work at new ways to interact together, including trying to do more fun and creative things with one another.

Working with scarcity

Some of us have a strong "charge" with the issue of scarcity, which, as we have seen, is an integral part of the old-story mindset. Therefore, however hard we try, we never seem to have enough love, money, health or fun! We are always struggling in our lives.

Working on this issue via our journal writing, we may perhaps come to see that "poverty consciousness" or not-enough-ness runs through all strands of our life and that it also constituted the predominant mindset of our family while growing up. In other words, we realize that the story we were raised with was soaked in impoverishment, with everyone around us always moaning about how terrible the world was and how there was never enough of anything. Thus, the world of our childhood was one where glasses were always half empty.

So, having seen this, what can we do about it?

Plenty of things. First, we recognize that we want to change this debilitating pattern. We might go and read books by people who write about abundant consciousness to give us a new intellectual felt sense about it. We might also seek out the company of people who exude *joie de vivre* and positivity and who feel inwardly rich, for as I have already pointed out, we can always learn a lot from being in these kinds of people's presence. We might also want to go out into nature and admire beautiful vistas, or listen to music that connects us to the beauty and magnificence of life. We can talk to the universe and again ask for its help, and we can meditate on abundance and create an affirmation for ourselves, such as *"I live in a sufficient world where there is an abundance of everything that I need."*

We can also close our eyes, go inside and ask our unconscious what other strategies it may have in mind for us, as very often the processes that we imaginatively find ourselves creating for ourselves work much better than the ones given us by others.

So please always be adventurous and trust that, as you continue to familiarize yourself with the landscape of your unconscious, it will always send you promptings of what it is you need for your greater health and wholeness at any time. And also what you don't need!

The question here is about our being willing to take the time and effort to connect with our inner life and to listen to the way it wishes to communicate with us.

Deep memory work

But all this may not be enough to shift certain patterns. Intimations of a deficient world may still come creeping back strongly and we may begin to suspect that our experiences of scarcity have deeper origins. Perhaps we are called to confront earlier memories of impoverishment that have nothing to do with anything we have ever experienced in this life. How so?

It is interesting that the deeper teachings in all the great world religions all talk about reincarnation. There is an almost universal human belief in this as a concept, and it is certainly one way of understanding and explaining the sense that we sometimes have of carrying very deep memories, not only of experiences from this life but also from other earlier lives or incarnations. It certainly follows that *the more we aspire to ascend into the higher soul echelons of our humanity, the deeper we are often called to descend into our blockages or unworked-through chunks of karma; these may relate to past difficulties or traumas in this life or, in this way of thinking, our previous lives.*

All this is not an issue if we live shallow and superficial lives. If we don't aim high, we're not called to go deep. I'll tell you a story about a woman I worked with many years ago in my capacity as a past-life psychotherapist.

A case history of impoverishment

This very loving and deeply good human being felt utterly enveloped in a shroud of scarcity. She seemed to have set up her life to ensure that nothing "good" ever happened to her, financially, emotionally or in any other sense. However, she had managed to convert her sense of impoverishment into good works; she was deeply concerned with the problems of poverty in the world and had helped set up an aid agency in Yemen to address this. Neither inner work nor traditional psychotherapy did much for her. Her issues, it seemed, had little to do with past experiences in this life.

She was sent to me and I did some deep memory work with her. In one session, she was able to touch into an old memory of a life where she lived in a part of the world where everyone – including her – had died of a famine. In a subsequent session, a further trauma came up, of an incarnation where she lost her only child to hunger. Her experiences felt so real, she told me, that they could have happened yesterday.

The issue of not-enough-ness or deprivation was consequently deeply programmed into her genetic memories. In subsequent sessions, she did a lot of screaming and releasing, and very slowly her blockages, or sense of deficiency, began to melt and new gateways began opening for her that hitherto had always been closed.

This took the form of a lot of "good" things starting to happen. In the course of six months, she was awarded a medal for her services to humanity, she was left money by an aunt who had died and she met a man who loved her and whom she subsequently married. In addition, her health began improving quite dramatically and a lingering depression that had hovered around for many years began evaporating.

Would these "openings" have happened if she had just worked on her own and not done deep memory release work? My reply is that I don't think so.

I tell you this story as all too often what keeps us marooned in our old mindsets, and prevents us from experiencing the abundance in our lives that our hearts yearn for, is the fact that we may be more deeply wounded than we realize. Identities that we take on – such as "the loner", "the loser" or "the victim" – often are our way of trying to cope.

It is only when our old blocked patterns are allowed to drain away that many of us feel sufficiently released to be able to smell the flowers, appreciate the value of play and thus allow ourselves to enjoy the truly good and natural things of life.

Human collective wounding

I would like to take this idea one stage further and remind you once more that as you and I are all part of humanity, and as humanity as a whole is wounded, it makes sense to consider that each of us carries some of those wounds. My old friend Roger Woolger puts it like this in his book *Other Lives, Other Selves*: "It is as though each of us is born with a portion of the unfinished business of humanity at large, which it is our personal and karmic responsibility to complete in one way or other."[22]

The historian Chris Bache says much the same thing in *Dark Night, Early Dawn: Steps to a Deep Ecology of Mind*:

> Each of us carries within us the collective diseases of our time. If our society
> is ill, each of us has a share in its illness, some more than others, perhaps,
> but we are all implicated in varying degrees…Thus, if our society is racist,
> sexist, violent, consumed by greed, these diseases live in the collective soul.

Just as a disease that lives in a physical body may manifest itself by attaching to one particular organ, so a disease in our collective soul may manifest itself disproportionately in the lives of specific individuals.[23]

This is the kind of *deeper* healing work that many of us are challenged to take on if we are truly to start making a difference in the world.

EXERCISES

- Describe the story or stories handed down to you when you were a young child growing up. What kind of values were you given? How were you taught to see the world? With humility or disdain, with fear or love? What beliefs were handed down to you and did you "swallow" them? Was it very "old-story" or was there some soul around? Were you made to feel good about yourself as you grew up or did you feel you had to conform to the story that your parents or caregivers subscribed to and so you had to put the "real you" in the closet? Answer this in detail.
- Was there conflict in your early life in any way? Was there any trauma? If so, what was it centred on and how do you think it affected you?
- On a scale of 1 to 10, how attached to your past do you feel you are today? If a lot, how does this make you feel in terms of your desire to "go for" new ways of living? If very little, how well do you think this bodes for you successfully moving forward into a more soulful, new story?
- How did you then, and how do you today, "get on" with your parents" story?
- What do you most appreciate about yourself?
- What do you find hardest to accept about yourself?
- From the perspective of desiring to make certain radical changes in your life, what does this imply and what challenges does this bring up for you?
- What changes would you like to see happen in your life? Would you like a more loving partner, a new, more "holistic" career or lifestyle? Do you want to learn to meditate, to downsize, do more to help other people, become more "green", etc.? Write down all the changes you'd like to see happen.

EXERCISE for objective self-viewing

This is a very important exercise and needs to be practised regularly.

- Sit down quietly on a chair and be aware that you have a body. How does it feel? Stiff? Supple? Tired, etc.? Perhaps low in energy or high in vital energy. Just observe.
- Be aware, then, that while you have a body, you can observe it.
- Now, do the same thing with your feelings. How are you feeling? Happy? Sad? Just be aware. Spend some time looking inside at your feelings. Just observe.
- Now look at your thoughts. What are you thinking about right now?
- Now be aware of something very important: namely, that you can both have feelings and thoughts, *and* you can stand apart from them and observe them. Same with your body.
- So be aware that it is possible both to *observe* and also *to disidentify* from what is going on inside you, i.e., that while you have a body and feelings and thoughts, you can also stand back and observe what is going on with them.
- So, for example, if you observe yourself feeling angry, you don't necessarily have to act it out.
- You can observe it. I observe I feel angry right now.
- Say to yourself, "I know I have a body and feelings and thoughts, but who I am – who the true me is – is neither my body, feelings nor thoughts."
- "Who I am, who the true me is, is the one who can observe me, observe how parts of me manifest, observe how I feel and think and what the state of my body is, at any time."
- So, for example, if you know you have a grumpy side (meaning you can easily get into slagging people off) or a side that is too free with money (meaning you can spend it too promiscuously) or a very judgemental side (meaning you can be very critical), then you can observe these parts of you or these "sub-personalities" when they emerge, and thus they don't have to be acted out or they don't have to run you, in that you can choose to stand back and not activate them.
- If you can observe whatever is going on inside you at any time, you can be the master of your life, for you now have choice as to what course of action you take in any particular situation.

(Most people live their lives at the mercy of whatever aspect of them happens to be driving them at the time.)

- Let us do this once more.
- Be aware you have a body, feelings and a mind.
- Observe each of them separately and what is going on with them.
- Now stand back and identify with the observer and say to yourself, "I have a body, I have feelings and thoughts but who I am is not my body or how I feel or what is going on in my mind at any time."
- *"Who I am or who the true me is, is the one observing me, so who I am is the observer."*
- So say to yourself once more: 'I have a body, I have feelings and thoughts but who I am is not my body, feelings and thoughts. Who I am is the me that observes them. This me is changeless and timeless."
- "I choose to live as the Observer me, the me that does not change as I go about my daily life, and from this observing-of-me place, I can live my life much more intentionally as I now can choose how I operate and relate to people and choose how I respond to what is going on in the world around me."
- "I needn't always react to my outer world as I used to! I am ME."

EXERCISE to connect to the universe

- This can either be done quietly in a meditative setting or out of doors if you have nature around you.
- Close your eyes and be aware that soul is everywhere. It is in you and me and in trees and bees and in the sky and animals and the earth.
- If you have a dog or cat, be aware that animals also have souls and look at them from that perspective. If trees are around you, be aware that they too have souls. You can talk to them: "Hey tree, I see your aliveness. I acknowledge your beingness. Let me receive nourishment from you."
- Now close your eyes and be aware of the soulfulness of all life and that you are connected to it as well as being a tiny speck within it.
- Affirm your interconnectedness with all of life.

This exercise will be developed further in subsequent chapters.

CHAPTER 9

Daily Life as a Gateway to Sacred Practice

To the poet, the philosopher, to the saint, all things are friendly and sacred, all days holy, all men divine.
— RALPH WALDO EMERSON

Every single person is sacred. Sacred means special, precious, a treasure of true beauty. That means you.
— AMY LEIGH MERCREE

Living Our Daily Life as a Sacred Practice

Let us now get down to the real nitty-gritty. Our challenge is simply this: how do you and I get to live our daily lives so that instead of our being a desacralizer – a scrubber away or a destroyer of soul – we instead become a re-sacralizer, a restorer of it?

While there are 15 specific things that I will outline here to help you in your mission, having our lives be a sacred practice is essentially about how much care, reverence and awareness we are able to bring into whatever it is that we happen to be experiencing or engaging in at any time, be it what is going on inside ourselves or outside in our environment.

Of course, it is possible to grow our sacred self or our soul life away from the world by avoiding or escaping from it, and this used to be man's spiritual path in the past, when initiates would go and work at their trans-formations in temples, jungles and caves undisturbed by civilization and its discontents.

While this way of growing soul is certainly valid, it is no longer relevant as a path for the twenty-first century, for the simple reason that it excludes society, and today the most important thing is that we be effective change agents or ensoulers of the culture around us, especially in those areas where soul has been most stripped away.

So instead of, as in the past, learning about our soul self by retiring from the world's many discontents, we are being asked to recover soul in their very heart – in our banks and boardrooms, in our Londons and New Yorks, our Parises and Rio de Janeiros, in our families and friendships – in whatever areas of society we happen to be interacting with at any time.

In other words, every aspect of our everyday life – from brushing our teeth to preparing a meal or taking the dog for a walk, from spending time with a friend or partner to organizing our finances – becomes a potential soul-awakening practice. So when I prepared a lovely fruit salad for breakfast this morning, I chose first to thank the fruit for being there to give me sustenance and I did my cutting up of it very carefully. Then, when I worked with two clients, I chose to be as present and as connected to their higher purposes as possible. When I took myself for a run late this afternoon, I chose to bring the quality of joy into my exercise. When, later on, I worked with my wife to change the sheets on our bed, I chose to bring care and awareness even into this minuscule task.

All of this brings sacred space into expression and so changes the fabric of the space around us.

I tell you these things because the way many of us unknowingly desacralize is by our not putting enough care or awareness into what we do. We do things unconsciously or unthinkingly. We live our daily lives too sloppily, wholly unaware of the kind of negative energy we might be giving out and how pollutive it might be.

Living our daily lives as our sacred practice, then, is all about choosing to bring care and integrity and heart into whatever we do – yes, even into the tiny things! – and the more of our "observer self" we include, the easier this is! Among other things, this means that we try not to operate reactively or see that there is nothing subtly manipulative in what we do. We seek to share our blessings and speak our truth and we wish our world well and we praise people instead of blaming or reducing them (which we can do through our thoughts as well as through our actions.) If we live in this way, our own soul light brightens and we gradually grow in our capacity to be effective ensoulers of the environment around us.

We have to recognize, then, that little things carefully done – a vase of flowers beautifully arranged, a meal cooked with love, a garden watered with mindfulness, a lecture delivered with care – are in fact big things; and, realizing this, we can choose to stand firm in our full humanity right in the middle of the rajassic and tamassic realities not only feeling immune from their often negative influences, but also having a transformational effect upon them.

In effect, this means that we can choose to regard everything that comes our way – be they disappointments, losses, illnesses and crises, or good fortune, gifts and successes – as opportunities to further work on ourselves so we can grow more fully into being who we truly are, and in so doing create more sacred space around us. This is what happens if we take care to live our lives symbolically, which we discussed in Chapter 7.

Here are those 15 specific things that will support us on our mission:

❶ Live more mindfully

This is key. As I've just pointed out, what primarily characterizes rajassic and tamassic man is his mindlessness or unconsciousness leading to his capacity to desacralize, which is precisely what the system encourages and feeds on, and what allows our planet to be despoiled.

And a big antidote is mindfulness – becoming more aware of what is, being more conscious of the consequences of our thoughts and actions and choosing to live with greater precision with regard to whatever we happen to be engaging with at any time. The more mindful we are, the more we inhabit observer consciousness and as we have seen, the more mastery we have over the way we live, and thus the less susceptible we become to the many negative and seductive pulls of the rajassic and tamassic worlds.

However, becoming mindful does not come in a day; we need to work at gradually developing it. Another way to describe living our daily life as a sacred practice means we try to bring a meditative or a contemplative spirit into everything we engage with.

▒ EXERCISE

Ask yourself: do I need to be more mindful? Do I have mastery over my life and do I operate from a still place (even if there is a lot going on), or am I always rushing about anxiously? What would be the benefit of my doing mindfulness or meditation training? What are three things I can do to help me be more mindful? Write them down.

▒ AFFIRMATION

I choose to live my life with greater mindfulness.

② Eat more healthily

The kind of food we put into ourselves is very important and has a powerful effect on the way we think and feel as well as the quality of energy available to us. In the words of Goethe: "*Man ist was man isst*", meaning "We are what we eat." Put simply, rich food – too much red meat and a lot of sweet things, additives and alcohol – is eminently conducive to mindless rajassic and tamassic states. As is fast food.

The consciousness we put into the way we eat is also very important. At Findhorn, I was taught always to bless the food on my plate and thank it for being there for me, and to eat slowly and savour my food as opposed to gulping it down.

It is of course well known that the more healthily we eat, and the more natural our diet – vegetables and fruit, ideally in season and maybe grown near where we live – the healthier we will be. Unlike some things in life, over which we have little control, we can choose to eat healthily and it will affect our lives very radically if we do so. It will also incline us to be more mindful and hence more open to new ways of looking at the world.

EXERCISE

How do you relate to food? Make some notes. Are any neurotic patterns being injected into your relationship with food? Do you overeat or are you always on some kind of diet? Do you have a healthy diet? Are you addicted to certain kinds of food? If your eating habits are unhealthy, write down some simple guidelines for yourself that you can use to change them, as well as guidelines for the kind of diet your inner self (that you are starting now to develop) is informing you would be good for you to have.

AFFIRMATION

I choose to bless my food and at all times only put healthy food into my body.

③ Look after your body

"If anything is sacred, the human body is sacred," Walt Whitman told us, and I fully agree. It is our true sacred temple and as well as needing to have the right food put into it, it also needs looking after – much better than many of us do. (Rajassic man, who so often lives in his head, can be dismissive of his body, only returning to remember it exists when he has sex!)

It is easy to take our bodies for granted and to ignore and mistreat them, or not exercise them properly; conversely, we sometimes also turn them into ridiculous shapes to satisfy our narcissistic desires. All bodies are different and we need to get to know our own and be more intimate with it, become more aware of its strengths and vulnerabilities and the particular kind of food and exercise it requires. If we look after the physical side of our lives, our body will look after us!

EXERCISE

How would you evaluate your relationship with your body? Is it good or not good? How would you rate your ability to care for your body out of 10? Is there anything you feel it needs and which you are not giving it? For example, do you need to sleep for longer, do more exercise, do yoga or tai chi, not stress it so much, have a better diet, etc.? Make a list. What are five things you can specifically do differently that will honour your body?

AFFIRMATION

I have a body that I value and cherish. I choose to listen to it, respect and honour it and work at always deepening my relationship with it.

4 Do a sport you love

Doing a sport we love and committing to it can be an immensely soulful activity. (Think of those many stories of kids on the street in gangs who have been rescued from a life of crime by taking up, say, boxing or football.)

In this arena, I was very fortunate; my father, who had been an athlete, used to take me for runs when I was a little boy and I haven't looked back since then. I represented my university in three different sports and it put me in a good space for academic work. Today, I still view staying physically fit as a matter of great importance and for six days a week, I always make room in my schedule either to play tennis, bicycle or swim. It is never a burden and always a delight and I think it is a myth that as we get older, we should do less exercise. Sport gives us many things in addition to exercise. It can enable us, if we so wish, to practise stretching ourselves beyond our old parameters of what we consider comfortable. In tennis, I always play to try to win, not because I have to beat my opponent, but because I like to do my very best – access states of excellence. On many occasions, even if I have lost, as long as I have touched into that mysteriously mystical place that players call "the zone", in my mind I will have won, and that always makes me feel happy. Therefore, I like playing against opponents who will test me and stretch me, for if I can be stretched physically, it also helps me expand metaphysically. If the sport we choose is a team one, it teaches us the virtues of cooperation and ensuring that our ego self is subservient to what is in the best interest of the larger whole. For all these reasons, I see sport very much as a soul-expanding exercise.

If we do a sport we love (it's no good doing one we don't!) it keeps us fit, produces endorphins that give us joy, and can wrench us out of our old comfort zones and at times take us into very mystical places. Certainly, if I look at my own life, one of the most powerful ways of accessing soul, finding my bliss and keeping "spiritually fit" has been through sport. It has also served to soften me and make me more flexible generally, which is why I so highly recommend it.

EXERCISE

Do you do a sport? If not, why not? Are you willing to make more space in your life for sport and for finding one that gives you pleasure? (If so, you may well find that you are giving up activities that do not serve you anyway.) How might your life change if you made a commitment to finding and engaging in a sport you like?

AFFIRMATION

I choose to devote time and energy into taking up (or carrying on with) a sport I love and doing it passionately.

⑤ Treat everyone you meet with integrity and kindness

How we relate to those around us is always a question of choice, and in the old rajassic story we often treat other people in terms of whether we think they see the world through the same lens as ourselves, or whether we consider them "important" to us or not. Thus, we are always putting people into boxes (class, religion, nationality, cleverness, etc.), which does not allow us to view them either intelligently or kindly. Either they are "above" us or "below" us, "our kind of person" or "not our kind of person". Thus, we never really *see* them.

This needs to change and these old boxes we slot people into need to be broken open. Whoever someone is, be they a king or a pauper, we need to relate to them in a kindly, positive and respectful way. The Dalai Lama once said that if there is one thing required to help heal our world, it lies in our choice to treat our fellow human beings kindly. This theme will be further developed in the chapter on friendship.

EXERCISE

How do you treat people in general? Do you make an effort? Are you interested in them and do you treat them kindly, or do you slot them into boxes of one kind or another? Make notes. Are there any areas here where you feel you need to change? If so, write down these changes and also how you think you can best implement them.

AFFIRMATION

I choose to relate to everyone I meet from a place of cheerful and unconditional respect and goodwill.

6 Consume less and conserve more

Consuming, as I have already pointed out, is something that many of us indulge in excessively. It is encouraged by the system, which prefers us to be consumers as opposed to human beings. Consuming, therefore, intrudes into all areas of our lives, even into our relationships, where we can also gobble each other up!

What underlies this habit is our insufficient appreciation of what we have – not sufficiently recognizing or respecting something's or someone's preciousness – with the result that we get tired of things or people easily, and we want to get rid of them so we can have something new and which we feel is better. This attitude of "we can just chuck it away" needs changing.

What is the antidote? It is more self-awareness. More mindfulness, which in turn leads to a greater desire to conserve. We need to cultivate more appreciation and gratitude towards what we have together with a willingness to give up our casual "let's just throw it away and get something new" attitudes.

EXERCISE

Are you more of a consumer than a conserver? If so, what changes are needed in your life to tone down your excesses? What areas of your life can you bring the spirit of greater conservation into? Write them down. What can you do to help you make the shift?

I choose to live as a conserver, not a consumer.

❼ Recycle, don't dump

This links in with my last point. Rajassic/tamassic man is a notable dumper of waste, whether it be physical or emotional. It is all symptomatic of unconscious or mindless living and is why our planet has become so polluted, in every sense.

Just as we need to sort out our physical waste and put it in the correct recycling bins, so we need to do the same recycling process with our emotions. We must stop dumping our pain, anger or resentments onto others and instead work them through inside ourselves. Let us find out how to turn our anxiety into kindly concern or our anger into love. People don't need to be filled up with our emotional garbage any more than our oceans need all the hundreds of thousands of tons of plastic we've carelessly chucked into them, which gets eaten by the fish and then comes back into us when we in turn eat those fish.

If we start acknowledging our carelessness, then we have the choice to transform these habits – and behave more mindfully. Remember: man and planet are interconnected. Stop dumping.

■ **EXERCISE**

Ask yourself: how do you treat your physical and emotional waste? Do you dump or recycle? If the former, how can you change this, and if the latter, do you recycle *carefully* enough? Make notes on what you can do to make changes in this area.

■ **AFFIRMATION**

I choose to take great care in the recycling of both my physical and my emotional waste.

❽ Cultivate gratitude

Experiencing gratitude is so important that I will continue to stress this quality throughout this book. The more we cultivate it, the more we begin appreciating not only what we already have, but also the richness and beauty of the life that is all around us.

Because too many of us view ourselves and our world from within too small a radius, we often tend to take for granted and to exclude the many blessings in our lives, while at the same time we are always comparing ourselves with others – seeing them as richer, prettier, younger, cleverer than us, which is inherently depleting and disempowering not only for us, but also for others (people around us can feel the force of our thoughts). For you and me to feel gratitude, we need to be open to experiencing the inherent generosity of the universe, which also helps open us up to its healing power.

I practise gratitude as an everyday mantra. It is my daily prayer. I say: "Thank you, great universe, for all the many blessings in my life," and then I list them, feeling each of them in turn and allowing my heart to take in how fortunate I am in that I have good friends, good health, enough food, a roof over my head, a profession I like and that earns me money.

Saying thank you to the universe makes my heart feel full. It connects me to the experience of life's abundance. Too many people today only emphasize what is wrong with everything and hence can be much too prone to opening the gateways leading to despair and desolation.

Recently a dear friend of mine had a stroke. Many of us went to commiserate with him. "Please don't feel sorry for me," he told us. "I am very fortunate. I have had a good life and I am continuing to do so. Now a few things have changed and certain things I could do, I now can't. I accept this and I am so grateful that I still have all my mental faculties and actually am even more grateful for the life I still have, now I realize that I nearly lost it." *That* for me is true gratitude.

EXERCISE

Are you grateful for the life you have or do you give too much focus to the life you feel you don't have or should have? In your journal, write down ten things you are grateful for and then spend some time feeling gratitude for each of them. Let it really sink in and feel your way all around this quality with your imagination. Take time with this exercise. It is very powerful and you will feel very good having done it. It is especially important to do if for any reason you feel dispirited.

AFFIRMATION

I am grateful for the gift of my life and I choose to live with as much appreciation of it as possible.

⑨ Never do harm

So much of what the rajassic and tamassic mindsets encourage and stand for does harm. Wars do harm. Hate and prejudice and bigotry and scapegoating and narrow-mindedness and fascism and fanaticism do harm. Projecting our dark side onto others does harm. Stupidity and mindlessness do harm.

If we are to stand for anything, it must be to be agents of harmlessness, to stand for peace in the world, goodwill to our fellow human beings and respect towards our planet. We need to understand that living from a place of harmlessness is very powerful and creates a spirit of love and goodwill that can spread. Being harmless is not being ineffectual. It is the very opposite.

▊ EXERCISE

Look carefully at your life and ask yourself: is there anything I do that is harmful? If so, what is it? Remembering that looks can kill or cure, ask yourself: do I hold any harmful attitudes or values? Does my work do harm in any way? Do I harm those I love because I am not sensitive enough? Most important, do I harm myself by not taking sufficient care of myself and by neglecting the world of soul?

Then ask yourself: what can I do to live more harmlessly? Write down eight things and then spend time visualizing yourself doing them.

▊ AFFIRMATION

I choose to live from a place of harmlessness that imbues everything I think and feel and do.

⑩ Cultivate prayer

We have already looked at the importance of prayer. "More things are wrought by prayer than this world dreams of," says the dying King Arthur in Tennyson's *Morte d'Arthur*. And I fully agree. Prayer, which at one level is simply focused positive thought, can – if, as I emphasized, we truly work at connecting to the source we are opening our hearts up to – achieve a huge amount.

As we have established, prayer is the process of intentionally making a connection with a higher source, which in turn opens up gateways to the soulful worlds. I repeat once more here: we can pray for ourselves; we can pray for other people, and we can pray for the world, either generally (e.g., "I ask that there be more peace in the world") or more specifically (e.g., "I ask that help be sent to people living in that particular village that has been buried in a landslide"). The beauty of prayer is that it serves to deepen our connection with higher sources of energy and so helps liberate us from the stranglehold of our egocentricity; and in so doing brings us closer to our soul self.

Many times in my life I have found myself in difficult situations and I have prayed and have felt gateways begin to open for me. It is best to not be too specific in what we ask for but rather request that what transpires should simply be in the best interest of whatever or whoever we are praying for. I say this because we might pray that someone we love doesn't die of their disease, when perhaps death is precisely what their souls are requiring.

Personally, I have always found set prayers in prayerbooks unhelpful because of all the rigmarole about compulsory religion that they were associated with at school.

EXERCISE

Is there something that you need or that is troubling you? If so, quieten down, experience yourself reaching out beyond your personal boundaries to the larger life around you – to what you might call "God" or "Higher Power" or "Source" or the "Cosmos" or "Infinite Love and Intelligence" – and just put your needs out there.

Perhaps start with asking for what you feel you require personally, then think of someone you know who needs help and ask that help be given to them, and then think what the world around you requires and pray for more love or more peace, or specifically – if this is something you feel strongly about – that there be greater harmony between nations. We might pray for those agendas that are especially dear to us. While someone who works with conflict resolution might pray for peace, an environmental activist might pray that extractivists wake up and realize the folly of their ways.

AFFIRMATION

I pray for abundance in my life and for greater abundance in the lives of all human beings.

⑪ Have animals around you

Life on Earth has many "kingdoms" and all of them have souls. As we have seen, there is soul in trees and flowers, streams and oceans, stones and crystals, and very much in animals. They can be hugely important gateways for us.

The relationship between ourselves and animals as fellow inhabitants of our planet is particularly special because they can be wonderful friends to us as well as teaching us a great deal about how to live and how to love. I have a particular connection with dogs and my love for my little King Charles spaniel has a great capacity to open my heart.

Just as loving one person can help open our hearts to holding all of humanity in an affectionate embrace, so loving a particular animal can also help open us up to appreciating all animals; and goodness me, this is so needed today. The extractivist mindset is so closed to the animal kingdom; it is utterly unconcerned over how much our overfishing is depleting the fish stocks in the oceans, or how much global warming is threatening the lives of polar bears, or how the greed to sell ivory is resulting in elephants and rhinoceroses becoming endangered species, or how the destruction of our rainforests is threatening the habitat of the wildlife that lives there.

I am reminded of a magical dolphin who many years ago used to live off the Irish coast. People with mental disorders would go and swim with it, and they would become healed through being in its playful presence. My sister went to swim with this dolphin and said it was one of the most significant experiences in her life.

I suggest that if you don't have an animal living with you, you perhaps consider getting one. The truth is that we need them and they need us; as they are an integral part of our planet's ecology and, the more species we allow to die out, the more our planet's health is threatened.

▨ EXERCISE

What is your relationship with animals? Are they important in your life? Do you have a pet or pets? If so, do you feel you have a good relationship with them? If you don't, is there an animal you would like to have, and would you be willing to make an effort to get that animal?

▨ AFFIRMATION

I choose to embrace the animal kingdom and hold all animals lovingly inside my heart.

⑫ Stay informed as to what is happening in the world

This is important. If our daily life is to be our sacred practice, we need to keep ourselves informed about what is going on in the world around us and not play the role of the ostrich who buries its head in the sand saying, "It is all too horrible, I can't bear to look."

This is the escapist way. It is also defeatist. It says: "I can't make a difference to life, so why should I bother to acquaint myself with what is happening in it?" Choosing not to be in the know simply allows the controlling forces of the system to continue to exercise power over us. The better informed we are – and here, we need to take trouble and ensure our news is not the false or biased news that seems to be increasingly prevalent today – the less likely we are to be overly affected by some of the more negative currents swirling around us.

▨ EXERCISE

How informed are you of what is happening in the world? Do you put enough effort into this? Are you willing to put in more effort to keep abreast of world news? Make notes.

▨ AFFIRMATION

I choose always to keep myself informed about what is going on in the world around me.

⑬ Feed your soul with what delights your heart

We have already looked at the politics of ensoulment and how important it is that this deeper dimension of ourselves be effectively fed. As a result, we must never ignore the importance of not only making space to engage with what delights us, but also of working at expanding the surfaces of our being so that more of the world that before used to exist *outside* us now resides *inside* us: this means that there is not only more to enjoy in life but also greater capacity on our part to do so.

One of our challenges, therefore, is to move away from a tendency to over-focus on doing things that we feel we *should* do (which, as you will be seeing, often comes from a guilt about really enjoying ourselves) towards instead giving ourselves time to partake in activities that we *love* doing.

Sometimes these two can link up. Right now, for example, I am spending many hours each day finding that what I *should* be doing – that is, completing this book – is also what I am *enjoying* doing, so I am finding that writing is good nourishment for both my heart and my soul. We will be exploring this issue in more detail as we follow the next chapters through the book.

EXERCISE

Ask yourself: am I sufficiently feeding my soul with what makes my heart sing? If so, how? Write down all the things you are doing and ask yourself if there are even more things you can do. If so, write them down as well. If you are not nourishing yourself in this way, then why not? Write down some things you can do to rectify this situation.

AFFIRMATION

I choose to feed my soul with activities that make my heart sing.

14 Choose the company of people wiser or more awake than yourself

This is so important as too many of us spend too long in the company of people just like us, narrow and one-dimensional, modelling old-story viewpoints, and so we are always having the same conventional and often uninteresting conversations where our old prejudices and limitations are continually being reflected back to us. In such environments, it is difficult to grow soul.

We need, therefore, to seek out the company of people who will stretch, challenge and inspire us and constantly remind us, through their example, to be more curious about the world around us, that there may be more to it than meets the eye, and many more enjoyable, meaningful and creative things that we can do with our lives.

EXERCISE

Do you spend enough time in the company of people wiser or more awake than you? Would you like to? If so, what can you do to bring this about and what do you feel the consequences would be?

AFFIRMATION

I choose to spend more time in the company of those more enlightened than myself in order that I might learn from them.

⑮ Be generous and allow in the generosity of the universe

Life, at its core, is inordinately generous. Just look at nature and observe how seeds travel in the wind and replant themselves everywhere at no cost, or the way fruit trees give of their produce to us without any demands. No interest is asked of us.

If pears and apples and oranges do demand anything in return, it is that we savour them; and similarly, flowers might require that we appreciate their beauty and don't pollute the Earth that they grow from. For me, this is a good model for how we also are challenged to live, namely, to be open and willing to give and share of ourselves, especially if we have particular gifts or qualities in excess.

However, it is equally important that we learn to receive and thus allow ourselves to take in the generosity of the universe, a) because it enables others to experience the gift of giving – and it really is a gift – and b) because it allows us to keep our tally in balance. People who don't let themselves receive often allow themselves to feel depleted and when that sets in, victimhood can often beckon!

My experience is that rajassic/tamassic man often has a problem with both giving and receiving. (Remember what I said about scarcity and poverty consciousness?) He doesn't tune in to life's inherent fruitfulness. He doesn't understand or trust in the idea that what we throw out on the waters of life will come back to us many times over. Rather, he is scared that if he gives he won't have enough left for himself; and by the same token, he is also afraid of opening up to life and receiving because he doesn't trust that good things will flow towards him. This pattern underlies many of our "substitute" behaviours that we looked at earlier.

On the other hand, people who are able and willing to give and receive in a generous-hearted way will find that the universe will flow through them and work for them, and their lives will become rich in very many ways.

▮ EXERCISE

Look at yourself. How do you relate to what I have just said? Are you generous? Are you a "giver"? Do you feel good sharing, or giving things to others? Or do you hold back? Also, ask yourself: how good are you at receiving? Which are you better at? Are any changes needed in this arena? If so, write them down and see what would be required on your part in order to implement them.

■ AFFIRMATION

I live in a generous universe and I choose to share my generosity with others and be open to receive theirs in return.

Choose to live abundantly

If we can manage all of the above and bring soul into these various areas of our lives, then we are truly living our daily lives as a sacred practice, which in turn means that we feel pretty full or pretty abundant for most of the time. Furthermore, this abundance has nothing whatsoever to do with our old-story (rajassic/tamassic) understanding of the word, which is all about living extravagantly, having the best food and wines, the top hotels, expensive holidays, all the money to do whatever we want.

Extravagance is very different from abundance. The reason why we desire all that razzamatazz is because we are probably not getting the "real thing". Many of those who spend millions on houses and yachts and travelling to exotic corners of the world and holding parties in extraordinary areas of the planet, to show everyone how rich and important they are, often feel compelled to have all this pantomime as a substitute for not feeling abundant inwardly, for not feeling good enough, which is generally a result of not having enough soul in their lives. (I do understand this as over the years, I have had several such people as my clients!)

From a sacred or soul perspective, we can have all the material assets we desire, we can have servants bow and scrape to us, we can eat in five-star restaurants every day, fly first class to any destination we desire and exercise power as head of some prestigious organization; but if our inner world is all higgledy-piggledy, if we are not at peace with ourselves, if we only live on life's surfaces, if we don't surround ourselves with good people who understand and love us, if we find it hard to accept and feel good about who we are, in no way are we living an abundant life. We are just someone with plenty of money who at a deep level feels impoverished and covers it up with a lot of outer stimulation.

I like what Joseph Campbell, the great mythologist, once said in an interview when asked about how the 1929 crash affected him. "I didn't feel poor," he said, "I just didn't have any money. People were so good and kind to each other at that time. Life felt very vibrant." *That* for me is abundance.

But don't get me wrong. I am not saying that we have to be poor and can't be wealthy to be abundant; this is certainly not the case, and as you will be seeing later, I have nothing against material wealth so long as it is earned honestly. Rather, I am suggesting that genuine abundance comes from the choice and ability to live a soulful life, full of joy, creativity, love, laughter, thoughtfulness and meaning, where we share of ourselves and work on our blockages instead of repressing them or allowing them to fester.

There's nothing sacrificial about this kind of life, as all we are giving up is what we don't need and what prevents our deeper humanity from being able to emerge. The sacrifice is *not* living this way.

EXERCISE

Be aware of where your life is abundant, as you understand the meaning of this word thus far. Write down all the areas where you experience abundance and then also sense where or how you feel you block it. Then write down what you feel you need to work at, in order to have more genuine abundance in your life.

AFFIRMATION

I choose to bring the spirit of abundance into all areas of my life.

CHAPTER 10

Gateways to the Heart

A heart filled with love is like a phoenix
that no cage can imprison.
— RUMI

The present threat to mankind's survival can be
removed only by a revolutionary change of heart
in individual human beings.
— ARNOLD TOYNBEE

The Alchemical Properties of the Heart

It is now time to explore what I have described as being absolutely central to living our lives in a sacred fashion and our ability to feel abundant: namely, having an open and unobstructed heart.

When our inner hearts begin to wake up and we increasingly start seeing life through their lens, everything changes. Not only do the pathways leading to soul become more clearly demarcated, but our capacity both for productive inner work and for leading a joyful and creative outer life become greatly enhanced.

I see our hearts as being that dimension of ourselves that has true alchemical properties and so is capable of turning our "base metal" (greed, selfishness, arrogance) into "gold" (altruism, selflessness, humility). Conversely, if we are experiencing a lot of pain, anger or hostility and we feed these emotions into our hearts – that is, we open our hearts up to what we are feeling – they have the capacity, as it were, to "gobble our negativity up" and purify and transmute it. The great Sufi poet Rumi understood this perfectly and informed us that "through love" (a key expression of heart) "all pain turns into medicine". This is why the more we bring our heart into our inner work, including all our writing in our journals, as well as into the living of our outer life, the easier it will be to embrace all 15 of the points that we looked at in the last chapter.

Opening the heart

One of the main reasons why our rajassic/tamassic realities are so heartless and why our world today has become so desacralized (or de-heartened) is because the domain of the heart is seldom given any significance. The old story – the system – utterly negates it. At school, for example, we are taught to exercise our rational minds, not our hearts, and this tradition is continued at our universities. Thus many of us learn over the years to shove the tender, feeling side of our lives into our closets, to regard it as unimportant. This certainly was the case with me. The more lacking in heart we are, the more likely we are to be in thrall to the system.

When we take steps to activate our hearts, however, what we observe is that many of our best human qualities are suddenly given the opportunity to emerge into the light of day, often enabling quite significant shifts in our lives to start to happen. So, for example, when the courage inside our heart starts to peek through, much of our fear dissipates; similarly, when we touch into our love, our indifference to human suffering vanishes. My experience is that it is through our hearts being open that we can best hear the voices of our souls.

This is why if our hearts are damaged or dysfunctional, or, as is the case with many of us, have simply not yet begun opening, we are barred from connecting to large chunks of our humanity, and so we remain marooned in our old-story mindsets where our separative self continues ruling the roost. Even if a few filaments of joy or love or kindness or truth or other potentially "higher-order" qualities manage to percolate through, they will never be of a particularly high quality.

Having myself been on a "path of heart" for the last 40 years, and having taught many retreats on how best to awaken it, my experience is that as people's hearts start opening and as their deeper nature of love and compassion begins showing through, this is always accompanied by an improvement in their physical, emotional, mental and spiritual health.

As our hearts open more and as our sensitivities grow, we may also find ourselves becoming increasingly aware of the many evils and injustices that exist around us, which previously we had blocked ourselves off from. This can often make us feel very sad – for example, we may find ourselves tuning in to the consciousness of what it is like to be homeless and have addiction issues, or a refugee who has lost everything, or a woman who has been gang-raped. I am particularly appalled by the heartless and inauthentic face of politics. How much this face would change, I muse, if politicians only saw the necessity to work at opening their hearts and recognizing the importance of becoming more rounded and developed human beings. Sadly, this is not happening.

Only with heart can we truly begin to reconcile opposites and start befriending life. To think we can shift from a state of insufficiency to one of sufficiency or from scarcity to the experience of true abundance of being, without having some degree of open-heartedness, is like believing we can play tennis without a racket! In Antoine de Saint-Exupéry's wise words: "It is only with the heart that one can see rightly. What is essential is invisible to the eye."

The Heart Math Institute

With heart, we can sense into life's essence; we can see many things that our rational mind on its own will miss. The Latin word for heart is *cor*; if we choose to "follow our heart", we are allowing ourselves to be guided by the *core* of who we are – or by an "us" that is connected to our souls and that is wise, can see things much more clearly, and consequently is far better equipped to know how best to operate at any given moment.

In America, the Heart Math Institute has made a deep study of the heart, and scientists working there have recently discovered that it actually possesses a brain of its own and therefore has its own unique "field of intelligence". In their words: "When the heart rhythm patterns are coherent, the neural information sent to the brain facilitates its cortical function and the effect is experienced as heightened clarity, better physical health, improved decision-making and increased creativity."

The heart, then, is not just a metaphor. It is an actual information-processing centre, with all the body's functions dependent upon it. When activated, it gives us the keys to living a fulfilling life, and the electro-magnetic fields it generates are transmitted like radio waves, which, if coherent, can uplift and if chaotic can depress the environment around us.

That is why, when we are around people whose presence pulls us down, we can be assured that their hearts are either shut down or not in good working order.

Heart bequeaths mastery

When our hearts are functioning well, we can not only think more clearly, but also feel much better, act more efficiently and relate to others more effectively. We are more incisive, more intuitive, more visionary, more mindful, more capable of going right to the core of whatever it is we are seeking to explore – all important attributes for the successful emergence of a more compassionate culture.

Not only does the heart not fuzz out the mind (this is "false news" propagated by those who fear the heart's power) but on the contrary, it does much to complement it. When intuition and logic fuse – or when our hearts and minds work together cooperatively – we are at our most effective. As Osho, an Indian sage of the twentieth century, explains:

> The mind is only a servant. The master is the heart…all that is valuable comes out of the heart and it is the only possibility for you to be bridged with your being…When you have a heart that is alive, your mind's quality will also change. Then you can go to the mind; you can function through the mind. The heart will give you a feeling that you are a master.

In other words, when we start opening our hearts, we also begin connecting with the deeper dimensions of our minds, with the result that our mental faculties are also enhanced. And at one level, what is mastery if not the sense that we are all grounded in and belong to the cosmos, that we feel naturally empowered in our being and that we all have a life purpose to fulfil, together with a responsibility to treat our fellow human beings and our planet with respect? Here, it links in with abundance.

People who genuinely feel masterful don't need to put on a show of being tough, nor do they feel pulled to denigrate others, or threatened by other people's success. Having heart, then, enables us to be much more fully connected to who we really are, to the world of our *being* – to our true innerness. We are much more positive; we feel much more whole. We also find ourselves much more connected to the natural world (as opposed just to the societal one) and one of the many consequences is that we emit an aura of strength, which others pick up on and respect. Martin Luther King wrote a great deal about the relationship between the head and the heart and came to the conclusion that what lay behind many people's mental rigidity or their lack of real intellectual vigour (a characteristic of many an "old-story" person) was actually a closed or inactive heart.

My experience of people whose hearts and minds have evolved and grown more integrated over time is that their days of operating out of a "black or white" or "either/or" mindset have come to an end. In addition, open-hearted men and women feel they have less and less to prove and tend to be much more invested in wanting to support others as opposed to proclaiming their own wonderfulness. (The open heart is a wonderful antidote to the narcissistic wound!). When we can begin feeling with our intellects and thinking with our hearts, the gateways into soul begin opening quite rapidly.

Can you see, my friend, how the opening of our hearts is a central ingredient to almost everything that we have been discussing thus far?

Yes, the path into our higher soul self is for many of us through our hearts.

Heart as our "secret weapon"

I like to see the heart as being humanity's great secret weapon of mass construction! I say this because with heart we have the capacity to make enormous differences in the world, and those men and women who have achieved important breakthroughs in their various fields, or who have done significant things to help make the world a better place, have always been people with heart.

I remind you once more: the reason why heart gets such a negative press from the rajassic and tamassic worlds, and why big-hearted people are often referred to demeaningly, is simply because heart presence, just like soul presence, is regarded as a direct threat. Generally, the accusation against big-hearted people is that they tend to be all soppy and sentimental.

In actuality, this is a myth. Nothing could be further from the truth. An open heart makes for power. Open-hearted people tend to be naturally caring and compassionate. Interestingly, it is when our hearts are closed that we can incline towards soppiness.

Yes, my friend, the reason why you and I need open and awake hearts is because *this gives us huge strength*. I will develop this theme in more detail in my next chapter, but here let me quote you something that that great visionary and futurist Pierre Teilhard de Chardin says in his book *The Future of Man*: "There is more power inside the awakened heart than inside the atomic bomb."

So seek out people who already have a lot of heart. It can be very empowering for you. I've said this before but it is so important. In the same way that we can catch people's colds or pick up their depression, so we can also "catch" heart qualities, as everyone emits a radiation of where "they are at".

Be open to both "peak" and "trough" experiences

Our hearts, just like any other muscle, need exercising, and they get a great "workout" when we are present at some extraordinary event like, say, the birth of our child, or if we fall deeply in love or have some transcendent or "peak" experience where we draw close to the upper reaches of our soul nature, as all experiences that feed our soul also nourish our hearts. Our challenge is to see if we can keep our hearts open and ensure they do not snap shut after the specific experience has left us.

As you have seen in the chapter on soul, painful experiences can also have strong heart-awakening effects, and when we are going through them, it is important that we allow ourselves to *experience fully* what is happening for us: that is, take our suffering deeply into our hearts and not try to "numb out" to shut down our feelings.

If you can consciously engage with your heart as you do the journal work we have looked at, it will be much more effective. I say this because our hearts are built to assist us in the journey of becoming more fully human, and they are therefore able not only to absorb our pain but, as we have just seen, to also transmute and recycle it. So the more we allow ourselves to have strong feelings – be they joyful or painful – the more these can serve as a "food" to nourish and thus exercise and stretch our hearts.

Indeed, anything or everything that touches us deeply may serve as a heart-opening catalyst. A few weeks ago I visited a very old and dear friend in hospital dying of cancer, and seeing his poor body wasting away, ravaged by this brutal disease, wrenched my heart open. I loved him so much that it hurt. *We all need at times to love until it hurts, as that stretches our hearts.*

Stretch your heart

So just as intellectually we may stretch our minds through study, so we can also do the same to our hearts through embracing qualities like love, kindness, compassion and joy.

However, in doing things that *stretch* our hearts, we must take care not to *strain* them, for while stretching expands, straining damages and can close the heart down. The kind of things that strain our hearts are exhausting ourselves, stressing ourselves, staying attached to our misery, indulging in being depressed, engaging in excess struggle (which our egos like to do to prove to us how good they are at overcoming obstacles), or drawing people into our lives who suck our energy and try to use us!

Heart attacks don't come out of our hearts being well exercised, they come out of the opposite. Jung made a remark to the effect that "any part of ourselves we do not own becomes our enemy"; we can speculate, therefore, that the fact that sometimes our own hearts choose to attack us may well be their way of showing us that they exist, and that they are demanding greater recognition and better care!

Care for your heart

We need to care for our hearts at all levels. This includes respecting their physical dimensionality through the right diet and regular exercise that we enjoy, as well as not engaging in toxic activities like smoking, excessive drinking or taking stimulant drugs.

We care for their emotional dimensions by choosing to engage with and deal with our feelings as opposed to suppressing them. Opening up to divine levels of consciousness is also hugely important. In Jung's words: "The approach to the numinous is the real therapy. And as much as you attain the numinous experience, you are released from the curse of pathology." In other words, the more soul we have, the less neurosis. I will be returning to this theme later on.

Engaging in regular meditation is another important "heart food" (as important as regular watering is for flowers). If too much static is going on inside us, our hearts prefer to hide away, for they also have a vulnerable side to them and need protecting, and are not going to "open up" unless it is safe to do so. The more we take care of our hearts, the stronger and fuller they become and the more we can then use them to help care for parts of ourselves also in need of healing. And hearts delight in this. For example, when in my psychotherapy practice I work with someone's "wounded child", I may ask them to imagine they are taking this wounded part of themselves into their inner hearts and feel it being surrounded by love and compassion. Conversely, I may ask them to imagine bringing heart presence into areas of themselves that may be hurting. In working with the spiritual heart, I may ask people to imagine that their God, or Love, resides in their hearts or – even better – to visualize themselves residing in the heart of God's Love!

Service your heart

Our hearts also love to be of service, and so finding a cause that touches us and evokes our passion and then committing to that cause is a source of great delight for them. (I often think a great many of our malaises today, including boredom, anxiety and depression, comes about because our hearts are not being sufficiently used in this way!)

Having a relationship with someone who knows how to love us and who challenges us to open up and love them is another very important heart food. But, as I will be stressing in the chapter on friendship, our challenge is to open our hearts not only to those who are especially special to us, but to regard every person we come across in our daily lives as special. This is not only empowering for them but it also does wonders for our own heart.

Each of us needs to find his or her particular heart "reconnectors". Often, they lie in things that we love doing and which are true for us. Our hearts also delight in being fed titbits by the mind. I am currently rereading *War and Peace* (which I do every 20 years or so) and, as I have Russian blood, my heart is absolutely delighted by it. I know myself well enough to know that it always opens when I am working with someone, when I am hanging out with my darling daughter, when I am meditating or am hiking out in nature. Today was a beautiful day and I took time off writing this book this afternoon to go to the beach, bringing with me the *Lyrical Ballads* by Coleridge and Wordsworth. Reading them and lying in the warm sun, my heart sang.

The Importance of Love

Hearts are best associated with the quality of love. The Russian philosopher Pitirim A. Sorokin in his great book *The ways and power of Love,* suggested that "[l]ove is the most powerful educational force for the ennoblement of humanity" and I couldn't agree more. Indeed, doing things to activate its greater emergence in our lives naturally has a profound effect upon our hearts.

Our problem is not that there isn't enough love in the world – actually there is plenty – but that believing in the old stories, we don't know how to generate a sufficient *quality* of it; that is, the kind of love that both heals and ennobles. Talking about higher-grade love, Sorokin goes on to tell us:

> Love is a life-giving force, necessary for physical, mental and moral
> health. It is the most powerful antidote against criminal, morbid and
> suicidal tendencies, against hate, fear and psychoneurosis...By its very
> nature love is goodness itself. Therefore, it makes our lives noble and

good…Where there is love, there is no coercion, where there is coercion, there is no love. And the greater the love, the greater the freedom.[24]

So close your eyes, sit back and imagine yourself being that love. If humanity could only learn to awaken this deeper love, the rajassic and tamassic realities would evaporate in a puff of smoke.

EXERCISE to get to know your heart

Sit on a chair with your back straight. Close your eyes and consciously choose to connect to your heart, and by this I mean your inner heart right in the middle of your chest, not your actual physical heart.

It is helpful if you put your hands over your inner heart and imagine a pair of lungs inside it. Quietly breathe in and out for a minute or so, all the time focusing your full awareness on your heart.

Be aware that your inner heart is your best friend and is where your soul speaks to you. Affirm your desire to link ever more deeply to it. So speak to it – say: "Heart, I choose to bring you much more fully into my life. I wish to be guided much more by your love and wisdom. I am sorry if for whatever reason, I have ignored you or marginalized you. I thank you for all you do for me in regulating so much of my life."

Now spend a little time feeling gratitude towards your heart. You may feel a warmth begin to come over you, or a feeling of softness or tenderness. If so, allow it. Allow anything hard within you gradually to unclench and soften. Stay in that tender place and visualize what it would be like if you treated yourself more tenderly and less harshly. Do this exercise once in the morning and once at night. It can be especially powerful if you do it outside in nature.

EXERCISE to connect with the quality of love

Hands on heart again, breathe in and out through the lungs you've planted inside your inner heart. Be aware that love lives inside it and ask it to reveal that quality to you. Now imagine a time in your life when you felt a lot of love and bring that memory into the present.

Speak to your heart – say: "I choose to allow the love inside you to come forth and pervade all of my being." Feel yourself giving love to yourself. If there is some part of you that you do not accept, for example, your "angry child", your "loner" or the you that can be selfish, or perhaps some aspect of how you look, imagine you are embracing that part of you with love and allow your heart to grow bigger and bigger until it infuses all of you. Say to yourself: "I choose to rest in the heart of love and bring love into all those parts of me I exclude or refuse to accept."

Then think of someone you know who needs some healing or love sent to them, imagine your heart opening and see yourself beaming love towards them. Then think of someone else and do the same thing, and be aware that the more love you give out, the more love will come back to you.

Close your eyes and now visualize yourself spending a whole day doing all the things you do – getting up in the morning, dressing, eating breakfast, going to work, meeting people – from a heart place. Be very specific in imagining all the small details of this. This is a powerful process to create new sacred patterns in your life.

EXERCISE to bring healing heart energy to your body

Find some gentle music that you like and which you can dance quietly to. Stand up and start moving gently to the music and as you do so, imagine your inner heart coming alive once more. Feel it expand in its radiance in the centre of your chest. Now imagine the energy of your heart moving down your shoulders and going through your hands, and then, still moving gently to the music, imagine this loving, healing energy flowing out of your hands. Begin stroking your hair and thank it for existing, then thank your eyes for the gift of sight, your ears for the gift of sound, your mouth for the gift of taste and your nose for the gift of smell. Continue this and gradually move all the way down your body, giving loving energy now to your neck, shoulders, back, pelvis, stomach, arms, legs, feet and so on, thanking each of these parts of you for the service they do you.

Now do the same thing – still continuing to sway to the rhythm of the music – to your inner organs. Imagine the loving and healing energy of your inner heart now flowing through your hands to your brain, to your physical heart, lungs, kidneys, liver and so on, again thanking them for the good service they have done you in your life. If there is a part of you that is unwell or weak, say your lungs or your kidneys, then give specific energy to that part.

When you have finished, lie down on the floor and imagine that your heart embraces all of you, that your heart's love is coming increasingly alive in every cell in your body, and give thanks quietly for the gift of your life.

▨ EXERCISE to bring heart into all areas of your daily life

Write down this affirmation:

"I choose to live with heart and bring heart into all areas of my daily life."

Say it to yourself a few times and make sure this is what you really choose. Then make the choice to act upon it by remembering, when you cook, to do so with heart, and when you go to your office or go for a walk or spend time with your family, to also bring heart into those activities. If you do a sport or activity like running or yoga or tennis, imagine yourself doing so with heart. In this way, heart energy can start infusing your mindfulness and it can slowly morph to heartfulness.

To begin with you will need to do this exercise intentionally, but the more you practise it, the easier it will grow; it will eventually become second nature.

▨ EXERCISE to nourish your heart

Write down things that you can specifically do, or not do, to better nourish your heart. Also, ask yourself: do I do enough things that *delight my heart?* If not, write down how you can structure your life differently to ensure your heart a) is better looked after and b) gets more pleasure.

If you choose to focus on your heart and really absorb the contents of this chapter, much can change in your life and your inner work will begin very much to deepen.

And don't worry that all this focus on your heart will take you away from your mind. It won't. The mental side of our lives tends to be well established inside most of us and will not vanish easily.

CHAPTER 11

Gateways to Power

The day the power of love overrules the love of power,
the world will know peace.
— MAHATMA GANDHI

This life is yours. Take the power to choose what you
want to do and do it well. Take the power to love what
you want in life and do it honestly. Take the power to
walk in the forest and be a part of nature.
Take the power to control your own life. No one else can
do it for you. Take the power to make your life happy.
— SUSAN POLIS SCHUTZ

Perceptions of Power

Nothing can happen without the power to make it happen, and if you and I are to work at living more abundantly and soulfully, we will need not only a lot of love, determination and psychological maturity, but also a lot of power. Indeed, having power is very important and it serves as a central gateway that can potentially lead us into important new, soulful spaces and places.

Sadly, many people don't think of power along those lines and either tend to pursue it relentlessly or, conversely, regard it with a somewhat jaundiced eye. What we forget, however, is that power exists at many different levels, and the kind of power the world needs today to usher in a new and improved society is of a very potent kind, but very different from that wielded by rajassic and tamassic man, where all too often it is used for selfish or destructive purposes. No doubt this underlies Lord Acton's famous derogatory remark about "power tending to corrupt and absolute power corrupting absolutely", and consequently might explain why many decent people who regard themselves as being "good human beings" often don't want to have much to do with it.

Revisioning power

This, however, is a great pity, a) because we can't really accomplish anything much without power, and b) the problem is not power itself, but the way we relate to it. Anything can corrupt us if we use it unwisely.

Yes, my friend, it is the same power that determines whether we hurt someone or whether we heal them, whether we disempower or empower them. As we saw in the early chapters, power can be used for dark, manipulative ends to gratify our selfishness, vanity and greed; but conversely, it can be used in the service of our altruism. Simply because it is all too often used for bad is no reason for us to walk away from it. On the contrary, there is all the more reason for us to start finding out more about it and exploring how we might bring into expression a higher-grade power that might help to offset its misuse.

What we badly need to understand is that the way power manifests itself at any time is determined by the *quality of consciousness* behind those using it, as well as by what it is being used for. For example, if utilized by conscious human beings who have worked at opening their hearts and who hold a positive vision for humanity, it can potentially be a great gate opener and can even move mountains.

A few years ago, I gave a lecture entitled "Soul Power" and the next section is taken from it.

Soul power

Power can be used in many different ways and for many different things, and its nature radically shifts when someone who is connected to their soul life begins employing it specifically to aid in some ensouling activity. Then it assumes a transforming presence and becomes subtle and soft and often doesn't look like power at all as we know it.

But don't be deceived. It is still power and it is actually much stronger. It has a higher ampage. A good name to give it is *soul power* – or even *higher power*, as it comes from a higher or more evolved source.

I feel qualified to say a few words about this kind of power, as on many occasions, in particular when I am doing my work – giving lectures, teaching spiritual retreats or doing one-to-one sessions with people – I have felt that this higher power has sought me out! What I mean by this is that whenever I am engaged in some form of soulful service work – trying in some way to live my life as a sacred practice – I very often experience an empowering force flowing through me and assisting me.

For example, a few weeks ago I had been teaching a week-long retreat, and over that entire time I was aware of a delightful energy presence accompanying me that not only seemed to guide me as to what to do, but also filled me with joy, aliveness and vigour so that working with a group of 25 people felt like the easiest thing in the world.

The other interesting thing about this power is that it also seems to flow through me into the participants on my retreats and also empower them. But what I am crystal clear about is that it is not my power but rather a gift that is being temporarily "lent" to me on particular occasions.

The generosity of the universe

If I am teaching a retreat on a subject like love, I tend to notice that people will feel empowered in the area of love; if on joy or courage, then the empowerment will focus on these arenas. It makes my work feel like the easiest and most fun thing I could ever be doing, although if looked at objectively, it is actually extremely challenging working non-stop and single-handedly all day for a week with a large group of people, many of whom have many strong psychological blocks. So I am very grateful to this wonderful "helping presence" for being with me and supporting me.

At one level, I see it as the generosity of the universe regarding me in a kindly fashion because I am trying in my little way to do something to assist it. Put another way, it seems that when I am doing my best to have my daily life be my sacred practice, or, in Buckminster Fuller's words, am trying to honour my role as being the "re-ordering function of the universe", what happens is that the universe graciously steps in and gives me a helping hand.

Power as abundance

I have a good friend who is a very fine musician, and he tells me that even when he feels tired or nervous before a concert, the moment he is up there on the stage, he also is aware of a similar empowering presence being with him and helping and inspiring him; his fatigue and nerves immediately vanish. The word we both use to describe how we feel when we are doing our work, and why we love doing it and feel so privileged to be doing it, is *abundant*.

What is interesting is that I do not feel this way if I am not doing my soul work. Recently, for example, I went out to dinner with some acquaintances; it was all very much small talk and I felt very sleepy throughout the evening as I was operating at a whole other level. Quite rightly, the empowering current decided for that evening to leave me well alone!

The Force is with us

So I ask myself this question. What if more of us learned to work with this higher or sacred power? Surely extraordinary things could be accomplished in all sorts of different ways if thousands of us invoked it.

I say "invoked" as I think this sacred dimension of power needs consciously to be "called into expression" and that there are three main criteria for making this possible. Firstly, we need to be sincere; secondly, we need to be working on ourselves along the lines already explored; and thirdly, we need to have some kind of soulful itinerary – some positive difference-making agenda – to commit to. When all these factors line up, then what I will call "the Force" is truly happy being with us!

Yes, my friend, I am talking about that self-same presence that Luke Skywalker brought down upon himself in that old Star Wars film when the Jedi warrior told him that "the Force" would be with him. And I think that the more we can have "the Force" working with us – or rather, for us – the more progress we will make personally and the more effective we will be in our endeavours to bring ensoulment into the world.

The importance of personal power

But let's not get overly carried away. One important thing to know about this soul power is that it is dependent upon our also possessing a degree of *personal power*, as this gives it a basic structure or scaffolding to enfold itself upon. Without a solid personal structure, soul power might literally "blow us away"!

And personal power is something that we *do* need to work on; we can't just "let go" into it. While of course these two kinds of power intermingle, personal power is something that is much more uniquely "ours" and that in most cases we will need to devote some effort to building up inside us.

My point is simply this. If, emotionally, you and I are wobbly and are always afraid and confused, higher power can't really use us, can't really work through us properly, as we don't, as it were, possess the emotional scaffolding to support it. The name of the game, therefore, must be for us to work both at de-wobbling and at strengthening ourselves so that there is enough structure to enable us to be used in the service of higher power.

Acquiring personal power

So how do we acquire this personal power? Well, we can't do so directly in the way we can develop, say, strong pecs by working out in the gym. Rather, it gradually grows inside us by our "working in", in many of the ways we have already been exploring, such as when we choose to take greater responsibility for our lives and not shy away from addressing our emotional problems.

To have personal power, we also need to understand why a lot of us *don't* have it and what some of the things are that we do or don't do that subtly disempower us.

What disempowers us?

Probably what most weakens us is that we live according to stories informing us that who we are is not an abundant, sacred human being, but a struggling "sin-filled consumer", whose main happiness lies in outer things. We've already explored this. There is nothing more soul-destroying than believing these stories, and what destroys soul also reduces our personal power.

We have also seen how the old story has conditioned us to relinquish our power or give it away to whoever in the system will have it. Doctors. Politicians. Bankers. Authority figures in general. And people are never loath to receive what we give them! Not only does this suck the life force out of us, but in handing over our responsibilities to others, there is no guarantee that what we give out will then be used for our benefit. (Do our investment advisers really care for us? Do our politicians really mind how we feel so long as we vote for them?)

This opens us up to playing the blame card, which in turn can lead us to feeling victimized, two hugely disempowering positions.

Disempowerment of women

This particular pattern of disempowerment is especially strong within the collective consciousness of women, who have suffered atrociously over the centuries at the hands of the patriarchal mindset, where we men, afraid of women's power, have invented thousands of ways to repress, abuse, marginalize, objectify and demean them. Our culture also loves to tell women not to accept themselves the way they are, and to be constantly comparing themselves with others, and to believe that they are only OK if they are perennially young and beautiful-looking! There is nothing more enfeebling than holding such beliefs.

Therefore, women are challenged to work through the many ways that they can begin to take back their power – or, put another way, re-sacralize themselves. (An extraordinary power always lurks wherever we have sacred space.) Today there is every evidence – especially as embodied in the Me Too movement – that a new feminine empowerment is arising, where women are saying "no" much more often and are steadfastly standing up for their rights. And this is terrific.

Disempowerment due to looking different

People who look different also have a lot of negativity projected on them, which can be disempowering. I have a friend in North America whose face was terribly disfigured in an accident; for many years, this wonderful woman felt very tortured as she took people's projections of "freak" to heart about herself. Having subsequently done a lot of work on herself, she is now wholly at peace with her looks and gives lectures to empower others in similar circumstances. Indeed, from my various talks with her, I have seen that "the Force" is strongly with her.

I recently saw a TED Talk by a young American woman who had had both her legs amputated below the knees when she was very young. She spoke about how this never stopped her working as an actress and athlete, and she also talked about how humanity needed to move away from its conventional views of what was right or wrong about a person and be open to include many different new human models. I fully agree.

How may we best connect with higher power and stay with our personal power?

Avoid what in our society disempowers us
Since higher power can't properly "come through us" if our personal power is waning, we need to be mindful of doing things to keep our personal power strong. And as we are only as strong as our weakest link, we need to be aware where in our lives we are vulnerable. Perhaps we need to stay away from certain scenarios or certain people. It also greatly helps if we "face our demons" head on and ensure we are as physically, emotionally and mentally fit as possible.

Let go
The emptier we are of our "stuff", the more space higher power has to enter us. Therefore, do all the inner work that earlier on I suggested will

help you let go, i.e., visualizations, and dancing to drumming music and then lying on the ground and imagining all the old negative patterns flowing out of you.

Be "in the now"

Being in present time or "in the now" is very empowering as it focuses our attention very acutely. So sit quietly and, first, meditate on higher power and ask it to come to you. Many of us don't receive things because we don't do enough asking. So start talking to higher power. Say: "Hi, Higher Power, come and visit me today please!"

Then imagine yourself existing fully in present time. Say to yourself: "This is it right now. There is no past or future; only this moment. I choose to exist fully in present time and higher power is overlighting me."

You can do this process with your eyes open or closed. Just remember: there is "only the now". Say to yourself: "There is no before and no after. I am inhabiting this present moment with all the force of my being."

Really make an effort to focus on this. If you manage ten minutes to start with, that is fantastic. As you get a handle on it, you will be able to meditate for longer; try taking it up to 20 minutes. This process is tremendously empowering. Eventually, if you practise it, you will be able to go about your daily life still remaining in "present time", which will add an extra dimension especially if you link it in with your newly discovered "objectivity" and make it all a central part of your sacred practice.

Befriend and affirm your personal power

So learn to love and cherish your personal power. Be grateful for it and affirm it. Know that you are not going to abuse it and that you will grow in strength by giving value and recognition to what is true, brave, noble and beautiful about yourself. Here are some powerful affirmations that you can use. Read them carefully and with each one imagine that:

■ AFFIRMATIONS

I am a loving and powerful human being and I choose always to live in this remembrance.

I choose to open to higher power and allow the Force to be with me and to guide me.

I choose to open up to receive the great power of the universe.

I choose to live in the now and experience the power this gives me.

I affirm my abundance and strength emotionally, mentally, physically and spiritually.

"I choose to connect to my inner power and realize all my dreams and visions.

A higher power is always guiding and protecting me.

I am a loving and abundant human being and every day I am opening my heart more and more to the awesome power lying inside it.

Write down a few of these affirmations, those that really appeal to you, and put them up in places where you can see them. Read them frequently and allow their message to reverberate inside you.

Empower others
The more we choose to support or empower others, the more what we give out gets reflected back to us. I will develop this theme further in the chapter on friendship.

Take a stand to be who you are
Taking stands for what we truly believe in is very empowering and warrior-like. The late Tibetan Buddhist teacher Chögyam Trungpa Rinpoche defined the stance of the spiritual warrior as "never being afraid to be who we are".

What this means is that we don't apologize to anyone for our being exactly as we are and we don't pretend to be someone or something that we are not. Thus we do not compromise ourselves or say things just to please people (which was something I personally used to do a lot in the past as I didn't like people disapproving of me).

At a societal level, it is about our choosing to live the truth we are taking the stand over, even if it is difficult and even if certain people won't like it and we don't always feel like it. So it means that if, for example, one of our stands is to commit to truth, and mine is – I feel this is so important in this post-truth world we are now in – we don't keep our mouths shut; we confront untruth.

Just recently, a very old friend of mine wrote an autobiographical book based on an enormous lie about how he had earned his money, and while

I knew why he did so, I still confronted him on it very directly. He found this very uncomfortable and let me know I was no longer a friend of his. In terms of a rajassic morality he was right in that I had betrayed him as a friend – given away his guilty secret. However, in the light of the new, more truthful life game I now do my best to play, the rules are different, and in this world, *he* was the one who had betrayed himself and his family in perpetrating such blatant dishonesties about himself. Yes, I am sad we are no longer friends, but I am glad I did not back down.

Let us say our stand is for human rights or for women reclaiming their power. What this means is that if we see human rights being abused or we come across situations of women being marginalized or taken advantage of in some way, then we choose to intervene – do something about it.

Stand-taking gives us enormous power and will often bring the Force to be directly with us.

Protect yourself

Protecting ourselves is vital, especially as the more we "go for" truth, the more we may find ourselves having to confront the rajassic and tamassic forces at their darkest. And that can greatly discombobulate us. I often ask for protection in my work and at times like to visualize myself being surrounded by a ring of light or a cloak of fire that allows nothing negative to get through to me – if anything tries to, it gets burned up. Protecting ourselves in this way is very important. We can also ask higher power to protect us.

Stretching and risking

Whenever we have the courage to venture into new terrain – somewhere we've never been before – be it in our inner or in our outer life, it is always empowering as it means taking a risk and potentially going to the edge. And it is so often at the edge where new gateways are to be found. So when we intentionally choose to stretch ourselves – for example, when something scares us but we do it anyway – we can find ourselves accessing a lot of power.

There are many ways that we can stretch ourselves. We can do so intellectually or soulfully or artistically – take up some new work, learn new skills, start expanding ourselves in whole new areas that we have never explored before. The more we do this, the more we ascend into what, a little later, I will be referring to as "higher-order realities", where we may find ourselves capable of accomplishing things that would have been quite impossible for us in our old mindsets.

So, my friend, never give up on things and never stop trusting in the essential goodness of life. If you live from this space, the Force will look after you and may even start endowing you with whole new capabilities. Here are some of the differences between old-story and new-story power.

Old-story power	New-story power
Love of power	Power of love
Need for control	Need for mastery
Disempowerment of others	Empowerment of others
Brute strength	Subtle strength
Holding on	Letting go
Unconsciousness	Consciousness
Giving power away	Taking power back
Using power irresponsibly	Using power wisely
Power struggles	Power resolutions
Codependency	Interdependency
Profane power	Sacred power
Lower power	Higher power

EXERCISES

- Make notes on what you see as being your current relationship with personal power. Do you fear it or embrace it? How much personal power do you think you have?
  Where are you vulnerable and what areas do you think you need to work on more to become stronger?
- Do you feel you might still be stuck in "playing" any of the soulless old-story power games? If so, which ones? What can you do to change things? Make notes.
- Do you feel that "the Force" has ever been with you?
  If so, what were you doing or not doing on those occasions to draw it to you? Are you willing to do more to try to invoke it? If so, what would you need to do?

- Do you feel you are someone who empowers others?
  If so, how, and what do you observe are the effects? If not, why not, and do you want to change this? If you do, list some of the shifts you feel you can do in this area.

EXERCISE to meditate on a personal and higher power

- Close your eyes and connect to your heart. Imagine you have lungs inside your heart and breathe in and out of them. As you do so, be aware of the centrality of your heart in your life and that it is your best friend.
- Dwell on this for a moment.
- Now I want you to remember that there is a lot of power inside your heart. Just imagine being a space for higher power to connect with you. Say to yourself: "I choose to open up my being and allow the Force to be with me and enter me and guide me."
- Now stay centred on the idea of the vast power inside your awake and alive heart. Say to yourself: "Who I am is a beautiful, radiant, powerful and soulful human being. Higher power is working through me to make me this way."
- Now feel the mindfulness that this power is giving you and stay centred in this mindfulness for five minutes.
- Now begin to visualize yourself living a full day centred in this place of powerful mindfulness. See yourself getting up in the morning and getting dressed in a powerful way, eating your breakfast, greeting your family in an empowered way, perhaps driving to work in this same spirit. See yourself acknowledging other people in ways that empower them, and if there is someone who you feel you have a disempowering connection with in some way, see if you can change the game around and visualize yourself empowering them.
- Work with this affirmation: *"I am living an empowered life. A higher power is working through me and influencing the way I deal with all areas of my life."*
- If you like to do exercise – if you swim or run or play tennis or go to the gym – visualize yourself bringing power into your sport; as in this way, you ground it in your physicality and thus your power becomes more embodied.

CHAPTER 12

Gateways through Our Dark Side

*Everyone carries a Shadow, and the less it is embodied
in the individual's life, the blacker and denser it is.
At all counts, it forms an unconscious snag, thwarting
our most well-meant intentions.*
— CARL JUNG

*Perhaps all our dragons and demons are only there to
help us realize how brave and beautiful we really are.*
— RAINER MARIA RILKE

Gateways Lie in Our Shadow Side

'If you want to be enlightened," Carl Jung once said, "don't sit up in the light but go into your Shadow." This may be surprising to those who believe that gateways only reveal themselves when we are expressing the nobler aspects of our nature, but it is true. As you saw when we explored the Dark Night of the Soul crisis, entrées into the deeper echelons of soul may also present themselves when we are called to confront and work with areas of ourselves that are the least lofty and where we experience the most shame and distress!

Not unexpectedly, this kind of exploration into our dark sides is not high on the agenda of rajassic man, which is one of the reasons why his worldview remains so narrow.

Shadow projection

So let me remind you once more what we often do if there are sides of ourselves that we suspect may exist but which we don't want to look at and own. Let us say, for example, that we are manipulative, sleazy and self-centred but would prefer to see ourselves as honest, virtuous and selfless. What we do is find people to act as "hooks" onto which we can project or hang our negativities, as in this way we can appear to ourselves as whiter than white! However, if we wish to evolve our humanity, if we wish to grow soul, such behaviours need to be knocked on the head. Not only do they stunt our growth and keep us caught in illusions about ourselves, but they also damage those we are projecting onto since all thoughts, especially negative ones, carry a certain potency.

The truth is that, if we are to engage effectively with inner work, we will have to accept two facts about ourselves: first, that we all have a Shadow side – yes, even saints do – and second, that one of the most important ways to grow our humanity is by recognizing this and working to bring our Shadow into the light of day – that is, become aware of it.

What Is the Shadow?

So what exactly is our Shadow? Very simply, it constitutes those parts of ourselves that we are "in the dark" about, that we don't know we possess. The Jungian analyst Dr Ann Belford Ulanov describes it as "that which is darkness to our light, unknown to what we call familiar, that which comes from the other side of our motives, from the other side of our virtue and from the other side of our vices."

So, for example, my tendencies at times to be disorganized, a trifle grandiose and sometimes lazy about doing housework are *not* my Shadow; I am all too aware of these shortcomings of mine, so if I am able to catch myself and see these traits about to pop up, I try to do something about them. "Stand back," I say, "I won't let you run me today!"

What my Shadow is – what our shadows are – is what we are *not* aware of about ourselves, what we are unconscious of. Remember what I said about the unconscious earlier on? It includes both the less and the more evolved parts of ourselves, which we could describe as our lower or dark unconscious and our higher or light unconscious. Our higher unconscious could be our kindness, generosity and altruism that we may be unaware of possessing, while our lower unconscious could, for example, be our manipulativeness, our self-destructiveness or our cruelty.

Becoming aware of our Shadow

One excellent way to become aware of certain aspects of our dark Shadow is to see if there are people of our own sex that we have a negative charge with as, unbeknownst to us, we may well be projecting onto them some part of ourselves that we don't want to see.

GATEWAYS TO THE SOUL

Just recently, for example, I've observed that the "closed-off" side of a friend rather annoys me. I always find I want to say to him "Look here, matey, open up!" What I am starting to realize, however, is that the reason why I have this "charge" with him is because it is about *me*, not him, and that despite in many ways being very open and unprivate, I can also be quite secretive and closed down, and I really don't want to see this about myself! Thus our Shadow side, both its more and its less evolved aspects, includes everything about ourselves that we are not yet aware of and consequently do not yet integrate into our daily lives. I will focus on our dark Shadow in this chapter, as in subsequent chapters we will be looking more at the light Shadow.

Negative Shadow projection

What our dark Shadow projections, then, allow us to do, is to deny things, split off from seeing things or repress things. This is a very, very damaging way of operating and actually takes up a lot of our vital energy as well as being potentially devastating for those who get projected upon in a negative way.

Also, most of the time neither projector nor projectee have the slightest idea what is going on other than that both may feel depleted. Earlier, I described how my dear dad, unbeknownst to himself of course (the projector seldom realizes what he is doing), projected his weak-willed side onto me and continually reprimanded me for not having enough willpower, as in this way, he could hold the image of himself as being the all-powerful and invincible alpha male.

However, for this I paid a big price in terms of my self-confidence, as these negative projections began very early on in my life when I was unable to recognize them and so defend myself (if we see what is going on, there are things we can do to prevent it), with the result that over the years I have had to do a lot of repair work to heal myself.

What happens when we get negatively projected upon – we can also say "regarded in a reductive light" – is that we will often internalize the projections and incorporate them into our own self-image. This is often what will have occurred with people who have low self-esteem.

If we look back over our history and think of the enormous price that black people have paid over the years, as a result of all the negativity projected upon them about being inferior, or what women have had to put up with in terms of their being continually objectified by men, or of the damage done in terms of homophobia or anti-Semitism or Islamophobia, we see the true viciousness of projection. The problem is that it is so insidious. Often, we don't know we are "enshadowing" (projecting our Shadow towards) certain people or certain races because we are so unconscious of the many prejudices and agendas that we carry inside us.

When I was young, my father also instilled in me the absurd thought (God knows where it came from) that small men were always out to get you! "Beware of small men," he used to say a lot, "they'll always do you in!" Well, I took on this negative thought quite unconsciously and over the years, men less tall than myself (quite a lot of men; I am quite tall) would pick up on what I was projecting onto them and stay well away.

Withdrawing projections

It was only when I realized the negative story going on inside me that I could choose to withdraw the projection. And it didn't happen overnight. But as I began to let down the drawbridge that I had put up to keep me distant from shorter men, the result was that they began coming into my life. And I am pleased to say that two of my closest male buddies today are around five feet tall!

Intentionally withdrawing our projections, then, is as central a part of inner work as is realizing what projections may have been levied on us so that we can start releasing them. Both processes can be challenging, a) because we are often as unaware of the negativity we are spewing out as we are of what we are receiving, and b) because the negative effects of both will have sunk deeply into us. However, the more we grow in self-awareness and the more our soul life starts sprouting, the more conscious we become of these kinds of things and the easier it is to let go of attitudes or beliefs that we realize do us no service.

In my own personal journey, I've found that each new shift up into the light – each entry through a new gateway – has required me to do a correspondingly deeper exploration of my dark side.

Yes, my friend, often inner work is about working with our same old issues, only now from a new level. When Jung, in his eighties, was asked about his relationship with his mother, he said that he still had to do a lot of work in this area!

The Importance of Shadow Work

Why working with our dark Shadow sides is so important is a) because our negative projections create deep fissures in the health of the society around us – they play a large role in the desacralizing process – and b) because we cannot properly "grow our soul life" if the murkier aspects of ourselves just get pushed aside or ignored – this does not make them go away. What is needed is for us to come to see our dark projections and gradually work at releasing, recycling and reintegrating them.

For example, we may not recognize that deep down, we are angry and aggressive. But that doesn't mean that other people won't pick this up about us. Our unrecognized Shadow sides will always seep out of us. I am sure you will have encountered people who outwardly are all smiley and sugary, but when in their presence you notice yourself feeling awkward, you sense a cold wind seeping out of them somewhere and you feel like withdrawing. What is happening is that you are picking up their dark Shadow, which they may be wholly unaware of.

A sensitive woman can often tell, for example, if a man, underneath his external civility, is projecting lustful thoughts onto her. This is why it helps to be conscious of what we may be hooks for in terms of other people. For example, very attractive women will always have lustful thoughts aimed at them by a lot of men, just as very rich people will always have certain people projecting envy onto them. If one knows what to expect, it is much easier to choose to not take on a projection.

Put simply, the fact that we may deny possessing certain negative traits and that we repress them – push them down into our unconscious, pretend they don't exist in our personality – in no way means that they are not spilling out of us all the time and continuing to pollute the environment around us.

The Shadow of war

As I said earlier, wars happen for many social, economic and political reasons, but one key one is that they are a reflection of the suppressed aggression within millions of people around the world. They will not vanish until we learn to recycle our hostilities and fill our hearts up with peace. I repeat: we fight our wars in the vain hope that goodness will reign supreme if we can only kill off evil: the evil that we have disowned in ourselves and projected outside of ourselves onto those whom we have designated to be our enemy of the moment.

And it is not only individuals who project. So too, do tribes, races, religions and nations. Just think of the kind of Shadow projections that continually go on between the Israelis and the Palestinians!

But we don't only kill in war. As Herman Hesse put it:

'We kill at every step. Not only in wars, riots and executions. We kill when we close our eyes to poverty, suffering and shame. In the same way, all disrespect for life, all hard-heartedness, all indifference, all contempt, is nothing more than killing. With just a little witty scepticism, we can kill a good deal of the future in a young person."

Shadow projection in relationships, families and organizations

It is often in close relationships that we become most aware of our Shadow sides, especially when the relationship sours and each side accuses the other of doing exactly what they themselves do.

A few months ago, I worked with a new client regarding his marriage problems. He presented a picture to me of himself as a loving and dutiful husband and his wife as a conniving banshee. "If only she would change," he moaned, "everything would be fine." He was completely unable to recognize his own selfishness and manipulativeness. To his limited and naive way of thinking, he was all goodness and light and his wife all badness and dark. When I met her and worked with her, I saw that in actuality, it was totally the other way around.

I came clean with the man. "You have to "get it" that so much of what you see in your wife, and so project onto her, actually exists inside *you*."

After a few more sessions, these realizations began to sink in and as he started to own his own murkiness – and this took a lot of courage as it is always horrible to confront these noxious sides of ourselves – instead of everything exploding as he feared, not only did he begin to feel happier as a person but their relationship rapidly began to improve.

How? Because the projections began fading. The truth is that we cannot properly have a mature intimate relationship with someone unless we stop playing the game of being the proverbial pot calling the kettle black.

Most families also have their Shadow side. This constitutes what does not get discussed or acknowledged but instead gets shoved under the carpet. If never addressed, these repressions simply get handed down through the generations, with each family member acting them out in their own way. The so-called "black sheep" of the family is the person onto whom all other family members project their negativity, and who they blame for everything, so that they can feel all pure and innocent! Needless to say, this is extremely damaging for the designated one.

All organizations and institutions also have their dark or "inferior" side – the part or parts that they disown or invest least energy in – which can often be the organization's soul (light Shadow) or its need to respect the importance of creating a space for good relationships to thrive. If this is not seen and acknowledged, it can result in the Shadow fighting back.

I once worked with a woman who successfully sued her firm for ill-treatment and received a large settlement. The organization received much unwanted negative publicity. Had it not initially rebuffed her, had it instead respected her, listened to her complaints and done something about them at the time when she first voiced them – in other words, had it been willing to face, as opposed to deny, its dark side – this would have been greatly in its own interest.

Our dark sides

I stress once more: *we all have dark sides*. There is a collective dark human Shadow composed of the sum total of our inhumanity, which I spoke of earlier, and which all of us in one way or another "plug into". Put simply, there is a potential murderer, rapist, manipulator, bandit and terrorist inside you and me, and you and I may also possess the capacity to be manipulative, aggressive, destructive, mean, selfish, cruel, demeaning, critical, greedy, dishonest, calculating and vengeful. But we can only do something about these things if we are willing to accept and recognize this, if we are willing to give up the illusion of how "nice" we are!

Personally speaking, I think I have become a wee bit more genuine as over the years I have acknowledged sides of me that are lustful, demanding, manipulative, deceitful, controlling and even in certain circumstances – say, if someone threatened the life of my wife or my daughter – capable of killing. This acknowledgement means that these sides of me won't spill out unconsciously.

This is also why I have stressed the importance of our not being judgemental in our assessment of ourselves, as this blocks our taking proper responsibility for handling the ugliness that lies inside us all.

So if I am working with a client and they suddenly alight upon some despicable part of themselves and they go into moaning and groaning about what an awful person they are, I tell them to stop, stand back and just see this despicable part of themselves in an honest way. "If you want to work creatively with your Shadow," I will tell them, "then recognize it and feel it fully but don't judge yourself; it will get you nowhere other than being mired in an even stickier quagmire of self-loathing. Inner work begins when you choose to take your Shadow side into your heart and start experiencing it fully."

Dr Jekyll and Mr Hyde

There is a lot we can learn about our dark side by understanding the significance of the story of *The Strange Case of Dr Jekyll and Mr Hyde* by Robert Louis Stevenson.

Dr Jekyll is the embodiment of rajassic man – all nice and inauthentic, wanting to be seen as "good" and doing the right thing by society. Mr Hyde is his other, more primitive and tamassically wild half, whom he has cut himself off from all his life but whom he has also been secretly fascinated by (we are always obsessed by what we repress), so much so that he creates a drug to bring "this other side of himself" to life. However, because this other side has always been repressed and so never allowed to exist, when it actually appears, Mr Hyde is ugly, deformed and shrunken, devoid of all morality, only catering to his animalistic appetites – and later to his murderous impulses – as, sadly, no integration has ever occurred.

The point about this story is that both sides needed the other for there to be completion. Dr Jekyll on his own was too disconnected from his body – his own innate life force – and was too insipid, and Mr Hyde on his own was too violent. Had these two halves joined forces, had there been some integration, the chronically repressed Dr Jekyll would have had more life-energy available to him, more chutzpah, and by the same token, the wild Mr Hyde would have had a connection to a more civilized way of behaving. The Jekyll–Hyde amalgam would have been a more whole human being. And as we have already seen, the more whole we become, the more open we are to the generosity and abundance of the universe being able to flow into us.

Our dark Shadow sides, therefore, always have something valuable to contribute to us, and as we just saw, this is a job that our hearts, with their innate alchemical capabilities, are specialists in. In Shakespeare's great play *King Lear*, the Fool is one aspect of the King's Shadow and it is he who always speaks wisdom to his master. Had Lear taken his advice and not succumbed to the flattery of his two elder daughters, he might have avoided the fate that ultimately befalls him. The story of Don Quixote echoes a similar theme. His "other half", Sancho Panza, is endowed with a certain streetwise intelligence, serving as a necessary balance to counter his master's tendency to be somewhat disconnected from the "real world". Without Sancho Panza, Don Quixote is lost.

We need to be grateful, therefore, to external figures who grace us by embodying some aspect of our Shadow, for they offer us the gift of letting us see ourselves for who we really are and potentially re-owning our projections. None of us as individuals can go forward and work at creating a healthier society unless we discover, confront, own and work with our dark side.

Rajassic culture and the Shadow

Basically, then, among the many things that are wrong with our rajassic worldview is that people are inherently disinclined to confront their Shadow side and are always trying to push it under the carpet. I remember when I visited Bali many years ago and bought some paintings from local artists, that what particularly stood out for me was that they did not exclude the dark side. It showed in all their work.

One beautiful mandala I have, painted by an artist called Batuan, depicts a holistic lifestyle where people play, pray, work and sleep. However, that is not the whole picture; these activities are presented against a scene showing people bowing down to false prophets and others dressed in terrifying-looking masks. The aim is to remind us that life has a dark side and that this always needs to be taken into consideration.

I had the honour of meeting Batuan and found him to be the most delightful man, full of joy and wisdom and laughter. "I am like this because I don't deny my dark side," he told me. "In fact I always honour it. I always acknowledge that evil exists in the world and unless we confront it, it will gobble us up. People who deny the existence of evil or who negate their Shadow – they are often stern and rigid." I could not have agreed more.

The issue of evil

For me there exist two distinct kinds of evil: obvious and non obvious. The former makes little attempt to hide itself. It is out in the open. Here, think Hitler, Stalin, Saddam Hussein, Auschwitz, Darfur. Non-obvious evil is less straightforward and recognizable; initially it may not look like evil at all and so it can do even more damage because we don't recognize it for what it is.

For example, when we have political systems that disregard the well-being of the very poor, that mistreat immigrants, that engage in policies that utterly negate what is in the interests of the larger world community, that peddle outright lies and espouse conspiracy theories deliberately destined to obfuscate and, at the same time, do nothing to address the ever-worsening world problem of climate change, we can rightly say that in their extreme tamassicness, these systems are evil and must be confronted as such.

In his book *Faces of the Enemy*, Sam Keen suggests that "we often create evil out of our highest ideas and most noble aspirations", and I fully agree. A good example of this was some years ago when Tony Blair took the UK to war against Iraq. He was clearly not aware of his extreme narcissism and his insecure Shadow side whereby, to compensate for feeling subtly inadequate, he wanted to be loved and appreciated by George Bush, as well as be welcomed by all and sundry as a great conquering hero saving the world from Saddam Hussein's supposed evil. Had he been more aware of the world of his unconscious, he might have done things very differently, with the result that the Middle East might have been spared much bloodshed and misery. But these things can happen when people in positions of power fail to acknowledge the Shadow issues inside them that prompt them to do many of the inappropriate things they do.

Hannah Arendt talks about evil's banality, suggesting that it is without depth and "can outgrow and lay waste the whole world because it spreads like a fungus on the surface." For me, unobvious evil does just as much damage as obvious evil. Perhaps much more!

The gift of Shadow and the need for evil

However, perhaps the murky side of life exists for a purpose. Perhaps that purpose is to test us and challenge us. And where tests and challenges reside, so too do gateways into the sacred.

I look at it like this: if there was no murky side, how could we have the chance to be courageous? If there were not forces both inside ourselves and out in the world continually trying to seduce and bamboozle us, how could we develop the courage and strength to work to try to rise above them? If no one was ever in an ailing state, how could we develop our capacity to be caring and compassionate?

If there were never any oppressive or evil regimes, no Stalins or Hitlers or totalitarian systems, no genocide or war, there would be no freedom fighters performing heroic acts. If the evils of the apartheid system had never existed, would big-hearted warriors like Nelson Mandela ever have had the opportunity to come into their own? If no one suffered, would the Mother Teresas of this world have had the opportunity to come forward to "bring the Christ to the poorest of the poor"?

We are back to the questions we asked ourselves earlier on about the sacred path and whether we will make the choice to wake up. Certainly, if I look at my own relationship with my darkness and murkiness, I definitely see its presence as having been a spur in assisting me in my mission to try to evolve and, in my tiny way, try to be a cheerleader for a better world. If I look at those people onto whom I have in the past projected my dark side, I realize that I am challenged not only to reel back my negative projections, but also to open my heart to them and embrace them in the spirit of unconditional friendliness, to recognize their innate humanity.

I will leave the last word to Jung: "Everyone carries a Shadow and the less it is embodied in the individual's life, the blacker and denser it is."

■ EXERCISES

- What thoughts and feelings has this chapter brought up for you? Is what I have said familiar or is it unknown?
- Can you have a sense of some of the things inside you that you like to deny, split off from or project out onto other people? If so, what are they; or, put another way, what do you think you particularly deny about yourself? Make a list.
- What are some of the consequences of your denials?
- What do you think were some of the Shadow sides of your own family as you were growing up? In other words, what got suppressed or pushed under the carpet? Joy? Intimacy? Authenticity? Sex? The world of the intellect? Emotions? Work? Black people? Muslims? Rich people? Poor people? Or other things? Write it all down. Do you think you have personally taken on any of these Shadow issues in your own life? If so, which? How do you feel this has affected you?
- Have you been the "black sheep" of your family? If so, how has it affected you? If not, has there been a black sheep in your family, and if so, what has it done for them to be assigned that role? Is

there anything you can do right now, to bring them some healing?

- Is there anything you feel fanatical about? If so, write it down and know it will probably be some aspect of your dark Shadow. Also comment on how this has made you behave and see the world.

- Is there someone of your own sex who you have a big charge with; that is, who upsets or angers or scares you? If so, might it be indicative that some aspect of your own dark Shadow is being activated? If you believe this is the case, write down what it might be and explore it. If there is more than one person or one thing you have a charge with, also explore this.

- If we can use the word "enshadow" to describe the process of projecting negative images out onto others, do you feel that in any way you have ever borne the brunt of other people's Shadow projections or enshadowings? For example, if you are rich, have poor people enshadowed you, or if you are poor, do you feel rich people have looked down on you? If you are black, have you ever felt demeaned by white people, etc.? Make notes about what you feel the consequences have been and what you think you can do to shake off these Shadow projections.

- Who in your life have you used or do you still use as a hook to hang your Shadow on? Write their names down.

- Now work at taking back all your projections by imagining yourself reeling in the negative thoughts you have sent out to them over the years, and bring them back into yourself. Then spend time tuning in to the love and kindness in your heart and see these feelings start to dissolve those negative thoughts.

- Now visualize yourself sending out positive energy to these people. See them as souls. See them through the lens of your loving heart. If there are several people, do this process meticulously with each one. It is very important. It will both free them up and liberate you.

- What Shadow scenarios out in the world most disturb you today and do you feel inclined, in some way, to "take any of them on"? If so, what do you think you can do. Make notes.

- Be aware that Shadow issues will always come up and you always need to be ready for them and ready to work with them. The further you journey up into the higher worlds, the darker will be the Shadows that you may be required to face.

CHAPTER 13

Gateways into Other Realities

*I feel more and more every day, as my imagination
strengths, that I do not live in one world alone,
but in a thousand worlds.*
— JOHN KEATS

*Another world is not only possible. On a quiet day,
I can hear her breathing.*
— ARUNDHATI ROY

*This "world" lost all reality because I had abruptly
entered another world, infinitely more real...*
— RENÉ DAUMAL

There is another world but it is in this one.
— W. B. YEATS

Understanding Levels

Let us pause for a moment and take some time to look at everything that
we have so far been discussing from the perspective of *levels*. The first
point I want to make is that an existence where we seek to live more soulfully or abundantly — where we attempt to have our daily life become our
sacred practice — is one that exists at a *higher level* than the mindset I have
been describing as being the rajassic way or the "old story".

A Gandhi operates at a higher level than does a Trump. Higher soul
self exists at a higher level than the separate self. The "game" of healing or
"saving" the planet is "played" at a higher level than the extractionist games.

Also, what is natural or normal at one level is not so at another level.
So, for example, while we may indignantly scream at the terrible actions of
world leaders — for example, Syria's Bashar al-Assad — and say "How could
you treat your own people in this way", his behaviour is completely in

keeping with the level he operates from, and thus with the kind of values he is drawn to. While you or I might find his actions repugnant, he will not have awakened to a level where the suffering of his own people has the slightest impact upon him, as what is most important to him is his own survival and his remaining in power.

All dictators live by a not dissimilar story. Their value systems are undeveloped and consequently, what might trouble you or me deeply simply does not concern them. And of course vice versa. Planet-centric awareness is still light years away from such people.

Levels divide us

What most divides us, then, from one another is not so much our perceived differences – skin colour, sexual preferences, race, religion or nationality – but the levels we operate at. The lower the level, the more our differences become a cause for separation; the higher the level, the less important this is. For example, for your average jihadist, who operates at a very low level, someone believing in a deity different from the one they subscribe to eminently justifies that person's murder. Conversely, for people who are seeking to make their daily life their sacred practice and who believe that the most important thing linking us is our shared humanity, how someone looks, what class or race they belong to, what religion they subscribe to or what their sexual preferences are, are of scant importance.

In other words, what is central and what is peripheral to us depends upon our level of consciousness, upon how evolved or awake we are or how connected or disconnected we happen to be to our higher-order soul self. One can say that we are "asleep" to, or have not yet awoken to, levels that we have not yet attained. This is why the fanatical white supremacist simply cannot understand why issues that are so important to him may not be so to other people.

I know this may seem obvious, but let's spell it out again: If we take someone who operates at a level where status and having power and making money for themselves and their clan is central to them and therefore more important than anything else, to expect them to be concerned about climate change or the plight of immigrants is like believing that cows can jump over the moon!

The levels we operate from, then, determine what we believe to be important. The lower our level, the more linked in we are to everything that I have been arguing is wrong with our world, and the harder it is to understand that higher, more abundant levels of consciousness might exist. This is why the system likes to keep us stressed and conflicted, as it keeps our levels low and thus makes us more dependent upon it.

Energy availability

The level we primarily operate at also affects the quality of energy available to us. It determines whether it is a high-frequency, alive kind of energy, or low-frequency and sluggish.

In the tamassic world, where, as we have seen, there can be a big tendency to be taken over by the *wetiko* spirit, the energy will most probably be dense and heavy and it can affect our health and well-being if we live at that level all the time. In these twilight worlds, we aren't drawn to "natural highs" – nature, inspiration and mystical insight – but rather to extremely unnatural ones.

Can you see now how important our levels of consciousness are? When I first went to Findhorn, the reason why I felt so uplifted and so aware of the humanity I had in common with everyone I met was because the community lived according to values and stories that celebrated our interconnectedness. And this impacted strongly on me. Consciousness-wise, it raised me up. Had an old-story mindset existed there, I would probably only have been aware of the many differences I had with those I encountered and would have been propelled back into my mythic elitism!

One of the basic differences, then, between people who still subscribe to the old story and those beginning to live into the new one is that the former not only operate with a heavier energy, but also labour under many more limitations. Thus, their creative or imaginative capacities will always be limited by the realities in which they primarily dwell. Resistance to the possibility of a new culture existing can be so strong and is therefore why certain people experience change as being so difficult.

Transformational presence

People who occupy what I will describe as the *higher echelons* of consciousness, that is, very highly evolved people who are much more fully awake to who they are than you and I, generally have a strong presence and as I have already pointed out, they may possess the capacity radically to raise the awareness of those they come into contact with. I will tell you a little story to illustrate this.

A few years ago, while travelling to New Zealand to see my young daughter, I spent a few hours in transit at Kuala Lumpur airport, where my path crossed with that of a young Buddhist monk from Thailand. To all outward appearances we had little in common, but this beautiful, pure young man radiated a presence that was full of deep sweetness and it affected me very strongly.

Although our encounter only lasted a few hours, it was intense; I left to catch my plane feeling very deeply moved, and with the sense that I now had a new "special friend" in my life. I felt closer to him than I had ever felt with the old schoolfriend with whom I had just spent three days, who I had known all my life. How was this possible?

It was possible because my new friend had a very open heart and the world he inhabited was a deep and soulful one. In fact, my new friend represented how we all ought to be – and indeed, could be – if we were to work on ourselves! I went deep with him not because we had an especially meaningful intellectual conversation, but because he inhabited a world that had a natural profundity to it; in his company, I temporarily "caught" this depth off him.

One could say that his presence lifted me and consequently opened an important gateway for me. His elevated humanity gave me permission to open to more of my humanity, to bring more of my soul out of the closet. After he had left, I looked around me at everyone in the airport. Because my heart was now so full of love, they felt like my brothers and sisters. No separation existed. This is how the consciousness of very awake people can potentially affect us and how we are challenged to see the world more and more of the time.

Different worlds, different levels

What gives us meaning at any time and how profound our experience of it is, then – or, put another way, how we see the world – is determined by the kind of reality that we primarily inhabit. Imagine two people, sitting side by side gazing at a sunset but who operate on very different levels. They both may look similar and you might think on first seeing them that they are similar. But they are not.

For one person, the experience is an epiphany; for the other a total bore. What divides them is the levels they both operate at. These differences are expressed beautifully clearly in a letter written by William Blake to a Dr John Trusler in 1799:

I see everything I paint in this world but every body does not see alike.
To the eyes of a miser, a guinea is more beautiful than the sun and a
bag worn with the use of money has more beautiful proportions than a
vine filled with grapes. The tree which moves some to tears of joy is in
the eyes of others only a green thing that stands in the way. Some see
nature all ridicule and deformity…and some scarce see nature at all.
But to the eyes of the man of imagination nature is imagination itself.
As a man is, so he sees…[25]

Human Development and Evolution

Don Beck is a geopolitical advisor and theorist focussing on the appli-
cation of large-scale psychology, including social psychology and evolutionary psychology and its effect on human socio-cultural systems.
With his colleague Christopher Cowen, he developed a structured
evolutionary model of human development that consists of eight levels
or "worlds", and which they called Spiral Dynamics. In their model,
the first five levels are all variations of what in my lingo I refer to as
the rajassic domain. The sixth level represents a huge shift, as the first
stirrings of the deeper soul self together with a new sense of planetary
awareness now starts to come into existence.

In levels one to five, the emphasis to start with is primarily on
surviving – having enough food, water, safety, sex and warmth. People
perform rituals to appease spirits and have allegiance to clan leaders.
When a rudimentary separate self starts emerging distinct from the
tribe, at these levels it is primarily about seeking power and glory. The
emphasis is on having as much pleasure as possible without regret or
remorse. Even when life at the higher spectrum of these levels begins to
have more meaning, direction and purpose, it is still all about personal
advantage and responding to incentives like money and political gain; the
world being regarded as a chessboard with winners gaining pre-eminence
over losers and scientific materialism, neo-liberalism and capitalism's
unacceptable face (as, for example, is so beautifully portrayed in the film
The Wolf of Wall Street) reigning supreme.

From the sixth level onwards we see the first flickers of those soulful
qualities, values, beliefs, stories and mindsets that I have been arguing we
need to take up in order to try to "save" or heal our planet.

Here, the story changes radically: here, as I said, the soul self starts
to emerge and people begin to believe that they need to live sustainably,

think ecologically and not pollute the planet. Some of the intentions characteristic of people starting to find gateways into this world, include the desire to:

- create more meaningful relationships
- care more deeply about their development as human beings
- achieve more equality for women
- be more optimistic about the future
- move away from the emphasis in modern culture on "making it" and on spending on expensive and luxury goods
- support worthwhile causes.

But Beck's level six is not the end of the road into soulfulness. Rather, it is the beginning. When we touch into the highest levels, seven and eight, we start showing a capacity to take on multiple perspectives on life and our true reconciliatory capabilities begin emerging. We see that differences and pluralities can be integrated into interdependent natural flows. Knowledge and competency supersede power and status. *This is the world of the ultimate synthesis of people, nations and organizations and it is seeking to pull those of us who are open to it up towards it. It is this domain which at the end of this book, I argue is going to "overlight" sufficient numbers of us to be able to carry humanity through to the next step in our evolution.*

Work at this level, has to be meaningful to the overall health of life. People who reside here find themselves able to see and honour many perspectives, including – and this is a very important point – those of the so-called "lower realities", that is, the domains of the old story. They realize that the name of the new game to be played is not to turn against and reject the past and make the old order wrong, as they realize that fragments of it still reside inside them. Instead, the aim is to try to fecundate the lower realities with higher-order heart and mind states and so try to help the rigid "ancien regime" to begin evolving! This needs to occur at a personal as much as at a societal level. We cannot reject and grow away from our past. We need to respect and take it up with us to the new level.

Beck's level eight recognizes that there is not one way to achieve greater harmony in the world, any more than there is one way to God.

And there exist even more evolved worlds still, which are also calling "down" to us or beckoning to us from "within" ourselves. And if we do the work required to open up gateways into these worlds and start receiving their blessings and generosity, then we will be able to make huge strides in consciousness.

I say this as these are worlds so profound that men and women who aspire to these levels no longer need to make choices as to whether a course of action is the correct one; their souls have become so fully attuned to the intelligent forces of evolution that they cannot but do what is aligned to the deeper well-being of the larger cosmos. The "Force" is well and truly embedded within them. People touching into these levels begin finding whole new sensibilities growing inside them, often including the escalation of their psychic, intuitive and creative abilities together with a deeper recognition of their belongingness within the heart not just of the planet but of the whole cosmos.

⟋⟍

I stress again that it is not the case that human qualities such as love, compassion, wisdom, courage and a desire for truth, justice and equality are entirely absent in the first five worlds, but rather that *at these levels, these qualities do not yet exist at a high enough grade or in a sufficient concentration to have a transforming effect on people's lives or in the life of our society.* Imagine drinking fresh apple juice very diluted with water; at this level one can hardly taste the apple at all, but it is unarguable that the juice is in itself delicious.

Peaks and troughs

While in the first five levels we are *particularly* vulnerable to being corrupted (remember what I said about our *wetiko* virus), in truth all eight worlds are susceptible to allowing tamassic ingredients to begin growing in their midst. Yes, even great gurus and saints and sages, who exist in the highest echelons of the new-story realities, can be seduced and are capable of regressing. I am sure we all know cases of very wonderful human beings who have fallen from grace, brought low by sex, drugs, fame, money or power.

What is also interesting is that in the same way that an evolved person can be *pulled down* off their perch and be "laid low" – we can call it a "trough experience" – it is also possible for someone who inhabits one of the lower levels to have a "close encounter" with a higher-order reality and experience some very transformational experiences, and consequently experience themselves being temporarily *pulled up* into a much more evolved world. We call this a "peak experience".

The effect may often open a person's heart and for a certain period of time, they are propelled much closer to their authenticity and may even be given a kind of sneak preview into the realization that in truth all of life really *is* interconnected. I use the word "temporarily" because whether we are being propelled up or precipitated down, we will tend only to spend a short time at our new level of consciousness. Our visit may only last a few days or even just a few hours. How, we may ask, is this kind of movement between reality levels possible?

Fluid worlds

It is possible because all the worlds or realities are very fluid and always interpenetrate each other; no domain is absolutely watertight. While there will always be a particular reality that will be more central in our lives at any time, we are always susceptible to being influenced by realities just above and just below where we primarily reside.

For example, I remember when I was at university, in the days when I was still very immersed in my old-story, ultra-snooty ways, going to hear an Indian master speak and then spending a weekend at his ashram and being very inspired by his worldview. I temporarily ascended into a more awake world. But it was only fleeting.

The experience lasted perhaps a couple of days; then it slowly wore off and my old rajassic separate ego self grabbed hold of me again. Indeed, aged 20 and spending a lot of my time being very seduced by the worlds of glamour and chicness, my immersion in old-story values was still so great that nothing could have shifted me. We cannot change until we are ready to. There is a delightful old Hindu saying that goes "When the fruit is ripe it falls from the tree." Not before.

It is important to remember this!

Today, I think that many of us feel poised in a kind of midway place between our past tugging at us, telling us to continue doing things the old-story way, and future, higher-order realities beckoning us to move forward into terrain as yet uncharted.

The suffering world

There is another world or dimension of being that is also very important to understand, which is not included in Beck's methodology. I will simply call it the Suffering World or the Underworld. While there is only one of these domains, it again has different layers or levels, and how we experience it, should we tumble down into it, depends on two important criteria: firstly, *how deeply we fall into it* – its depths can be very murky indeed – and secondly, *what level we fall from*. If we fall into it from, say, a low level, we will have much less capacity to deal with the many challenges it presents us with than if we tumble into it, say, from level six.

Why? Because in the higher-order realities we generally have more capacity to deal with life's challenges in a more coherent way, as we will have started doing serious inner work on ourselves and consequently our soul life will have begun germinating and our emotional, mental and spiritual intelligences will have begun evolving.

That said, from whatever heights we tumble into the Suffering World from, and however shallowly or deeply we go into this domain, it is a singularly unpleasant space to visit. In my own life, I have had more than enough encounters with it.

We visit this world on those occasions when we feel terribly depressed or sense that life has no meaning in it and we want to die, or when we feel obsessed with hatred and a desire for revenge, or when nastily rejected by someone we adore. At its deepest levels, it is a truly dungeonous, dysfunctional, psychotic, dangerous and psychopathic zone where life is completely topsy-turvy. At these levels, we can liken it to Dante's Hell – or, in Jesus' words, a vale of "weeping and gnashing of teeth".

Often this world is characterized by extreme viciousness and violence. In its darkest regions, it is the realm of child abuse, torture chambers, Nazism, severe crack cocaine addiction, violent pornography and ethnic cleansing. Writers like Jean Genet and William Burroughs have been excellent cartographers of its despair-filled wasteland. Here, evil may have its abode; here, love is so degraded that we may even commit murder in its name. Many ISIS members and probably a lot of white supremacists spend time there. It is the world whose depths the Norwegian Anders Breivik no doubt plumbed when he decided to murder 77 children, and it is chillingly personified by the cannibalistic serial killer Hannibal Lecter in the film *The Silence of the Lambs* and by the slobby and gluttonous Jabba the Hutt in the Star Wars films.

Luckily, most of us neither plumb those truly terrible depths nor do we tend to take up long-term residence there – if we do have to visit the Suffering World, it is only occasionally and temporarily.

States and stages of consciousness

What do I mean when I talk about visiting a certain world occasionally or staying there all the time? This is an important distinction and here I am grateful to Ken Wilber for clarifying it very well in many of his writings.

We need to recognize that there is a big difference between a *state* – the experience of *temporarily* "dropping down" or "moving up" into a reality whose worldview *temporarily* impacts us, and a *stage* – which happens when we take up residence in a particular reality with the result that its worldview becomes embedded inside us: that is, we live it *all the time*.

When we enter a stage, it becomes the prime lens through which we see life and live it, in all our waking moments. I have described how I was temporarily elevated into a higher world as a result of being in the presence of the young Buddhist monk I met at the airport. What I touched into was a higher *state* of consciousness. It was not a *stage* – I did not continue to reside there. Most of us enter higher-order soul worlds first as a state and then, if we decide we like the scenery there, and are prepared to work to find the gateways leading to residency, we can over time transform our state into a stage.

Visitations by grace

When I talked about "peak experiences" I suggested that, whatever our level, we are all potentially open to being "visited" by grace: that is, to having higher worlds "descend" into us or open up their hearts to us and so temporarily embrace and uplift us.

Yes, my friend, as I said earlier, higher realities seem able to "reach down" and touch us, inspire us and open us up, and also to have an effect on people who might seem utterly "untouchable", in the same way that the downward pull of degeneracy seems able to "reach up" and infect anyone, including those whom we would have deemed were "beyond temptation"!

To feel graced, often a trigger is required, such as doing a particular kind of work, tuning in to nature, meditating on soul or falling passionately in love. Sometimes, however, there are no obvious triggers at all and grace just enters us with no particular warning, as it seemed to do for St Paul on the road to Damascus. However the experience comes upon us, even if it is short-lived, it can have an extraordinary healing effect upon us.

I remember, many years ago, being fortunate enough to spend a night in a sacred space where I was surrounded by the tombs of great saints. As

I sat in meditation, I was aware of a great luminescence all around me and over the following weeks I observed that a problem that had been irking me for much of my life had suddenly enormously diminished in nature; now as I write about this experience many years later, the problem has entirely vanished from my life. There is no doubt that very, very high-frequency energy has great healing capabilities and is why our being able to access the mystical domains of our human nature is of such profound evolutionary significance.

Interpreting graced experiences

Regardless of how our graced experiences come about, how we *experience* and *interpret* them – that is, the kind of lens through which we view and understand them – will be determined not only by the world or reality we primarily inhabit but also by the culture we belong to.

So let us say someone very highly evolved has an ecstatic experience. It could well be experienced by them as emblematic of the transcendental, infinite, selfless self, the divine consciousness that is in all the great spiritual masters and in you and me too, and which reveals a reality beyond death, suffering and space and time. While the experience does happen for them personally, they will know that in fact they have touched into a state of consciousness or a sacred presence far greater than their own little personal-ness.

If, on the other hand, someone less highly evolved who happens, say, to be a Protestant and who lives on the cusp between the old and new stories has the same ecstatic experience, they may well feel predisposed to interpret it in their familiar Christian terms; possibly as an encounter with Jesus or with an angel.

However, if someone who happens to be a Christian fundamentalist has this same visitation by grace, they may well interpret the experience as proof that *they* really *are* special, that *they* really *are* one of the "chosen ones" and that Jesus has come *personally* to save them!

Conversely, if this same high state manages to percolate through the defences of someone who lives a very defended or clenched-in kind of life and has no belief that anything "higher" or "sacred" exists, the peak or graced experience may be experienced as abject terror! "Help, this is happening but it can't be happening!"

In all cases the experience is the same but how it appears to us is conditioned by where we are at and the culture we belong to.

Step by step into higher humanity

It is important to remember that we graduate into higher-order worlds of soul or into our deeper (or higher) humanity step by step and in different ways. Some of us seem to take big leaps and then take a long time to integrate them. Others advance more gradually, going, say, five steps forward and two back! However we progress, as we learn to take our inner work increasingly seriously, and as it deepens with the result that our consciousness gradually expands and our sense of possessing a higher soul self continuously opens up, we become more and more drawn towards the idea of a new vision for our planet and a desire to serve that vision with all our heart and soul.

As we evolve, we also observe that the kind of "games" we feel moved to "play" (the way we choose to live our lives) also naturally shifts and matures – things that used to hold little importance for us now hold plenty and vice versa – and the "rules" also become other than how they used to be.

We note too, that the fuller and more abundant we become as human beings, the less pull the system has over us.

By the same token, the denser or more tamassic the reality we inhabit, the less awake we are and the less freedom we have, the more control the system has over us. We realize, therefore, that while we live in a culture that is largely composed of that system, that it is eminently possible to remain above it as its observer, being "in it but not of it", that is, seeing it but not having its tentacles intrude into us, as we will have mainly detached ourselves from those areas of our lives where it can have a hold over us.

So as our planet grows increasingly confused and topsy-turvy and as breakdowns of one form or another occur all around us, we are challenged to open up our heart and soul life and develop our inner clarity and strength, not simply out of a need to survive the chaos (although this is very important), but also to ensure that we may exercise a transforming influence upon it.

We gradually come to see that operating out of the higher-order realities enables us to achieve things that we could not do while residing in the less evolved worlds. To give an example, an activist working to save the whales or someone standing up for human rights can achieve much more working out of a higher world. I have also observed that my own work has become increasingly effective as I have very slowly evolved.

No bypassing

As I mentioned earlier, it is very unwise to think we can bypass realities, and if we attempt to enter worlds or go through gateways that we are not yet ready to face, it can often be at our own peril.

Also, if you and I are fully to embody a world – to embrace it as a stage – it is important that at least 90 percent of our self transitions into it. If this doesn't happen and too much of ourselves gets left behind, we can feel split. What often transpires is that we may become intellectually mature – that is, our minds evolve and go through the gateway – but our emotional self remains behind and we stay emotionally juvenile. Often, it is this immaturity that can be our undoing and that renders us vulnerable to being pulled off our perches – which has certainly been the case with certain well-known spiritual teachers – which is again why doing the inner emotional healing work on ourselves (especially with our inner child) that we explored earlier on, is so vitally important.

Honouring, not rejecting, our past

When we start operating at higher-order levels, we are instinctively pioneering new ways to be and to live in the world. However – and I will continue to make this point as it is so important – this must never mean that we ignore, reject or demean or feel ourselves in any way superior to people who still primarily function in old-story ways; or, conversely, feel moved to wage war against those parts of ourselves that may still remain immature.

On the contrary, we must try to see how, without our being in any way self-righteous, those people, or those less awakened aspects of ourselves, can be helped to evolve. As our consciousness expands, or as more dimensions of who we are start coming into play, what happens, as I mentioned earlier, is that we feel increasingly committed to trying to inject higher-order values into the fabric of our old culture. In other words, we come to see that endeavouring to live our daily lives as a sacred practice has to include our consciously choosing never to reject Krishnamurti's "sick society" but rather explore how we can best imbue it with sacred energy to help it transform – support it become more functional and holistic. So for example, a more enlightened scientist will not decry a colleague for still holding on to a materialist view of science, but will explore ways and means to seek gently to coax that colleague into possible new ways of viewing their field.

One reason why Hillary Clinton lost the US presidential election in 2016 was that she proclaimed herself a superior kind of person and dismissed all those who resonated with Donald Trump as just being a bunch of redneck "despicables". By evoking their hostility as opposed to giving them a voice (as Trump did), she gifted him the election.

Best and Worst of Worlds

We are now clear about the relationship between the values we embrace and the level of consciousness we inhabit, and the fact that none of us can be expected to exhibit features of a reality that as yet we have no comprehension of. We have also seen how we can be "pulled up" or "pulled down" by various states, and also that the way we will experience whatever we encounter, depends on our overall level of development: that is, by how much or how little "integrative or imaginative capacity" we possess.

While I talk about our being firmly ensconced in a particular reality, of course this can never be effectively quantified. It is hard to measure consciousness and my general take is that those who love to parade how wise and awakened they are tend to be less far along the path than those who don't. But I will mention that just as it is important that we never consider a temporary "Aha! Wow!" peak experience to be evidence that we are enlightened, so we should also never interpret a temporary descent into Dante's Hell as evidence that we are doomed to dwell in the Underworld for ever, even though at the time it may feel like it. In fact, as we saw in the chapter on the Shadow, the more we start engaging in playing the "awakening game", the more we realize that we cannot hope to begin discovering what may be best about ourselves without also having to confront what is worst.

▧ EXERCISE

- ▪ What thoughts has this chapter brought up for you and do you think you have learned anything new? If so, write down your thoughts.
- ▪ How do you feel you evolve? Step by step or do you take huge chunks and then spend a lot of time integrating them? Comment on the challenges either stance gives you.
- ▪ Have you ever descended into the Suffering World, or had a peak experience and ascended into a domain of grace? If so, write about your experiences.

- What can you specifically do, or perhaps not do, to develop your capacity to have peak experiences? Write some guidelines to yourself.
- How liberated from the system do you feel you are? Are you able to be "in the world but not of it"? If this is hard, what aspects of the system do you find hardest to disentangle from and why, and what are the challenges this provides you with? Write them down.
- Are you starting to live the way your heart and soul desire for you? If so, what are you doing that works and opens up gateways, and if not, what do you think you need to do more of? What area or areas of inner work are hardest for you?

CHAPTER 14

Gateways into Friendship

Friendship that flows from the heart cannot be frozen by adversity, as the water that flows from the spring cannot congeal in winter.
— JAMES FENIMORE COOPER

I will scatter myself among men and women and as I go, I will toss a new gladness and roughness among them...
— WALT WHITMAN

The Importance of Friendship

Choosing to make space to relate in a gracious, respectful and friendly way to everyone we come into contact with is a central aspect of having our daily lives be lived soulfully. As is valuing the importance of good friendships.

As we've seen, love can be expressed at many different levels, and exactly the same holds true for friendliness and friendship. Not all our friendships are necessarily soulful, which is why it is so important that we all work at opening our hearts up more. When Thomas Hughes said "Blessed are they who have the gift of making friends, for it is one of God's best gifts; it involves many things, but above all, the giving out of one's self and appreciating whatever is noble and loving in another", he was defining it at a level that I think we should all aim for. However, not all of us are able to go there. If we primarily operate at rajassic levels, that is, we live in Don Beck's worlds two to five, we won't be able to "do" friendship along these lines. I am not suggesting that at these levels we don't value friendship and don't appreciate having friends, nor that we are necessarily unfriendly. But if the self that we share with others is limited to being our separate and not our soulful self, we probably won't yet know how properly to appreciate "whatever is noble and loving in another" or to give of our nobility to others, as our range won't yet have included such vistas.

The limited nature of old-story friendships

From a rajassic viewpoint, therefore, friendship tends to be somewhat conditional and to lack depths. It may be conditioned more by similar tastes, faults, interests and backgrounds than by any kind of sharing of "beingness".

I myself have some of these friendships, especially with some of my old mates from school and university. And it is not that I do not appreciate these friendships. Because I do. However, it would not be true to say that they nourish me deeply or that my soul feels fed by them. For example, one cannot have a level-six friendship if one's friend is more familiar with conversing at levels three, four or five. Similarly, if a very highly evolved person were seeking to be a friend of mine, he or she would need to adjust their levels down to where I am at.

If we find that we exist at a higher level than our friend, then, as I stressed earlier, we should never feel superior to or better than them – as the simple truth is that we are not. Butterflies are not superior to caterpillars. They're just at a different stage of their evolution. Rather, we should always try to meet someone at the level or levels we sense they are comfortable with and in no way try to force "depths" onto someone who we sense is not open to them. But before I say more about friendship, let me say a bit about friendliness.

The importance of friendliness

Friendliness is not the same as friendship. Friendliness is more open and can include – indeed, it ought to include – almost everyone. It may lead to friendship or it may not; indeed I am not for one moment suggesting that everyone must be our friend. However, I see no reason why – unless someone has just done something dreadful to us – we cannot relate in a friendly, good-natured, respectful and well-meaning way to everyone whom we encounter, whoever they may be, and without it mattering what level they are at or how different from us they may be.

I think the demonstrating of friendliness is so important, a) because there is not enough of it in the world, and for this we all pay a price; b) because it is an adhesive that can connect us much more closely with people, and thus help create a more unified world; and c) because it allows for the possibility that it might morph into friendship. Also, most importantly, when friendliness emerges unfriendliness begins to dissolve. Thus, all the enshadowing we recently explored, all the dumping of our disowned stuff onto others, all our prejudices and scapegoating – all those symptoms of rabid unfriendliness can start to unravel.

Friendliness is like a food

Relating in a friendly way with people is nourishing for both giver and receiver, and because it doesn't have all the expectations that friendship does, one can be more carefree. Over the years, I have had five-minute friendly encounters – waiting in line, on a bus and so on – with people I've never known before or encountered again after, where unexpected depths have spontaneously peeked through magically as if from nowhere.

And it has felt so nourishing.

I also observe that people who walk around choosing to relate in a friendly way to others, and who always have a smile and a kind word to say, are much more likely to be happy people. It then follows that people who don't know how to be friendly, or who don't bother or regard it as important, often suffer as a result.

I rate being friendly to everyone I encounter in my daily life high up on the scale of sacred practices that I regard as vitally important. Wherever I go – be it walking down the road outside my house or travelling to a foreign country – I try to practise encountering everyone who comes across my path in the spirit of unconditional positive regard. People pick it up and smile back at me and it feels good.

Remember the delightful man I encountered at Kuala Lumpur airport? We probably wouldn't have connected with each other in the way we did if we had not both been on the friendly trail!

Honouring the outcast

I not only think it is important in the spirit of friendliness that we respect the cultural customs of those we are choosing to be friendly towards – for example, I have been told that we don't show the soles of our feet to Japanese people as in their culture, this is considered a grave insult – but also that we take great care to be especially friendly towards those who may feel cast out or excluded in a community – and here I include people begging on the streets, those with addiction issues, impoverished refugees and street people of all shapes and forms who have been made to feel like outsiders. If we take steps to be truly friendly, perhaps we can in some small way help reconnect them to the society that, for one reason or other, they have become exiled from.

And feeling like an exile, feeling alienated and that no one wants to know us, is one of the worst forms of impoverishment.

Some of us are perhaps challenged to take the spirit of friendliness a stage further, especially if we happen to have the concrete means to help those less fortunate than ourselves. We don't necessarily need to know who a person is in order to care about them and even, if we so choose, to take care of them!

I spoke earlier about Gandhi's attitude towards respect, and I see this as an integral part of friendliness. Why the projection of disrespect onto someone can be such a killer is because it serves to reduce a person to being nothing more than some part of them that we may disagree with, disapprove of or feel threatened by. And, as we just saw, it is very easy to take on the negative projectiles aimed at us and believe we really *are* how other people perceive us! I therefore consider the whole business of fault finding – which in our "sick society" exists in epidemic proportions – to be one of the most damaging, unfriendly and pernicious of all activities.

OK. Let us now move to friendship.

What is new-story friendship?

If I ask myself what I *really* want from those who are my dear friends, there are seven requests, and I think they define for me what a genuine friendship is about. I ask that my friends

1) love and accept me for who I am (and for what I am not), and allow me to enjoy their company without any ulterior motive and without my feeling I have to put on a special face in order to be accepted;

2) are fond enough of me and know me well enough to always tell me the truth as they experience it. At times, this may require that they challenge me and point out where and when they feel I am making mistakes, but they do so in such a way that I am always elevated and never diminished by their insights;

3) always encourage me to be me and enable me to share my innermost thoughts and craziest ideas without feeling silly, or out of place;

4) not only enjoy the good times with me but will not desert me and stop being loyal and supportive if the going happens to get tough;

5) allow me to love them for who they are, so that a field of deeper unconditional friendship can slowly start to grow between us. If we are in an intimate relationship, this will of course include sex, but if not, it won't (we can of course love people very deeply and have very deep friendships without being sexually involved);

6) have the courage not to turn away from working through difficulties if any arise between us (very often in close friendships, big Shadow issues can emerge);

7) can always be relied on to feed me the food of imaginative sympathy so that my heart and soul may blossom in their presence.

Of course not every friendship will give us all of these gifts and, as we saw earlier, we can have friendships with people that aren't deep and where soulful topics are not on the menu.

As I said, a lot of friendships are based on a collusion of habits or just social convenience. Yes, we can be friends with people because we both come from similar backgrounds and have certain things in common like having been to the same school, share the same political affiliations, work in the same profession, even have certain weaknesses in common! And there is nothing "wrong" with these friendships. They, too, need honouring. It is just that when heart and soul enter the equation, greater depths become possible and the friendship can start existing in a higher domain – Spiral Dynamics' level six or above.

The beauty of deeper friendships is that the act of being intimate with another person can bring out many wonderful qualities in both parties, such as love, loyalty, consistency, respect, generosity of spirit, kindness, compassion, humour, fun and honesty. It is on the wings of such qualities that we can move through gateways into the higher realms of soul.

Soul mates

I like the idea of our having soul mates, which I define as friends who accept the existence of soul and where our buddyhood is centred around a concern for each other's evolutionary growth as well as a strong desire to make a difference in the world. Our role in each other's lives is to support just these purposes.

I go to a lot of conferences and will often connect up with good soul mates at such gatherings, where we are often involved in projects together. I find these friends a huge joy to hang out with.

Soul mentors

Soul mentors are different. They are generally found in a relationship between older and younger people, where the older person acts as a kind of wise guide for the younger person. I think this is very important, especially in today's world as it grows ever more confusing.

When I was a young man, I suffered because I had no older person to help guide and mentor me on my path through life. Consequently I made many mistakes and took many wrong turnings. It was not until I was about 30 that I met someone who became a very important mentor for me in a relationship that lasted many years. Today, therefore, I have made a point of having a mentoring relationship with many young people and I find this very fulfilling, especially as I always learn so much from them. It is important that soul mentors in some way hold the next step of our human evolution in their consciousness and so can give guidance to young people from this place.

The evolution of friendship

Whatever kind of friendships we have, we need to remember that they seldom remain the same. They either evolve or they fade. Sometimes, at the start, they can grow very quickly, but if no effort is made by either party to build upon their early foundations, they can easily crumble away, which is why there can be a certain comfort in having friends whom we have known for a long time, as the dangers of this erosion occurring are much less.

That said, if we feel that the "something special" that once existed has now gone and that the old spark is no longer there, we need to accept this and not be overly sentimental. Ten years ago, I left the Gloucestershire village where I had lived for many years, and while I am still close to a few of my old buddies there, most have fallen by the wayside as there is no longer enough common ground to sustain us.

Circle of friends

I like the term "circle of friends". Those who are very close to us – our spouses, lovers, best buddies, some soul mates, family – constitute our inner circle.

However, there are also those who exist a little further out – close but not as close – and those who exist at the outer perimeters of our circle; those who are certainly still our friends, only we don't share really intimate things with them. Maybe they will come closer. Maybe not. Or perhaps they will just slowly drift out of our circle altogether and in so doing, make space for some of those hovering on its edge to move in more. We need therefore to allow our circle to be fluid and open and respect the way life unfurls, and to let go our attachment to having things remain the way they always used to be, which again is very much a trait of Beck's levels two to five.

For me, friendship needs to be a flow. All of us express our friendship at a different level, in a different way, and – back to gratitude again – we need to be grateful for what our friendships *do* give us, not be unhappy about what they *don't*! No one friendship will give us everything.

Sustaining friendships

For existing friendships to continue, however, they will need sustaining, and here it helps if we place friendship high up on our list of what we consider significant in our lives. I do. Many people don't and I feel this is a shame. Indeed, many of us sandwich friendship in between what we deem to be more "important" – things like, say, our work or our marriage or our children, which we then devote "quality time" to. But what this means is that we only have our exhaustion left for our friends, which I find a great pity and a mark of disrespect.

Agreed, the love we have for our friends is different from that which we have for our family, but it is also very important, and *I think we are all challenged to find imaginative ways to keep our friendship fires burning; I see them as a potential deep source of soul food, and the deeper they are, the more they can nourish us.*

But if we don't feed them in return – if we don't make efforts to stay in touch and meet and perhaps do things together with our friends and take time to explore if what we share might move to a new level – a friendship might wither when it could be growing. Here are some of the blocks that may stand in the way of our enjoying soulful friendships in our lives. See if any apply to you.

- We make no space in our lives for friends – we're too busy! Friendship exists low down on our scale of priorities.
- We fear or dislike the whole business of learning to interact with new people – perhaps because we grew up with parents who were anti-social, so we never learned friend-making skills.

189

- Our self-esteem is low and so to protect ourselves we project onto others that they don't like us, and so put up a screen that keeps them away. "I wouldn't be a friend of anyone who would want me as their friend" might be our negative mantra.
- We fear real intimacy (and real friendship implies intimacy) in case we might then lose it and we'll be rejected. The idea of rejection is so painful that we will sabotage a potential friendship and ensure it never gets off the ground so that we'll never have to face that possibility.
- Our friend-making and friend-keeping skills are both underdeveloped.
- We feel that only certain people, who think like us and come from a similar background, can be our friend. Thus we limit the possibilities of who might qualify.
- We fear that friendship means being swamped. Perhaps we had the experience of having had our boundaries continually invaded by our siblings or our parents. So to stay safe now, we ensure no one comes close.
- We are not willing to experience and work through the inevitable ups and downs that all genuine friendships experience. Consequently, we often break off friendships at the first sign of a cold wind.
- We lack discernment and want to be friends with everyone, so we end up close to no one.
- Our always-on-the-go lifestyles preclude friendships – we are never in one place long enough to build them.
- We see ourselves as a loner, an outsider, a character a little like Meursault in Camus' novel *L'Etranger*, which means we are not focused on connecting emotionally with other people.

If we want the soul food of having more friends and enjoying them at a deeper level, we must not only put time and energy into this project, but also be willing to confront and work through what blocks us. It can also help to spend time observing people who are popular and have many friends, and see how they operate. We may see that such people often tend a) to be friendly, b) to be authentic, c) to genuinely care about others, d) to be empathic and good listeners, and e) to have a capacity to savour and enjoy people and so make people feel good around them.

So, what if we worked on ourselves to try to develop these attributes! This last point is especially important, for the more we delight in people's company, the more the business of creating friendships and observing them grow becomes a delight itself and thus a very natural part of our daily lives becoming our sacred practice.

The importance of having heart

Having an open heart is a key ingredient in our ability both to be genuinely friendly and to have loving friendships, as open hearts naturally honour and embrace people. With heart, as we've already seen, we also have the capacity to reach out into other people's hearts and sense what they are feeling and needing *from inside them*, which in turn equips us to be better at knowing how best to be appropriate for our friend at any time in their life. This intuiting is so important. What is required of us right now? Does our friend need us to stand back and let them talk, or is it preferable that we come forward with suggestions? Do they need our arm around their shoulder or should we let them put an arm around ours? I say this because in a genuine friendship, there always needs to be a balance between giving and taking. If we are always doing the running or conversely, the taking, then there will be serious imbalances.

Growing friendships

For me, there is always something enormously satisfying about the whole process of "growing a friendship", where we gradually come to know someone better, to see new sides of them slide into view that had hitherto been invisible. I always see this process as a beautiful adventure.

At times, we may need patience, as everyone reveals themselves very differently, and for those who initially show little of their true face our challenge is to be accepting and gentle, so they can trust us enough to gradually start thawing; often the deepest friendships emerge with those who initially do not present themselves as open books.

The gift that friendships offer us is not only that they give us pleasure but also that they can stretch us and help us evolve. An example is when tragedies happen to those we love. Let us say, for example, that a very dear friend becomes very ill or has a severe accident. Are we willing to drop the many things we do that we like to call "so important" to be there for them fully in their hour of need? I feel that these kinds of action are hugely important – and, again, they test us.

While you and I don't have a choice in the families we are born into, we always have a choice as to who we want to be our friend. I am fortunate in that as I am neither rich, glamorous or famous, I never need to be suspicious that people want to be my friend simply to feed off some kind of mysterious "allure".

▇ EXERCISES to develop friendliness

- ▪ Ask yourself: Am I a friendly person or do I walk about immersed in my own little world, disconnected from other people?
- ▪ If you are disconnected, do you want to change and be more friendly? If so, you will need to work on choosing to be more mindful of the world of people around you – more interested in them – and tell yourself that you are not separate from them, but connected to them.
- ▪ You might meditate on friendliness and choose to radiate it whenever you go out, making sure your emanations touch everyone you encounter, in a non-threatening, open-hearted but (very important) non-intrusive way. If you do this, you will notice that it will automatically put a smile on your face and also on many other people's faces when you pass them. Your friendliness will help bring theirs also out into the open.
- ▪ You can also think: what friendly things can you do for people? Perhaps mow the lawn for the old lady who lives next door or take her dog for a walk when we take ours? All these little acts go to build up a field of friendliness around us, which not only serves to protect us from those swathes of negativity that are so powerful in the world today, but also helps to reduce them. Thus practising friendliness is a very important sacred activity that brings light into the world.

▇ AFFIRMATIONS

I choose to be open and friendly to everyone I meet.

I choose to smile more often at people I encounter.

I choose to be mindful when I meet people and listen to what they have to say.

EXERCISE to develop friendship

- With your notebook in front of you, ask yourself the following questions:
  - *Do I value friendship and make a space for it in my life?*
  - *How important is it to me on a scale from 1 to 10?*
  - *How adept am I as a friend?*
  - *Are my friendships deep or shallow?*
  - *Are any of them truly soulful?*
  - *Do I have many friends in my life?*
  - *Do I work at maintaining and sustaining my friendships?*
  - *Am I a friend to the Earth?*
  - *Do I do things to block out or sabotage existing friendships and so ensure they do not evolve and go deep?*
  - *Am I scared of deep intimacy with my friends?*
- Spend time contemplating yourself as a friend. How would you rate yourself? (Remember: no self-flagellation!) Make notes on how you observe yourself in this arena. What feelings come up as you do this?
- Now ask yourself: do I wish to change anything in this area? Do I wish to have more or closer or deeper or more varied or more sustaining kinds of friendships? If so, based on what you have just read, make notes on what you feel you need to do if you wish to make this happen.
- Look again at my list of what stands in the way of us having friendships, and see if any of the points in it apply to you.
- Now think about how your life might change for the better if you actually
  a) addressed your blocks to friendship, and
  b) carried out your intentions.
- See if there is anyone already in your life on whom you could practise your new intentions. If so, go out and practise them.

Now write down some more guidelines for yourself for improving the way you experience your friendships, and then create some relevant affirmations for your life. The affirmations on the following page might make a useful start for you.

◼ AFFIRMATION

I choose to make more space in my life for friendship.

I choose to take greater care to nourish and deepen the friendships I already have.

I choose to draw to me more people whom I could potentially be friends with.

REMEMBER: Energy follows thought. So hold in your awareness that your new intentions will draw new people and new opportunities for new kinds of friendship into your life, and choose to be open to them. Imagine your circle of friends both widening and deepening.

CHAPTER 15

Gateways into Courage

The most courageous act is still to think for oneself.
— COCO CHANEL

Success is not final; failure is not final;
it is the courage to continue that counts.
— WINSTON CHURCHILL

The Importance of Courage

When E.E. Cummings suggested that "it takes courage to grow up and be who you really are", he was expressing a profound truth. Yes, my friend, it sure takes courage to mature and to be moved to engage in inner work and find out new things about ourselves and come face to face with our dark Shadow. It takes courage to say "no" to life's many seductions, not to go along with the herd, and not to participate in the desacralization process. And when the conventional opinion asks us to say "yes" – and we know we'll get lots of Brownie points for doing so – and we instead stand up and say "no" and don't back down when we are made wrong for it, there's a lot of bravery involved.

I particularly think of brave journalists who risk their lives to report what is happening behind the scenes in totalitarian countries, knowing full well that if caught, they will be tortured and imprisoned. I think of activists standing up for democratic rights or for the protection of their homes in the face of development threats; of Aung San Suu Kyi in her dissident days, when she was the sole voice speaking up for human rights in Burma as she stood up against the fascistic generals. In her book *Freedom from Fear and Other Writings* she tells us: "The most precious thing is the courage acquired through endeavour; courage that comes from cultivating the habit of refusing to let fear dictate one's actions; courage that could be described as 'grace under fire' – grace which is renewed repeatedly in the face of harsh, unremitting pressure." [26]

If danger, or the things that frightened us, didn't exist, if we never had to confront the things we feared, would we ever have the chance to become courageous?

I doubt it.

Courage based on accepting what is

While external courage is easy to see and to measure, inner heroism is much harder to quantify. We don't get any medals for it and often we don't even recognize it ourselves or give ourselves credit for it, but I think this is the kind of bravery many of us would-be activists for a more soulful world are being called to develop today.

I have an old friend who, at time of writing, is dying of cancer. He knows he only has a few months left. But he is not showing an iota of self-pity or "poor me, isn't this terrible"! On the contrary. He is still choosing to live as full a life as he is able, playing music, teaching and writing poems. Indeed, as I now revise this chapter, I have just heard that he has died and the person who informed me, who lived close to him, told me he was writing and teaching and being cheerful to the very end. The point is that he knew that very soon he would be entering the great unknown, and he had the courage to accept what lay ahead of him. He accepted that having a family and children would not be his lot in life and that he would die young and his life's work would be unfinished; but there was no complaining. His life force, I am told, remained fiery to the very end. That's the power of courage.

I don't think any of us are going to start "outing" who we really are – truly make our lives into a sacred practice – without a certain degree of bravery, for in going through a gateway we are very often facing the unknown. What does our life hold for us if we don't engage in it in the conventional and non-courageous way that the system tells us we should?

The faces of courage

Courage has many faces. It has a physical face. We see this in those intrepid explorers who venture into terrains no one has been to before, and in those mountaineers who conquer the highest peaks. Emotional courage is present in those who dare to open their hearts to someone and tell them they love them even though they are not sure how they will be received. Those scientists who dare to come up with new theories of how the universe works, knowing that the establishment will be threatened and will oppose and attack them for it, are the intellectually brave souls; while spiritual courage is present in those choosing to stand up for soulfulness in a soulless world.

At root, courage is all about a willingness to engage in life with passion, to choose to participate wholeheartedly in the adventure of discovering who we are and, in so doing, being prepared to take ourselves to the edge over and over again as we refuse to allow the many constraining forces in life to hold us back.

It often involves us taking risks. Sometimes heroism can just rise up from us out of the blue. Here is a little story to illustrate this point.

Harry, a rather timid massage therapist at my old sports club, surprised me once by announcing that he was off to Buckingham Palace to receive a medal for bravery.

He had seen a little girl being pushed onto the railway lines at a station and had jumped down onto the line and thrown her back up onto the platform. He just managed to get back up before the train bore down on him.

But the really important part of the story is what he told me next.

I didn't think I was being brave. Something in me much bigger than me came to life. I knew I had to save her life and the moment I jumped down and lifted her up, I felt in a different world; I felt I had all the time and all the strength."

He went on: "I feel very changed from this encounter. I have felt happier than I have ever felt and in a month I will be giving up working here. I plan to do something more adventurous with my life."

What had happened was that Harry's brave soul had taken him through a gateway, a rite of passage, and he had accessed whole other dimensions of his being. In order to succeed in the mission that his soul had required of him, he was, you might say, temporarily lent some extra strength by "the Force".

Altruism, or the willingness to put our own lives on the line (which Harry did quite literally), for another human being – even for someone we don't know – is inside all of us, and that one way to find *who we really are* is to discover that particular gateway and choose to go through it.

The call to adventure

So can you and I find that altruistic impulse inside ourselves that is happy to put our lives on the line for others and that *wants* to break out of our conventional existences, that *wants* to embrace a higher consciousness, that *wants* to do good, that *wants* to serve, love and honour our fellow human beings and our planet and give up our at times overly safe, often unadventurous and perhaps our rather self-centred little lives?

The problem seems to be that the rajassic and tamassic realities take us over and hold us prisoner to their limitations and so these impulses seem to get squashed. In our society we are surrounded by trivia and superficiality; we are encouraged to be materialistic and to fill large patches of our time doing things that have very little deeper meaning. The effect of all this is to close us down to what is naturally heroic and noble about us. Given the right stimulus, however, courage *will* break through.

However, there are problems here – there is no guarantee that this stimulus will occur in such a dramatic fashion, or be as much a coincidence of timing and circumstance as that train, that platform, and that little girl. And we can't only galvanize our heroism out of the closet by means of children being pushed onto railway lines or wars or tsunamis happening. The possible cost is too great. Harry only made it by a hair's breadth; a hundredth of a second later might have been too late.

So we are all perhaps challenged to find our own ways to connect to our courage resources, to exit our overly "safe lives" and live a bit more on the edge, where the aliveness and the sacredness is to be found.

The courage of Erin Brockovich

Erin Brockovich, whose story was made into a famous film starring Julia Roberts, is a wonderful example of someone making the conscious choice to give their all in service to a cause dear to their heart; someone daring to be themselves, living on the edge and risking everything.

Erin was a young, working-class, penniless lone parent who knew that a large corporation near where she lived had polluted the environment and lied about it. She met many of the people who had become ill with cancer from the pollution, and became deeply touched by their plight. It prompted her to take up, single-handedly, the fight for their rights. She managed to infect a timid lawyer with her enthusiasm and got him to support her. Together, they took on this vast powerful corporation – David against Goliath – and they won.

By taking huge risks, Erin showed how much you can achieve if you have a powerful, unerring vision. Indeed, through her perseverance, Erin revealed herself to be much more powerful than the sum total of all the tamassic forces trying to hold her back.

What the film beautifully revealed was that, seen from a conventional perspective, these forces, represented by the corporation in question, initially looked very strong. However, when confronted by someone with a truly brave heart, the corporation could be seen for the weak, greedy, dishonest and manipulative entity that in reality it had always been.

I think each of us has a particular life destiny or soul purpose to fulfil. In this context, I am also reminded of Malala Yousafzai who chose to defy the Taliban's orders that girls must not go to school and got shot for her efforts but continued to live as her stance, and Greta Thunberg who, at sixteen, began lecturing world leaders on climate change.

What all these awesomely brave young women show us is that when one takes powerful and courageous stands for truth, that there is nothing that cannot be accomplished. We start drawing "the Force" to be with us so powerfully that we don't just believe, but we know that miracles really are possible.

Which they are. We just need to choose to live with an open heart, be unafraid of taking on challenges, and always be aware that it is the grit in the oyster – the so-called "enemy" that creates all the irritation – that is ultimately responsible for producing the pearl.

EXERCISE

- Look at your life and ask yourself: do I live it courageously? Do I live it adventurously? Do I ever take risks? If so, how and where? Where in your life are you most courageous and adventurous? Think about this carefully and make notes. Perhaps you will discover that you are braver than you believe.

- Now see if there are areas where you are timid and hold back. Where are these areas? And why? Make notes. Do you have ideas about yourself as being a brave or an unbrave person? Also ask yourself: do I have certain fears about "outing" my real self? If so, what are they? Are you afraid of what people might think of you? Are you afraid you will lose the support of people important to you? Are there particular problems or obstacles you fear facing? Make notes.

- Now, focus on your heart in the same way you did in earlier meditations. Again, imagine putting lungs in your heart.

Breathe in and out for a few minutes. I now want you to choose to breathe in the quality of courage to the count of eight, hold it for the count of five, then breathe out your timidity. Do this five times.

- Now think of a particular situation in your life when you were brave and bring that memory into the present. Then another situation. And another. Now say to yourself: "I am a courageous person. I choose to live my life with courage and take conscious stands for those truths I believe in."
- What cause or causes are you willing to take a stand for? List them.
- Think of an area of your life where you ordinarily would feel timid and imagine yourself being brave in this area. Now do this with another area. And another.
- Write the word "courage" on three cards. Leave one on your desk, pin another onto your mirror and put the third card on your fridge, so you are being reminded of this quality all the time.

EXERCISE A guided meditation

- Sit down comfortably, close your eyes and connect to your inner heart in the centre of your chest.
- And meditate again on the quality of courage.
- Let this quality come more and more alive in you. Perhaps think of someone you know or know of who is or was courageous – a Martin Luther King kind of figure maybe. Imagine them existing inside your heart and you drawing this quality out of them and into yourself. Now think of someone else and put them also inside your heart and do the same thing. Feel your heart fill up with courage more and more.
- Again, remember a time in your own life when you behaved courageously. What was happening? What were you doing that made you feel courageous? Now visualize another time. What were you doing? Bring these old memories into your present day and allow this quality to deepen inside you until you feel courage inhabit every cell in your body.
- Become courage.
- Now think of something you need to do now in your life that requires courage and which you feel a bit fearful about. Visualize yourself doing it courageously and observe how empowered you feel. Now go and do that thing literally.

- Affirm that the pattern of courage has been implanted in your unconscious and say three times: *"I am a courageous person. Courage always lives inside me and I always choose to operate courageously in my life."*
- Every morning when you get up, say this affirmation to yourself: *"Who I am is a courageous person. I choose to live this day with courage and have courage imbue all my interactions with everyone and everything I encounter."* Now visualize yourself going through the day in exactly that spirit.

CHAPTER 16

Gateways into Forgiveness

The weak can never forgive.
Forgiveness is an attitude of the strong.
— MAHATMA GANDHI

We must develop and maintain the capacity to forgive.
He who is devoid of the power to forgive is devoid of
the power to love.
— MARTIN LUTHER KING

The Importance of Forgiveness

The gateway of forgiveness is a very liberating one. If moved through properly, it is able to dissolve many of the hurts, regrets and resentments that keep us embedded in old-story consciousness. Not only does forgiving bring liberation and a sense of peace, but it is also a key component in the resolution of many different kinds of conflict.

Whether it is ourselves we feel we need to forgive or another person, or whether we are challenged to forgive in a more general sense, embarking on this undertaking will always open up whole new possibilities for peace and harmony not only in our own lives but also out in the world.

The gateway of forgiveness, however, is by no means an easy one to enter. Firstly, genuine forgiveness is difficult – it requires much more than our simply saying "I forgive you." Secondly, it seldom happens all at once; in fact, to be most effective, it generally needs to occur gradually.

Certainly our minds might recognize the necessity for forgiving, and yes, we can say to someone "I forgive you." However, unless in so doing we touch into the heart of what forgiveness is all about, that is, unless our words come directly from our heart, they will have little power and the gateway will remain unopened.

Obstacles around forgiveness

Forgiving is particularly challenging if our hearts have been very wounded. For example, there may be a situation where we want to forgive someone as we recognize the benefits it could bring. However, we may find it extremely hard to do so because the very circumstances that we need to forgive them for have so embittered us that they have caused our hearts to shut down.

Also, so long as our egos are still prominent and unhealed – and wounded ego, we remind ourselves, always "knows best", "likes to be right", and thrives on revenge and retribution – we may not feel predisposed to forgive. This is again why it is so important that we start moving into states where our soulful self plays an increasingly larger role in our lives.

As we start accessing more of our soul life, we realize that forgiveness is actually not so much something that we do, but more something that we are – or rather, a space that we enter into gradually, as we increasingly learn to open to those dimensions of our hearts that naturally desire bygones to be bygones. Often, when we start out, our capacity in this arena may be small, but as our hearts slowly begin to open, we may gradually become more adept at it. It is hugely liberating for all concerned, because it enables both the forgiver and the one being forgiven to cast themselves off the heavy hooks that they have become pinioned onto. (Resentment and hatred, for example, can often bind us as close to a person as love.) Indeed, the gateways of forgiveness and love are often situated close to one another, as in many instances the one or the ones we are needing to forgive are those whom we once used to love.

One problem we can potentially face is that since the act of forgiving has to involve our taking the one we are forgiving into our hearts, we may not want them there. Thus, we prefer to remain filled with our hatreds or resentments (or whatever emotions are uppermost) in the sure knowledge that those who we are resenting will continue to pay the price for the wrongs we feel they did to us – that is, will remain skewered by our negative projections against them. In other words, we may feel loath to release our hatred as it seems to be the only thing we have left.

Another difficulty is that if we have suffered serious sexual or emotional abuse or endured ethnic cleansing or years of warfare, we may have deeply internalized the negativity or violence thrown at us and will have identified strongly with it; we may even have come to believe that we deserved what we got and that there is nothing to forgive.

But the price of refusing to do so can be seen in this little story. In my couples therapy, I worked once with a husband and wife. The wife had discovered that her husband had once slept with a call girl while away on a business trip. He apologized profusely for this, his sole indiscretion in 20 years of marriage, and let his wife know he loved her very much – which was the truth – but his wife, whose insecure ego was anyway very vulnerable, simply wouldn't let her hurt go.

Rather than forgive, she plotted her revenge and did her utmost to destroy the entire relationship and everything that they had built up together as a family. Years later, I bumped into her again by chance, and she told me what a fool she had been: out of her desire for vengeance, she had destroyed her own life, to say nothing of the damage inflicted on their children, by getting rid of a good man whom she deeply loved. This is an example of what the wounded ego is sometimes capable of doing, and why *not* forgiving can be so destructive.

Our unwillingness or incapacity to forgive and our resultant feelings of victimhood, therefore, are often closely enmeshed, and in many instances, the choice to forgive is also a choice to give up our attachment to this posture, which I always feel is defined more by the position we take around painful events that have happened to us than by the nature of the events themselves.

Requirements for forgiveness

What work, then, is required of us, if we choose to forgive?

To start with, I think we need to be sufficiently connected to our feelings to be aware that we may well be carrying resentful thoughts inside us towards those who we believe are responsible for causing us grief in our lives. Secondly, we must realize that these thoughts are poisoning us and restricting our lives and that if we were to forgive and let go – for we cannot do one without the other – we might well feel a whole lot better and get on with our life more peacefully.

If the issue or issues we are dealing with are complex and therefore need greater clarification, it may be that we may need to enlist outside support like counselling to assist us.

In the chapter on the Shadow, we looked at the phenomenon of how we tend to project onto other people those particular "motes" that we refuse to recognize in our own eyes. We can make progress along these lines, and begin to open up to the possibility of forgiving someone or some group or tribe or race (or whomever); but we will find that this needs to be accompanied by one of the most difficult aspects of the whole process: we need to start to consider taking into our hearts that person or persons who were responsible for damaging us in the first place.

Interestingly, in the Christian Lord's Prayer, we not only ask for help to forgive those "who have trespassed against us", but equally, we ask for forgiveness for where we also might have trespassed – that is, where wittingly or unwittingly, we may have hurt or injured other people. This is important. Sometimes, we cannot forgive others because there may be things about ourselves that we also find it hard to forgive.

If we are trying to forgive someone and perhaps to suggest to them that they might also consider forgiving us, it can also be very helpful, if at all possible, to arrange a face-to-face meeting. This enables both sides to share their thoughts and feelings, talk things out and, very importantly, hear each other's side of the story.

Forgiving ourselves

Before we can properly love another person, we need to open our hearts and first love ourselves, and exactly the same thing holds true in the area of forgiveness. Even if we haven't ourselves committed some terrible atrocity, often unconsciously we may still have pinioned ourselves on all sorts of mysterious hooks for not being perfect enough. (Remember what I said about Christian guilt in our old-story religion?)

So if we can work through our feelings around being a "sinner" because we are not as "perfect as our Father in Heaven is perfect" and start accepting and honouring ourselves for being the way we are, then the forgiving dimension of our hearts has a much better chance to start surfacing and working in our favour.

Working with unforgivability

That said, there may be certain instances where we may genuinely feel we have done something "unforgivable".

A man once came to see me. He had just lost his only son; he had been run over by a drunk driver. Although the culprit went to prison, my client could not and would not forgive him, and constantly felt possessed by thoughts of revenge. "All I ever think about is doing the same thing to his son, so that his family can suffer as mine have done," he confided in me, "and these thoughts are killing me."

I could see that this man was closing off to life more and more and that he could not, on his own, move out of that deadening and vengeful, suffering world that he had sunk into. He was also starting to drink a lot, and once or twice had driven dead drunk himself. I feared he too might run someone over.

He needed extra help to move into a domain of being where forgiveness might be a possibility. He came on one of my retreats in Mallorca, and with a lot of work and support, things began to shift for him and a new viewpoint began to open up. He started to accept more fully what had happened and allowed himself properly to mourn – he had up until then been primarily in denial. He found himself starting to walk in this other man's moccasins and to realize that the person who had killed his son was not a bad person, that he had not meant to do it, and that he felt huge remorse.

We did a guided visualization in which he imagined his son sitting inside his heart. "It feels as if my son is telling me that he is fine, and that I need to let him go and give up my thoughts of revenge and get on with my life," he told me.

As he touched into these realizations, the presence of the "forgiving heart" inside him began to reveal itself very strongly. He began the long process of forgiving and therefore taking his son's killer more deeply into his heart. "Build on this process every day," I said to him. "Every morning when you get up, choose to forgive a little bit more. And do it your way; your heart will show you how." Six months later, he told me that he had twice visited in prison the man who had killed his son.

Forgiving God

Sometimes the "one" we need to forgive is the same one we may sometimes turn to or pray to to ask for help in this process. Sometimes we can get very angry with God (or "higher power", the force, Spirit, or whatever we want to call it), not only for not always giving us those goodies from life that we desire, but on occasion for seeming to deal us very tough blows. This can apply in particular to people suffering in natural disasters like earthquakes or tidal waves.

The argument people tend to use to express their anger towards a higher power generally goes along these lines: "If God is good, if God is love, then why did God bring this suffering into my life?" This is an important issue. I have encountered many people whose refusal to "let

God off their anger hook" has resulted in their closing off to everything and retreating back into worlds of fear and separation, where it is easy to become overly susceptible to the pull of the rajassic and tamassic.

Our anger also serves to stand in the way of allowing God, the higher force or however we think of it to be with us. In other words, if we feel resentment towards the Higher Power, we are not able to allow our hearts to open to this power's "other face" – the one of joy, love and tenderness.

If we are to move closer to the possibility of forgiving God, we also need to contemplate the issue a little more deeply. The idea that "God's goodness" is predicated upon Higher Power seeing to it that everything in our lives always goes the way we would wish is an egoic and childish view of how the universe works. We need to understand not only that higher power moves in mysterious ways that we may never understand logically, but also that death, devastation, tragedy and evil are all part of this process. Remember what I said about this whole process earlier on.

Forgiving God therefore requires that we give up our juvenile concepts of the divine. Instead we must be willing to open to the realization that purposes exist in the cosmos that are deeper and subtler than we will ever understand, and that what from our egoic self's viewpoint appears retrogressive may, from a much broader perspective, be progressive. If we are someone who likes to pray, we can even pray to higher power to help enlighten us and help us forgive God!

The need for global forgiveness

The hurt caused by wounds perpetrated upon ourselves personally is also mirrored out in the wider world. We see this rage and hatred manifesting itself very strongly in the enormous amount of bitterness between, for example, many Palestinians and Israelis; an unwillingness and inability on the part of both sides to forgive ensures that the conflicts between them grow increasingly difficult to resolve. Similarly, so long as many Muslims continue to despise Christians and so long as people in Iraq continue to find it hard to forgive Iran for having invaded their country, peace will continue to be elusive in that part of the world. Of course, we need peace initiatives instigated by our politicians and it is good that they take place. But if no strategies around forgiveness are ever set in place from the bottom up – that is, if there is never any impetus to work at letting go of resentments at a grass-roots level – then whatever politicians manage to achieve will always have its limitations.

I could talk about the lingering resentment between Serbs, Croats and Bosnians or how certain Irish people must still feel towards the IRA, how some Chechens feel towards the Russians or how Syrian people feel towards Assad, how Shi'ites feel towards Sunnis, and so on. The truth is that we human beings have treated each other quite abominably over the centuries. We have raped, tortured, pillaged, betrayed, destroyed, and ethnically cleansed, and as a result very powerful hate memories have grown up inside our collective unconscious. If this particular dimension of world Shadow is to be more fully transformed, a great deal of forgiving is called for in many different ways.

Entering the world of the heart of forgiveness

Forgiveness is not something static, something we just "do" and then it's over and done with. On the contrary, it is an ongoing process, and it requires that we try to live out of a place of unconditional acceptance both of ourselves and of the one or ones we are seeking to forgive.

The challenge is ultimately to enter into what I called "the world of the heart of forgiveness", which I see as a space of great love. Not only should we aim to try to relate from that space to those whom we are trying to forgive, but our intention must also be to seek to live it as a *stage* and not merely experience it as a temporary *state*.

When this occurs, forgiveness becomes more than just something we do. It becomes a reflection of who we are – a reflection of a new way of living that is tender and open-hearted and which we are continually radiating out as an integral part of choosing to live our daily lives as our sacred practice. And to ensure this occurs, we need to be continually working on ourselves in all of the many ways that we have been exploring.

▨ EXERCISE to forgive someone towards whom you feel great resentment

- Look inside yourself. Is there someone towards whom you hold great resentment, hatred or anger? If so, what happened to make you feel this way? What did they do or not do that so hurt you?
- Tune in to your heart in the middle of your chest and put these feelings there. How does your heart feel? What is the story there? You can either just let yourself experience these feelings fully, or you can write them down. Or do both.

- Observe: is there a desire for revenge or to hurt or destroy this person? Do you wish this person ill? Do they wish you ill? Is there a continual cross-current of negativity flowing between you? If there is unpleasantness and heaviness, write about it and experience it and take it into your heart.

- Continue to be aware of these negative thought currents and see how they are poisoning you both. Now see if you want to go on carrying them; if so, be aware of the price you pay for doing so.

- What do you want to say to this person about how you feel they hurt or harmed you? Imagine they are in front of you right now and speak your mind, or if you prefer, write down what you want to say in a letter.

- Get all those negative thoughts and feelings out. Shout them out if necessary, or bang some pillows. If there is a lot of anger, go and chop some wood!

- Now see if you would be prepared to consider forgiving them. Ask yourself: what would it feel like to have no more negativity flowing from me to them and if I no longer carried all those negative thoughts?

- If you would like to start to forgive them, make this affirmation: *"I choose to start forgiving* A *for* x.*"*

- Now that you have made the intention to forgive with your mind, begin to focus into that place inside you where all forgiveness emerges from, namely the deeper echelons of your heart. Ask your heart to open up that aspect of itself that forgives, and begin to see that person towards whom you feel such negativity through that lens. (Remember: our hearts are capable of both feeling the pain and the hurt and, at a deeper level, producing the love that will bring about a healing to the pain and the hurt.)

- Now look at or think about that person again in this new spirit and observe if there is a softening in your attitude towards them. If so, let it deepen.

- I also want you to look deeply into yourself and see if there may be a place inside you where you could also have done to someone what you feel they did to you. If there is, acknowledge it. If there is not, try to see the place they came from from a place of greater wisdom. Let your forgiving and loving heart tell you why they did what they did. Was it in relation to something you did? Was it out of their pain or some inadequacy? Was it stupidity? Was it out of a desire to hurt you because they felt hurt by you? Was it because they are a very unconscious human being? (Knowing the place someone "comes from" is very important, for the more sides of the issue we know, the fuller our forgiveness can be.)

- So: with your heart, try to get inside the thinking of the person you are seeking to forgive. As you do so, observe if your own vulnerabilities also might have contributed to you reacting or feeling the way you did.

- Feel your way all around and into the dynamic existing between the two of you and see if you would like to change it; see if you can recognize if there is something that you need to let go of. If so, what is it? To help you here, breathe in the quality of forgiving love to the count of six, hold it for four and then breathe out what you feel you need to let go. Do this five times.

- Now see if there is a bigger space in your heart to take in and include the person who you felt hurt you so much. Imagine drawing that person into your heart and saying to them: "I choose to start forgiving you for x and I choose to hold you inside my heart in a loving way. I visualize the pain melting away."

- The forgiveness process is now beginning. But it needs to be built upon. Three times a day I want you to send the person you are choosing to forgive "I wish you well" or other positive thoughts. Be aware that the more you hold them in your heart in a loving way, the more the forgiveness will grow. It may morph into tenderness or compassion. If they are still alive, you might try to make physical contact with them and meet with them, have an honest talk with them, tell them how you feel from a place of love not of judgement, and invite them to share how they feel as well. Do your best to relate to them in the spirit of that unconditional friendliness that we explored earlier. All this helps the forgiveness process to grow and invite in change.

- Also know that the more you choose to take your old enemy into your heart, the more you will release blockages inside both of you and the lighter you will feel. Remember, too, that the more you choose intentionally to relate to this person in a truly loving and forgiving way, the more likely it is that you will pass through a gateway into a new level of soul.

- Know that the gift of needing to forgive someone is challenging you not only to open your heart but also to keep it open.
- If there are other people or other situations you feel you need to forgive, follow the same process with them.

EXERCISE to forgive yourself

This is equally important.

- What did you do or say that you consider is unforgivable? Feel it or see it or write it down.
- How, up until now, have you expressed your anger towards yourself? Do you make yourself physically ill? Do you make yourself feel constantly guilty? What do you do to punish yourself? Can you see that self-flagellation only hurts you and generally keeps you marooned in a mindset of insufficiency? The world will not be a better place if you are hard and vengeful on yourself.
- Perhaps you can see that given where you were at the time, you couldn't have done anything different; or perhaps you could, but you simply made a mistake. (For example, perhaps you can't forgive yourself for, say, making a very bad investment or giving up a very good job or punishing your child, even though these things felt appropriate at the time.) So experience the price you pay for all those negative or self-chastizing thoughts coming to you from you, and see if you are willing to consider letting yourself slip out of the punishing noose you've put around your neck. Also be aware of how much your negative attitudes towards yourself bring a flatness into your life, deprive you of joy and keep you fixed in the scarcity/separation mode of the old story. Do you really want to continue in this place?
- If you could forgive yourself, what do you think you would get from it? Imagine it or write it down. What things that currently seem to be blocked off for you might return?
- Ask yourself: am I ready to forgive myself so I can move on in my life?
- If you feel you are now ready to start forgiving yourself, focus on your inner heart and start opening it to yourself. Let all of you be enveloped by it, and realize that your heart is by its very nature inherently forgiving. The more you open it in unconditional love and acceptance of you, the harder it becomes to continue berating yourself or making yourself "pay a price".

■ Write out this affirmation for yourself: *"I unconditionally forgive myself for x and I choose to hold myself steadily in the love of my heart. I choose to love and accept all parts of myself."* Say this every morning as you wake up and before going to bed at night, until you feel that your self-forgiveness has grown strong enough that you no longer need do so.

CHAPTER 17

Gateways into Joy

*He who can no longer pause to wonder and stand rapt in
awe is as good as dead. His eyes are closed.*
— ALBERT EINSTEIN

*Find out where joy resides and give it a voice far
beyond singing, for to miss the joy is to miss all.*
— ROBERT LOUIS STEVENSON

Joy, Pain and Happiness

When we experience authentic joy, it is a sure sign that we are accessing
a sacred space. Or as the great visionary theologian Teilhard de Chardin
reminds us: "Joy is a sign of the presence of God." Therefore, the more
we experience this quality, the more connected we are to higher power,
abundance and grace, and the more all vestiges of scarcity and separation
begin evaporating.

However, where joy differs from many other qualities is that it cannot
be directly sought; and, in particular, it does not come through our trying
to avoid pain. William Blake understood this only too well. In his poem
"Auguries of Innocence", he tells us:

> *Joy & Woe are woven fine,*
> *A Clothing for the soul divine.*
> *Under every grief & pine*
> *Runs a joy with silken twine…*
> *It is right it should be so*
> *Man was made for Joy & Woe;*
> *And when this we rightly know,*
> *Thro the World we safely go…*[27]

Rumi says much the same thing: "Be full of sorrow, that you may become full of joy; weep, that you may break into laughter."

Rajassic man never seems to get this, never recognizes that life is a play of oppositions and that just as light and dark are part of each other and give rise to each other (we see this in the yin–yang symbol where both are contained in each other), so too are joy and pain. This is why our old-story hedonist who devotes himself to seeking pleasure – trying to feel good by doing his best to dodge feeling bad (this avoidance mechanism being one of the traits most responsible, the Buddha tells us, for why we suffer most) – generally ends up with mission unaccomplished!

My friend, we have to accept that there will be times when sorrow descends on us and fills our heart and that these times cannot be avoided. Tragic things sometimes happen: we become very ill, our house burns down, our spouse abandons us or dies. As you have seen in earlier chapters, when these painful things occur, we are called to face them courageously, open our hearts to them and work with them. This helps open up a space where we may later feel joy.

So while joy is intimately connected to sorrow, there is also a strong link between it and happiness. Let us call happiness its first cousin.

But there are also significant differences. Whereas happiness comes more from outside us and relates more to our separate self – we are happy if we win the lottery, when we win the race, when someone tells us they like us, when life goes the way we want – joy is connected more with what is going on inside us – with our depths, with the domain of our soul self.

Joy, therefore, is subtler than happiness and, interestingly, can often emerge when there is nothing going on externally to make us happy, i.e., even when we fail to win the race or the lottery! In my experience it relates a great deal to being in a calm and integrated space inside ourselves, when we've done our inner work and our prayer and meditation and we feel at peace with what is and we aren't full of desires to have what we don't have (another great dampener of joy).

As Blake and Rumi both tell us, often if we allow ourselves to experience something that may be painful and we open our hearts to it and allow its alchemical force to work its magic, we may suddenly find a whole lot of joy bubbling up as if from nowhere.

Where is joy to be found?

Joy is not connected to what we possess in the outer world, that is, to fame, wealth and success, but much more to our relationship with ourselves. I say this as many people experience joy who possess very little or who may not be at all successful in the conventional (old-story) meaning of the word. This shows us that it is not so much a quality connected with *having* but more with *being*; not so much about what occurs for us in our lives, but more about how open we are to allowing ourselves to fully experience what occurs for us. It is therefore another of the faces of abundance that we explored earlier.

If I look at those times in my life when joy has come seeking me out, they have most often been when I have been aligned to my truth or in some way following my bliss – that is, doing things I love doing, which are appropriate for me to do and naturally dear to my heart. And of course, when we fall deeply in love with someone, our feet will seldom touch the ground as we'll be so busy jumping with joy.

Joy and nature

I observe that often not only my heart but also my body needs to be included for it to feel like the full joyful experience. I have noticed, too, that the more my mind is quiet and not clogged up with trivia or anxiety, the more likely it is that gateways opening to this quality mysteriously start emerging.

I remember one memorable long walk in Mallorca with a good friend. We climbed together up to a high point on a cliff and sat looking at the sea and the mountainous terrain around us and I felt joy creeping into my heart and expanding it. I felt the power of the earth, the strength of the wind, the warmth of the sun and the softness of the ocean and I felt huge gratitude for being alive, for being part of the great miracle of life. I felt humble and somehow blessed and utterly free from that nagging feeling that still at times can sometimes assail me, namely, that I have somehow to "justify" my existence (which can be such a big joy blocker!).

I felt connected to joy because I also felt connected to the intelligence of life flowing through me. The Force was with me and it was now revealing its joyful face. I felt, I am OK just the way I am and like the rocks and bushes around me, I am growing out of the earth. I felt big changes coming and in my little way I felt part of them, in relation to which my trivial niggles were so insignificant.

I felt in a holy space; I felt whole, part of something vast and unfathomable. *I felt very strongly that life is given us to be enjoyed and celebrated, and that if there is a God – if we have a Creator – then our Creator wants nothing more than to be invited into our lives to participate with us in our joyous celebration of it.*

Sadly, so many of us are defended against allowing joy to visit us. In Matthew Fox's insightful words from his great book on *The Coming of the Cosmic Christ*:

> When we cannot celebrate and reverence the cosmos, we fight it. Our problem is that we are cosmically lonely and the result of this is big ego trips and institutional violence…Believing in original sin makes us overly competitive. It builds empires and weakens our true spirit…Real beauty got lost when the cosmos was lost.[28]

That's why if we are still living the old story where we operate out of Don Beck's levels two to five, our mindsets are not going to be conducive to reverencing the cosmos and thus we're not going to be much of an "opening" for genuine joy to come stalking us.

Resistances to joy

The connection between joy and pain is the reason why, ultimately, our attempts to avoid pain never work, for we can't block off to just one thing: if we try to, we will find ourselves doing it to all things and it will mean that we do not let ourselves feel love and joy and affection. Beauty will also be invisible to us. And to live from a space of not being able to feel anything deeply, that is, to live numbly – which is a condition called "anhedonia", meaning "a fear of joy" – is actually the worst pain of all. We feel emotionally dead. I have met several people with this condition and they have to feign feelings all the time; it is truly a terrible curse.

For some of us, our difficulties with experiencing joy may be due to our having been brought up by joyless parents in joyless households. As this soul quality was never properly mirrored for us when we were young, we both desire joy and at the same time fear it – joy has been relegated to our Shadow. In such instances, there will be plenty of Shadow recovery work to busy ourselves with.

The threat of joy

The system as a whole is very invested in seeing that we remain joyless. Why is this? We've already answered this question. Joyful people are a threat, as they can't be controlled in the way that anxious, depressed or fearful people can. They have a freedom about them that is scary to the status quo; and, especially, they don't have all that emptiness inside them that they need to fill by excessive consuming, so in effect they can hold two fingers up to the system and say, "I don't really need you as I am pretty sufficient unto myself."

And it is true. The moment we experience real joy, we've temporarily transited out of the old story – gone through the gateways into a new one. This is why joy is such an important point of transition and why we need to devote energy to creating the conditions in our lives conducive to it visiting us.

And the old story – let's admit it – is pretty joyless. Most of our institutions and political systems are pretty joyless. Look at any politician or banker being interviewed on television. Do they exude the joys of spring? Very seldom. Wonkfulness seldom leads to joyfulness! They have to look earnest and serious and sensible – to convey the illusion that they know what the hell is going on, when most of the time, bless them, they don't!

I am afraid that a lot of this can be laid at the feet of orthodox Christianity, which, as I briefly touched on earlier, holds little that is joyful and therefore inherently sacred about it.

Joyless Christianity

Too many "devoted Christians" live with the idea that in order to be redeemed from being the "miserable sinner" one is told one is, one should not allow too much joy into one's heart, as that might mean losing sight of the fact that Jesus suffered on the cross for our sins!

I think that many of Jesus' true teachings have been distorted over the years – "churchified" is the word I use – by cold-hearted, stern and joyless theologians who took the words of the Bible much too literally. I particularly think St Augustine did a vast amount of damage by mixing up notions of original sin with sexuality – seeing one of the areas that we derive huge joy from, namely sex, as being "bad" for that very reason. What this did for our society was simply to open up the way for junk sex and pornography, which is utterly joyless; the more it is engaged in, the more we debase and coarsen ourselves.

I believe the true Jesus was a healer and shaman (a master of ecstasy) who loved women, who felt connected with the Earth and recognized its aliveness, intelligence and sacredness, and who preached joy, love and compassion and being of service to life. By contrast, the Christianity we have today is a very watered-down affair, in which people who may be mystics are automatically viewed as psychopaths and where man's innate creativity and imagination is utterly discounted. I think one of the great tragedies in theology over the last few centuries has been its divorce from dancing, music and painting; that is, from all the things that potentially bring joy into our lives.

The materialistic impulse

Something that also has the potential to kill joy in an instant is our separate or our ego self with all its materialistic inclinations. Let me tell you a little story about this involving myself.

I have always been a collector in a small way of African tribal art, and many years ago, a friend took me to visit a well-known dealer in this area who had a truly exquisite collection comprising many great pieces. I suddenly saw myself comparing my collection very unfavourably with his and I observed all the joy drain out of my heart. Instead of being able to appreciate his collection, I was reduced to thinking: "Oh dear, I don't have *enough* pieces; I don't have any *great* pieces."

"And your piddling little collection is so insignificant," my ego self whispered to me, "and it reflects very badly on you. No one will be impressed!"

I realized that I was suddenly full of misery. I had already started out on my soul journey by this point, so I had some sense of what had gone awry and how to work on it. As soon as I got home, I sat with my little assembly of tribal figures, arranged them all around me, and then took time to feel myself deeply into the presence of each figure. *I found they all had unique qualities to them as well as a mystery and a beauty that in all those years of owning them, I had never properly allowed myself to experience.*

As I did this inner work, to my amazement I felt each piece beginning to communicate with me and tell me about itself, and one small figure conveyed the message that it needed my respect and acknowledgement and that I shouldn't do all my comparing and looking at it in terms of its financial worth, as this was insulting! I felt momentarily ashamed; but then the true sacredness of my little tribal collection began to make itself known to me and I felt quite awed by the power and beauty of my figures. I had to confess that for all those years, without my being conscious of it (another of my many "hidden agendas"!), I had been looking at my pieces in much the same way my father looked at his art (he'd also been a collector): that is, primarily as "good investments".

I was reminded of that famous line in Oscar Wilde's *Lady Windermere's Fan* that "we know the price of everything and the value of nothing" and I felt very sad. I was one of *them*; I thought like that! Here was a whole new aspect of my Shadow side "outing itself", a side that, up to that moment, I had had no inkling of. It showed me that I too was unknowingly participating in the desacralizing process.

I never realized until then how potent and how reductive, what a desacralizing and joy-killing force the materialistic impulse can be if it goes awry.

I thought with sadness how in the early part of my life, I had also done much the same thing with women. Reduced them. Not allowed myself to see their depths. Never permitted real intimacy. Instead, I had objectified them and *that* was why I could never be content with the one I was with as there was always someone better over there! If I couldn't allow myself joyfully to experience a woman's *quality*, then at least I could make up by increasing the *quantity*! This mindset killed my capacity properly to enjoy my relationships.

Killing joy

These insights made me feel enormously sad, but it was good that this was all surfacing – I could now do something about it. I saw that I was confronting in myself one of the darker faces of the Western soul wound and that when we desacralize something or someone, one of the many side effects is the killing off or disallowing of whatever capacity for joy may be lurking inside us.

So *that* was why my joy had seeped out of me so suddenly, and why I had begun feeling so inadequate and envious. My misperceptions had drawn me down into those realities where scarcity, separation, deficiency and not-enoughness are integral parts of the landscape.

No wonder we've created the word "killjoy". The rajassic/tamassic mindsets have to do that, for the moment joy appears, their *raison d'être* vanishes. Over the years, then, I have come to believe that *what underlies many of our dissatisfactions with our lives is not that we don't have more money or a bigger house or more recognition or a "better partner" or all the things we believe are deficient, but that we can't enjoy and feel gratitude and appreciation for what we have.*

In doing this piece of inner work, all my joy flooded back and I observed that my huge gratitude for what I had far, far exceeded my sorrow for what I thought I didn't have. In fact, that sorrow fell away at once and has never returned.

We don't need to work *for* joy; we just need to work through all those patterns inside us that prevent it from shining out. When the storm clouds are no longer there, there is nothing in the way to stop the sun from shining.

EXERCISES

- **Ask yourself: How do I rate myself on the "joy scale" from 1 to 10? If your rating is low, what do you think you do or don't do that is a joy stopper? If it is high, what do you think you do or don't do? Make notes of what you have learned about yourself from reading this chapter.**
- **Are any of the following killjoys relevant in your life?**
  - *A pessimistic outlook*
  - *Overwork*
  - *Being a blamer or complainer*
  - *Negative religious beliefs*
  - *Too much doing and not enough being*
  - *An attachment to suffering*
  - *Carrying unresolved old wounds or traumas*
  - *A tendency towards depression and/or anxiety*
  - *Holding on to regrets and resentments*
  - *An inability to forgive*
  - *An image of yourself as being joyless or a miserable old so-and-so*
  - *Not enough soul in your life*
  - *Anhedonia*
  - *Being overly materialistic*
  - *Bad physical health*

Make notes on any that are relevant, why you think these things exist in your life and what you feel you can do about any of them.

- ■ Ask yourself: what gives me joy? Is it any of the following:
  - *Being with things that I find beautiful*
  - *Being out in nature*
  - *Being in love*
  - *Engaging in work that I love*
  - *Being with close friends*
  - *Doing a sport that I love*
  - *Intellectual pursuits*
  - *Listening to or making music*
  - *Meditation*
  - *Helping others*
  - *Being with my family*

Are there other things? List them all and then ask yourself if you give yourself enough time to engage in these things.

- ■ What might you do in the future to bring more joy into your life? Make comprehensive notes. Here, I will add that I think joy emerges naturally out of our living a balanced life, that is, a life that is right for us, where we make time to work through our fears, inadequacies, regrets, resentments and hates so that we are not full of negative energy, while at the same time making an effort to feed our soul self so that it may expand.
- ■ Feeling gratitude for what we have, and not feeling that we will be OK only if we possess what we don't have, or have more of it, is also very important. So take a moment, close your eyes and let yourself feel grateful for:
  - *Being alive*
  - *The blessings in your life (list them)*
  - *The friends in your life and those who love you*
  - *Having food, warmth and shelter (our basic needs)*
  - *Being on a journey to find your soul*
  - *Finding yourself in good health*
  - *Enjoying meaningful work*

And whatever other things you feel should be on this list. Take time in doing this.

EXERCISE to meditate on joy

- Close your eyes. Focus on your inner heart (where joy lives). Be aware of this quality existing there.
- Now recall a time in your past when you felt a lot of joy and bring this memory into your heart.
- Now recall another time. And another.
- Let your heart fill with these joyful memories. Allow it to expand. Let joy pervade your entire being. Let it expand into the environment around you.
- Just rest for ten minutes in the experiencing of joy.
- Now imagine yourself spending a whole day in joy: getting up in the morning, getting dressed, having breakfast, going to work, engaging with everyone at work, having lunch and bringing joy into your conversation, spending the rest of the day in a place of joy, and going to bed with a joyful heart.
- Now make an effort actually to spend a day in this mindset, choosing to take pleasure in all the little things you do. As you do this, you will see how very connected feeling joy is to choosing to live each day out of a mindful space.

AFFIRMATIONS on joy

I choose to live today with joy in my heart.

Even though difficult things are happening in my life, I choose to keep my capacity for joy alive at all times.

Joy inhabits every cell of my being.

I am grateful for all the many blessings in my life.

I choose to work out of joy and allow more fun and play into my life.

I choose to allow more space in my life to do things that bring me joy.

Joy informs all my thoughts and actions each day.

Remember: you cannot go looking for joy. If you choose to live appropriately, it will come looking for you.

CHAPTER 18

Gateways of Good Work

Work is love in action.
— DAVID SPANGLER

*Without work all life goes rotten but when
work is soulless, life stifles and dies.*
— ALBERT CAMUS

Work on and the universe will work with you.
— SRI NISARGADATTA MAHARAJ

The Importance of Work

We have been spending a lot of time looking at the importance of inner work, or work done consciously on ourselves to help us live a more meaningful and authentic outer life. In this chapter, we will explore how finding the right kind of *outer work* can also serve as an important gateway, not only to help us deepen our inner lives, but also to support our becoming an effective ensouling or re-sacralizing presence out in the world.

While I certainly agree that those who simply cannot find work or who are condemned to utterly soulless work should be assisted in some way, I am firmly of the opinion that with the exception of a few natural-born mystics whose work primarily lies in their capacity simply to "be" – to radiate goodness into the world – all of us need to find some kind of outer occupation that has meaning for us, regardless of whether we get paid for it or not. Without this, we will find it much harder to live abundantly or soulfully.

The price we pay for not working

One of the great tragedies of today is that due to fault lines in societies, many people are unable to find work, or conversely they work at a job that is soul-destroying. That said, I do believe that people who do not work, miss out on something that is intrinsic to what it means to be a human being.

In fact, I view not working at all – and by this I mean not involving ourselves in any tangible and concrete activity that engages us in some way with the world outside of ourselves – as being an even greater burden than doing a dehumanizing job. I have met such people and their suffering evolves around being denied human feelings such as excitement, pride in one's accomplishments, creativity and a sense of belonging, attributes that can only be developed through activities that involve cooperating with other people.

The importance of "good work"

I believe that having the *right kind* of work – or what E. F. Schumacher calls *good work* in his book of that title – is absolutely intrinsic to our well-being. Schumacher suggests that the purpose of work is essentially threefold: "It is to produce necessary and useful goods and services, to perfect our gifts and skills and to serve and collaborate with other people so as to liberate ourselves from an inborn egocentricity."[29]

I would just add that good work must also assist our personal evolution and in no way be detrimental to life. As Jesus once put it: "By their works shall they be known," implying, I think, that there are certain aspects of ourselves that we cannot find out about other than by way of the concrete work that we do.

Not only can good work (hopefully) put bread and butter on our table, but in the process we can also know that we are making some kind of positive contribution to society. In my opinion, the happiest people are those who have found a vocation that is right for them, that is honourable and has integrity and that also enables their hearts to sing.

Living in a cosmos always at work

When we engage in good outer work, we are simply mimicking the cosmos, which is always at work, always busy. It never stops.

Whether or not the world around us always *works* in terms of functioning harmoniously, it is always *at work*. By this I mean that if not interfered with by us, nature is always engaging with itself to advance itself. In his doctrine of the Reciprocal Maintenance of Life, George Gurdjieff talks about how every part of life essentially functions to serve every other part. This is well demonstrated by the ecosystems of our rainforests and oceans.

Nature, then, is always engaged in good work, which is beautifully reflected in the way we function. For example, if we cut our finger, thoughtful work will occur inside our bodies, enabling blood to flow and wash out the toxins while, at the same time, the appropriate healing antibodies are summoned to come to aid the specific wounded area. In a few days, we observe the skin "miraculously" growing over the cut. A very great healing intelligence is at work!

Yes, my friend, the whole of life is forever working at looking after its many constituent parts, and you and I are a very integral part of this process. However, because many of us have lost connection with – or not yet opened up to – who we really are, the work that we engage in today has become disconnected from the work of the universe (that's why the Force cannot always be with all of us), the result being that we not only contribute little to the advancement of life, but often, unbeknownst to ourselves, do a great deal to impede it.

Our great challenge is to learn to bring back soul into the world through finding a work that in some way helps advance human and global evolution.

The old model

To this end, we may need to start out by questioning the old work model so prevalent in the world today, whereby the most prestigious jobs that give us most "status" are those that earn us a lot of money, often regardless of *how* we earn it or if what we do makes a positive difference to our world. In other words, high-earning work in today's society is regarded as good work even if in Schumacher's reality, it may be very far from being so. Remember what I said earlier about the way we like to deify those who are financially wealthy regardless of how it is earned!

Essentially, then, what the old story around work does is elevate those who best fit into the soulless system and do its bidding. So, for example, let us say someone is a CEO of a large firm manufacturing munitions, and is earning a great deal of money. That person may come to be regarded as "superior to" or "more successful than" someone who is, say, picking fruit or stacking shelves, which is seen as "low work", or doing vital and highly demanding work for a non-governmental organization in the area of war or poverty and being paid a relative pittance. However, any of these people doing those jobs may well be operating out of a world six consciousness while the CEO is operating, say, out of level two or three.

These are examples of how dysfunctional our society is. *What we need to understand is that if our shelf-stacker or fruit-picker or peace activist has a quiet mind and an open, generous heart, their energetic contribution to the world may well be very considerable.*

Thus, it is important that anyone who is a low earner, or not in a job seen as "successful" or high-flying, learns to not see themselves through old-story eyes, as this can depress us and make us believe we have done something wrong, whereas it may in fact be the case that the "wrongdoers" are those who – tamassically speaking – have made the grade! What is most important is for increasing numbers of us to come to recognize the enormous importance of bringing soul into whatever we do, as well as to appreciate the huge damage that can so often occur when this ingredient is excluded.

Our planet needs deep, soulful, creative, courageous, joy-filled and self-aware men and women in all kinds of work. We need conscious people operating out of level six and above, not only as shelf-stackers and road sweepers, but as healers and teachers, environmental, human rights and peace activists, university professors, politicians, shop owners, cleaners, cooks, philosophers, social workers, scientists, midwives, doctors and so on: people who all understand that the spirit that underlies the work they do is just as important as what they do.

Expanding our sense of what is seen as "work"

We also need to include under the category of "good work" the profession of the parent looking after their young children, as well as people who spend their time cultivating their gardens or making beautiful music or painting beautiful pictures (even if they are not paid for it) or who devote time to looking after their elderly parents or who dish out soup to homeless people or protest around the world against climate change resisters! All these activities bring soul into the world.

Transformative work

Because of adherence to the old model, which associates work with money, some of you may also feel that if you don't get paid, what you do is not work. Here is a story about this.

Some time ago I received an email from an old university friend to tell me he'd retired. In it he said: "I am not working any more," but when I contacted him, I discovered he had merely retired from his paid job so he could put all his energy into raising money for two charities he believed in. He was not thinking of this as "work" because he wasn't being paid any more.

I pointed out that he was doing something really important putting in a lot of hours every day.

He admitted that he hadn't thought about it that way, then added that he had simply retired from one way of working in order to embrace a much more fruitful and enjoyable job. He concluded by saying, "And you know what, what I do now doesn't feel like work. Actually, a lot of the time it feels more like play."

I particularly resonated with that last comment. When we are fortunate enough to have a job that we enjoy (I know that, sadly, not all of us do), and when we see that it makes a difference, other dimensions start opening up for us; the Force starts to be with us and we start experiencing what we do as fun!

Work as play - and surrender

If I am honest, I never find the work I do hard. I am very fortunate as I love what I do. OK, perhaps some of this is connected to the fact that I am my own boss and don't operate in a suppressive environment with reductive people breathing down my neck! But it is much more than this. A lot of the time, the work I do feels closer to play because I enjoy being with people and trying to connect with them and help them with their challenges. It feels like an expression of my soul's purpose. Even the writing of this book is fun and not "hard", as it stretches me, makes me think, and I enjoy that. My mind loves a good workout!

If we can say that the Force is one of the expressions of soul power – as we've seen, when soul is present, this helping presence is "invited in" – we can also say that when this presence starts connecting itself with us, everything changes. This is the ingredient that brings in the experience of abundance, out of which is born a sense of play.

And when play emerges, another possibility also enters the equation: the possibility of surrender.

When the Force is with us, we are able – one can even say that we are called – to surrender to it and allow higher power to move through us and guide us in what we do. One of the most prolific songwriters of all time, Bob Dylan, maintained that he never had to work hard at his songs and that if he just "let go", most of them would just "come" to him as a kind of gift from the graced worlds.

Roger Federer, when playing his best tennis (his expression of going to the office) also seems to do so in a letting-go-and-going-with-the-flow way! It never feels a struggle, which is perhaps one reason why he so rarely gets injured.

But don't get me wrong. I am not saying the surrendering spirit means we shouldn't also put effort into our work and not be conscientious and industrious about what we do, which is certainly the case with both Dylan and Federer. Perhaps our challenge is to learn to embrace both polarities simultaneously, see them as integral parts of each other. In other words, we choose to move forward and "go for it", while at the same time we do so in a laid-back and going-with-the-flow way.

I think that you and I need to work not because we *should*, i.e., out of guilt, but because we *need* to for our bread and butter, and because we *want* to, for we know it will make a difference, and also because we *delight* in expressing ourselves and connecting with other people and thus feeling ourselves part of the larger work going on in the universe.

However, for some of us, this is easier said than done. We may first need to do some inner work around certain blockages, as some of us feel our work is only worthwhile if it involves great hardship.

The snag of the Puritan "work ethic"

If this is the case, then the "Puritan work ethic" may well be intruding. Just as we've seen that "churchification" has muffled our capacity for joy, so, in a similar way, its offshoot, the "Puritan work ethic", can distort our perceptions of work, keeping us hunkered down feeling that the more hours of struggle we put in and the more drained we feel, the more virtuous we are. In other words, our work, if onerous enough, can hopefully "redeem us" from being the miserable, "fallen sinners" that we believe we are! Remember the expression "I'm a stockbroker [or whatever], *for my sins*"!

Of course, this is all unconscious. And also a myth, for it has been proven that the most successful people in what they do are not necessarily those who work the longest hours. But it works well for the system as it keeps us tied into it and ensures we'll do lots more consuming to compensate for our misery! No wonder workaholism is so rife in our society. This is emphatically *not* how the work of the universe operates and *not* how we need to approach our work if we want it to be part of our daily sacred practice. So be clear if this particular virus inhabits you in any way because if it does, it will need addressing, as its presence will prevent you from having the helpful Force being with you to empower you.

"Real work"

Some people who start connecting with soul, and who become aware of what they don't like about the old work model, find they simply don't know how to bring a new, soulful approach into their current profession. Either it really *is* impossible or they have become so deeply embedded into the way they operate that they can't imagine any other way.

In this context, I want to share an extract from a letter from an old client who decided he needed to change occupations and, work-wise, reinvent himself. He decided to move away from being a senior financial analyst in a large merchant bank to becoming a Cotswold stone-waller.

People used to tell me that it was a pity I gave up a good job in the City to do what they call this "lowly" work of building Cotswold stone walls. They said I was doing so well. But I don't see what I do as lowly at all. On the contrary, I regard it as "high work" as it makes me feel very good! Just because a person earns well and has "good prospects ahead financially", as I admit I did, doesn't always mean that our jobs necessarily satisfy us at a deep level, and one of the problems with my old job was that it kept me in the office for too many hours and was too stressful and I lived too much in my head and had become too disconnected from my heart and my body.

I also felt I didn't really do much that made the world a better place and thus I felt out of kilter a lot of the time. I now look back and regard this high-earning job as "lowly work" as in no way did it personally elevate me as a human being! What I do now in my new career as waller is wonderful for me and it is not downsizing one bit as it enormously satisfies the ethics of my heart. Actually, it is about "going up in the world" in that my whole life has become enriched and expanded – I was too focused before on things that had no depth – and now a lot of the time I am filled with delight.

I am always out in nature and this makes me feel healthy and my work stretches me and ensures I do a lot of natural exercise so I no longer need artificial "workouts" in gyms! In my old work life, I was always stressed and anxious and I tell you, I wouldn't have been able to get through certain days if I hadn't sometimes used a lot of alcohol and pills! Now, I hardly drink.

OK. I don't have the big car and the perks and first-class air flights I used to, but who needs that stuff if one is happy inside oneself, and I am, and luckily my wife is not at all materialistic. Yes, I live much more simply, but the truth is I am happier living this way as I feel much mora connected to myself and to the earth and to things that feel real. I call this work "real work" in that now I earn money through doing concrete things with my hands as opposed to just talking on the phone and earning money by gambling on numbers which [sic] in no way fed my soul.

In my new job, I also need plenty of intuitive intelligence to listen to what the stones tell me about how they want to be cut and where they want to be placed so my walls can look beautiful. And making things beautiful is very important to me. It makes me feel at peace and in harmony with myself. What is also very important is that my relationship with everyone and everything in my life – and especially with my wife and children – has become much more authentic...

I cannot think of a better description of what my former client calls "real work" and what Schumacher referred to as "good work". What I find especially interesting is how, *in doing work that was soulful and that felt right for him, areas of his life outside his work, including his health and his relationship with his wife and children, also improved.* Here, I also think about how many clients of mine had their marriages destroyed because of the pressures of doing soulless work.

What's more, my client's description of the joys of stone-walling shows how mythic is the idea that some business coaches love to peddle, namely that we all need a good "work–life balance". Why separate the two? I say: does not our work constitute a significant part of our life? Should we then not "live" or put our "living" on hold when at work? Does our sacred practice stop when we are at the office? Similarly, when we are not at work, not doing our job – that is, when we are supposedly doing our "living" – does this therefore disallow us from engaging in inner work?

I say that work and life are integral parts of each other.

I like what the Tibetan Buddhist master Tarthang Tulku says about work in his book *Skillful Means*:

> Caring about work, liking it or even loving it, seems strange when we see work only as a means to make a living. But when we see work as the way to enrich and deepen all experience, each one of us can find this caring in our heart and waken it in those around us, using every aspect of work to learn and grow.[30]

This is exactly what my waller was doing.

Respecting the Material World

I need at this stage to say a little bit about money, as you may perhaps be thinking that I am somewhat ambivalent towards the material world and believe that being soulful and finding the right work for ourselves can only come about through our being church-mouse poor, and that all people who do high-flying jobs and earn lots of money must therefore be soulless!

If you've got this impression, this is certainly not my intention. On the contrary, I believe the material world is very important, that we neglect it at our peril and that many people in high-earning professions are actually doing much good for the planet. Materiality only becomes "evil" when – generally along with power and a need for control – it assumes too much significance and strangles out beauty, as it did for me in the story I just told about my tribal art.

The truth is that money is never the source of evil. *We* are, and it is not money's fault if it gets abused and becomes an instrument of our greed. And we abuse it for exactly the same reason that we abuse other human beings or we abuse our environment: namely, we fail to respect its inherent sacredness.

It is very important, therefore, that we come to see that money also has soul and needs to play a significant role in the whole ensouling process. When it is used to bring beauty, truth or healing into areas of our world that are ugly, dishonest or wounded, or when it pays for medicine to come to people in need (here I think of what Bill Gates's funds have done to help end malaria in the world) its soul becomes hugely luminescent. Yes, my friend, the same "financial force" that can get frittered away on empty ultra-consuming lifestyles and superyachts can also be used to pay for the housing and education of thousands of immigrants fleeing rogue regimes!

Financial abundance

So when I talk about living our daily lives as our sacred practice, relating to money from a soulful place needs to be an integral part of this process. If we don't have enough money to function properly – if we can't afford a car and so can't drive our kids to school – our resultant anxieties will wipe away any sense of inner abundance we might have acquired.

I think we all have a great responsibility not only to see that we have enough money for our needs (not our greed!), but also that we earn it ethically and we use it wisely. If we have psychological issues around it – if we are stingy, say, or we fear money or we believe it is "evil" and so push it away, or we are obsessed with it or fritter it away when we have it – then it is vital that we do inner work around these issues. To hold a higher consciousness around money – to be able to recognize the divinity within it – is one of the most important things we can learn to do, and also one of the most difficult because of all the temptations around it.

I therefore don't see financial abundance so much in terms of the amount of money we have, but rather in our ability to understand and appreciate it, and to be wise, soulful and conscious in our use of it. Those with excess funds have potentially a very precious gift to offer: namely, the capacity to be generous to those less fortunate than themselves. And many multimillionaires today *are* generous.

Work challenges

So what do we do if we are stuck in a job that we find very hard to ensoul and which in no way honours our bliss, but which we cannot give up because we need to feed our family, and we cannot find anything more suitable?

My advice is: try very hard to see if there is some opening somewhere to squeeze soul into, even if it is only in the way you relate to those who work with you; and at the same time, see if there is something else you can do *outside of* your main work that is more naturally soulful. A few chapters further on, I talk about the importance of being of service, so perhaps you can also find a cause to work with that in some way serves the vision of your soul.

I am not pretending it is easy to find work that is "good work", an expression of our bliss, and which also puts food on the table, but that said, if we really put effort into asking the universe for what we need, our prayers may well be answered. The universe *does* listen the more we work at becoming connected to it.

Doorways are also more likely to open for us when our creative sparks are ignited and when we exhibit sincerity. The more we start letting go our old rajassic thinking patterns and come to realize that we inhabit a universe that is much more magical, intelligent, alive, abundant and supportive of us than our separative self could ever dream of, the more spaces start opening up that enable miracles to happen.

▣ EXERCISE on work

- How do you evaluate yourself on the work front?
- Do you feel you do "good work" à la Schumacher's definition?
- Does your work fulfil you, and do you put your heart into it?
- Do you feel you ensoul your world sufficiently through your work?
- Is there enough play in your work?
- Do you feel "the Force" is sometimes or often with you when you work?
- Do you see your work as an integral part of your life and do you see that your life includes the fact that you need to work?
- Are you at all caught up in the Puritan work ethic or in the rajassic mindset around work? If so, how does this affect you?
- What would you like to change in your work life and what can you do to bring it about?
- What goals and aspirations on the work front do you have for the next five years?

▣ AFFIRMATIONS

I choose to find work that enables me to "follow my satisfaction".

I choose to work at finding satisfaction in the work I already do.

I choose to bring more joy and play into my work.

The work I do is good work that is able to serve my own and the higher purposes of human and planetary evolution.

I choose to bring greater self-awareness into the way I work.

▣ EXERCISE on money

- How do you view money? Do you love it or are there fears or anxieties or other "patterns" around it? Are you a saver or a spender or a squanderer or are you careful or miserly with it, etc.? Answer this question in detail.
- Do you think you earn enough money and, if not, what can you do to earn more?
- Do you bring soul into how you relate to money? If so, how? If not, why, and do you want to do anything about it? If so, what can you do?
- Do you feel you run money or does it run you?

- Do you feel you are deserving or undeserving of making money? Here, see if there are any unconscious agendas you can bring out into the open.
- Do you plan how you make, how you invest and how you spend your money?
- Do you give money to good causes? If so, do you give a lot or a little, and to which causes?
- Are there any changes you would like to make around either your perceptions towards, or your use of, money? If so, write them down in great detail.
- What can you do to implement these changes? Are you willing to do this? Write down your plan of action.
- Work with this affirmation: *"I choose to honour and respect money and see it as a powerful ensouling tool."*

CHAPTER 19

The Corporate World as a Gateway to Soul

If business does not change its strategy,
business itself may well be at stake.
— FRITJOF CAPRA

Businesses, because they wield unparalleled
wealth and power, are a key factor in the
equations that decide the future.
— ERVIN LASZLO

Deeper Purposes of Corporations

In this chapter, we will continue with our theme of outer work, only we will look at it specifically in relation to the way businesses function and the challenges that they face as we move further into the twenty-first century. It is particularly important that they transform and have more soul, not only because they potentially wield enormous power to do good, but also because, as we have seen – especially when those running them are possessed by the *wetiko* virus – they can also be very destructive for the planet.

I remind you again that corporate transformations can only occur if the men and women working for them do inner work on themselves and start having more respect for the well-being of their planet. In other words, unless they start becoming aware of their own "higher soul purposes", they will not be able to grasp that their organizations also possess them and also have a "deeper destiny" to act out, and that no business, be it great or small, can operate at a higher level than those running it. Put simply, if top management are men and women who abide by the rules of the old story, they will simply not "get it" that their business might have a purpose higher than or beyond simply making money for themselves and their shareholders!

The good thing is that increasing numbers of CEOs and top managers *are* beginning to realize this and it makes me very hopeful. For example, Bill George, a former chairman of Medtronic, has suggested that "the purpose of business is to contribute to a just, open and sustainable society", while the IBM founder Thomas J. Watson Sr has said that "companies were not created just to make money but to knit together the whole fabric of civilization." These are both beautiful statements indicative of higher-order corporate soul purposes.

I also very much like what Gail McGovern, president and CEO of the American Red Cross, wrote in a paper in the *Harvard Business Review*, entitled "Lead from the Heart": "Your job as a leader is to tap into the power of that higher purpose – and you can't do it by retreating to the analytical. If you want to lead, have the courage to do it from the heart."[31]

Heart power as an antidote to the limitations of old-story business

This is such an important statement as large chunks of our humanity reside inside our hearts. Therefore, the more open they are, the more access we have to our capacity to be wise, honest and authentic, to revere life, to have integrity, to experience joy, to be intuitive, to persevere and have a vision, to think in wholes and not in parts, to desire justice, to feel gratitude and to relate well to other people. These qualities are also conducive to a corporation being successful.

Just imagine: if men and women who are starting to open to Spiral Dynamics' level six and are being "overlighted" by levels seven and eight, if these people have senior positions in their firms, what their businesses might be able to accomplish!

In my experience 99 percent of the serious mistakes that take place within organizations – such as inadequate leadership, insufficient connection between departments, managers managing unwisely, inflexibility, too many improperly thought-through, short-term decisions, an inability to behave in environmentally friendly ways or to deal with complex challenges creatively, a repressive work culture, dishonesty, racism, sexism, homophobia, you name it – arise out of top executives being fixated at operating at levels two, three, four or five, where the prime god being worshipped is the god of reason, and the self you identify with solely is the separative one. Also, unless business leaders are made aware of their own Shadow side and how to work with it, they will have no clue as to how often and how destructively Shadow issues get played out in the corporate arena.

Those executives who never seem able to "think outside the box", who tend to relate badly with their peers, who are forever being critical, always have to be right and can never allow a space for anyone else's creativity to surface, are generally people who, dimensionally speaking, do their business mainly out of levels three or four. These are also the levels that characterize how a good deal of our British political "business" is being conducted today, where there is much dishonesty and little evidence of soul or authenticity present among either those in power or those in opposition.

Yes, my friend, the "assisting Force" is there and ready to help us and it is not only available to guide and empower individuals, it can also over-light corporations and even nations. Yet it can only begin to be with us and guide and direct us when the work we are doing is aligned with the greater soul well-being of our corporation, our nation and, ultimately, the whole planet.

Benefits of ensoulment

What I have observed in firms that invite in soul is that employees are happier, teams work more closely together and those at the top feel moved to communicate with those on the shop floor, while the latter also feel free to reciprocate and talk openly about their ideas and concerns. Corporate work can start having playful dimensions to it.

In this new environment, the quality of the firm's output also tends to rise, as the best starts coming out in everyone. So when problems rear their heads, people are able to take them on and work through them in the knowledge that a problem is always a challenge, a crisis is always a new opportunity – an evolutionary ally capable of stretching one to start thinking more multidimensionally.

Indeed, the more heart and soul there is in the workplace, the more meaning people derive from what they do, the happier, more nourished and sustained they will feel, and this in turn leads to greater success for the business. Yes, when the corporate heart begins to emerge and the firm's soul life starts being activated, the entire energy in a business begins radically to shift, and the workforce discover that they can achieve much more and with more joy and less struggle. Enheartened and ensouled executives come to see that having their businesses operate from an ethical base means that being sustainable, doing good and making a healthy financial profit are actually all on the same side of the fence. There are no contradictions.

Executives realize that firms that emit a healthy aura of honesty and heart are much more attractive to shareholders. In other words, an organization that has heart and soul is sexy! It makes you friends, it wins you business, it leads to greater effectiveness, people trust you and you earn more money.

Possessing heart and soul, then, is not just "something nice" that enables everyone in the firm to feel "happier and cosier" – although this is certainly a by-product. It is a core ingredient for a firm's success. Many of the companies going out of business today are those that do not think making these kinds of shifts is important, preferring to adhere to the old devil called "business as usual"!

13 characteristics of corporations that embrace more soulful ways of operating

1) Those at the top recognize that their firms have a higher purpose and are ever-mindful of the need to engineer the appropriate circumstances to enable it to emerge.
2) The workforce is content. A spirit of empowerment predominates. Nobody works out of a culture of fear. There is competition, yes, but it is healthy as it is also balanced with a spirit of cooperation. People on the shop floor experience being recognized and appreciated and therefore feel loyal and strongly moved to want to remain in their jobs and support the success of their firm.
3) The firm operates out of integrity. There is a minimum of negative game-playing and manipulation.
4) There is a healthy top-down/bottom-up flow. Senior executives are often happy to admit they don't know all the answers and are willing to listen to advice from those on the shop floor. Thus, a spirit of openness prevails.
5) People feel free to relate humanly with one another, and no longer does anyone feel they have to sell their soul to be at work. On the contrary, they realize that being at work helps them find it.
6) Communication breakdowns are minimal and if they do emerge, steps to remedy them are at once put into operation. Staff feel empowered to trust one another.

7) A spirit of respect prevails at all levels. Employees will respect not only themselves (not drive themselves into the ground) and their colleagues, but also the local environment and the planet as a whole. Should any employee, for any reason, go through a difficult time, they will be supported and not excluded.

8) Staff will no longer see the workplace as somewhere separate from "life" but rather as an integral part of it and therefore as a place to evolve as human beings. They will also feel "allowed" to take certain risks in the interest of doing things in a new way.

9) Everyone's shared humanity is acknowledged. There are no prejudices against anybody for their gender or sexual preference or for their skin colour, age, race or religion.

10) All messes, of whatever nature, are no longer pushed away or ignored. Rather, they immediately get sorted out.

11) As all organizations have a dark or Shadow side, space will always be made to recognize, acknowledge and "work with" the disowned side. Should issues of scapegoating ever surface, they are conscientiously dealt with.

12) Success is no longer primarily measured by how big an organization is and how much money it makes for its owners and shareholders. It will also be evaluated in terms of the happiness it gives those who work for it and its capacity to respect the local environment and give work to people who need work, as well as its ability to produce products that are required in the world and to support enterprises that it deems worthy.

13) Companies are much more capable of intuiting and designing their own blueprint for operating wisely and moving forward collectively, as opposed to primarily having to obey "orders coming from the top".

It must be remembered that while the existence of a "heart space" or "heart field" in a firm is conducive to having all of the above take place, none of these things happen by magic. They occur through a great deal of conscientious, conscious, soulful work on behalf of everyone. Many may feel stretched in the process.

Here are some additional features of how a soul-based, heart-centred business might operate if it were to put into practice some of the things I have just been describing.

Old-story ways of operating	New-story ways of operating
Scourge of Protestant work ethic	Joy of going with the flow
Analysis (rationality alone)	Synthesis of heart and mind
Leaving your heart at home	Bringing your heart to the workplace
Selling your soul to the company store	Growing your soul at the company store
Feeling stressed	Feeling stretched
Feeling disempowered	Feeling empowered
Superficial communication	Authentic communication
Fear of chaos	Embrace of chaos
Seeing crisis as a problem	Seeing crisis as an opportunity
Denial of firm's dark side	Embrace of firm's dark side
Culture of suppression	Culture of openness
Seeing work as struggle	Viewing work as love in action
Separation of work from life	Integration of work with life
Separation of work and play	Integration of work and play
Rigid closed mind	Flexible open mind
Cleverness (ego)	Wisdom (soul)
Thinking productively	Thinking creatively
Thinking egocentrically	Thinking planet-centrically
Thinking short-term	Thinking long-term
Operating separatively	Having the Force with one
Creating pollution	Clearing up any messes
High carbon footprint	Low carbon footprint
Dumping waste	Recycling waste
Operating unconsciously	Operating mindfully

Making Change Possible

In my experience, exactly the same things hold true when I work with executives of corporations as when I work with my non-corporate clients. One or two at once take to a more soulful way of seeing the world. They are excited to learn and are a pleasure to work with. Such people, I think, are naturally more evolved and are simply being reminded that for far too long they have been going against their own grain and have been caught up in a corporate story that limited them, and which they couldn't do anything about, either because they didn't recognize what was going on or because they didn't realize that other ways of being were possible.

Some of my corporate clients start out by being suspicious of many of my suggestions and may offer some resistance. A few have even got quite stroppy, telling me that "all this heart and soul stuff is a load of new-age baloney"! This is understandable, for it can be scary, if one has spent most of one's work life seeing the world with materialistic blinkers on, to suddenly experience them being peeled away.

This is why corporate soul work needs to be gentle and gradual and happen organically and why the blinkers need to fall away slowly. If one tries to force the pace, one may find, quite understandably, that people will clam up.

When initial resisters *do* start opening their hearts, however, and begin connecting to the good inside themselves and to their higher purposes and those of their businesses, it always brings up a lot of delight. Some may even have spontaneous "awakening" experiences; others observe a noticeable dropping away of old stress levels. Many begin to see that there really *can* be a connection between working and "feeling joy", that there really *is* no reason to separate work from life and that the idea of a higher power supporting one is a definite reality and not a superstitious myth.

When I work with businesses, I am never presumptuous enough to tell people how they should operate. Rather, I prefer to try to create a context whereby a firm's own collective wisdom, which may have been frozen, can start to thaw and so begin revealing itself in its true colours. When this awakening occurs – and it sometimes does so in surprising and interesting ways – increasing numbers of employees discover that they know exactly what needs to happen for the greater good of their business and that everyone in the firm – including those on the shop floor – is essentially a leader and shares responsibility for its success.

▓ EXERCISE

The more detail you can answer these questions with, the better.

- How effective is your business?
- Do you feel your business does "good work" á la Schumacher's definition? Does it support its employees, produce goods that are needed in the world and respect the culture of the country it is situated in?
- Does your business use excess monies to fund any charitable endeavours?
- Does your business pay its taxes honestly?
- Does your business do anything that harms anyone or the planet? If so, are you willing to confront these anomalies and make changes?
- Has your business ever had to enter the Suffering World or gone through a Dark Night crisis (see Chapter 5)? If so, how long did it remain there and did the firm grow stronger as a result? Or did it self-destruct and have you had to start all over again?
- How happy do you think those who work in your business are?
- Go through the list of the 13 points characterizing the new-story, soulful business and note how many of those points you think apply to your business. If some of them don't apply, make a note of them and ask yourself: are certain changes needed and are you willing to try to implement them? If so, what will your challenges be? What will you need to "take on" and what will you need to "give up"?
- Go back to my list comparing some of the characteristics distinguishing new-story corporations from old-story ones and note where you feel your business has made the shifts and where it hasn't. What does it say about your business?
- Is the culture of your business open to its workforce being able to work on themselves?
- What is your corporate plan of action over the next five years?
- What is your vision of what you would like eventually to accomplish?

CHAPTER 20

Gateways of Death

Everyone knows they are going to die but nobody believes
it. If we did, we would do things differently. Learn how to
die and you learn how to live.
— MORRIE SCHWARTZ

Fear of death has caused more suffering
than all physical diseases combined.
— LARRY DOSSEY

End? No, the journey doesn't end here.
Death is just another path we take.
— J.R.R. TOLKIEN

The Significance of Death

Death is perhaps one of the most significant of all gateways into a new story, especially if we sincerely wish to transform our lives and start living more soulfully, as this inescapably calls us to do a lot of dying to and detaching from our old mindsets. And this is never easy as, in our rajassic culture with its many rigidities and limitations, the idea of death in any form is a taboo we prefer to not have to look at.

In 2018, and quite out of the blue, I was suddenly forced to confront this particular archetype in the form of the possibility of my own actual physical demise, so I feel rather close to this theme and thus am only too aware how powerful a gateway into a new consciousness it can potentially be. Here very briefly is my story.

I had had a long swim and a hefty workout in the gym, and on returning home, I complained to my wife that I felt strange. My arms felt funny and she noticed I was very short of breath walking up the stairs. Being much more aware than me that I am not 25 any more (we all still like to hang on to our little pockets of self-delusion), she bundled me at once into her car and drove me straight to hospital, where I was immediately put into the emergency ward.

Three heart operations later, I am now as fit as a fiddle. But most importantly, I have been given a great gift by life in that I had been forced for the first time to come face to face with my own mortality, which is something that I confess I had never done *properly* before. Yes, I had read a lot of books *about* death and I have worked with many clients around this subject, but that is very different from contemplating the possibility of one's own demise. But now having done so, I look not only at death but also, interestingly, at life with renewed respect. I have never been so grateful for the fact that I am still around and have all my faculties intact.

Inappropriate living leads to inappropriate dying

Not only has this made me much more conscious of the fragility of life, but I am also horrified at how ill-prepared for our demise so many of us are, the rajassic story telling us as it does that the best way to live the so-called "good life" is to repress the fact that one day it will end. Death, therefore, is *the* great Shadow issue, which is partly why so many of us keep ourselves so occupied all the time – organizing our social lives, buying things (consuming), working long hours. What all these ploys do is distract us from ever thinking about the fact that one day we won't be here in our bodies any more. So long as we are always scrabbling about on life's surface and don't ever allow ourselves to go deep (death is not a shallow topic!), we remain in safe waters.

The truth is that it terrifies us, and no wonder; our old-story or our rajassic culture has no useful instruction book to offer us other than when we go, that's it, *finito:* nothing else. The sad thing is that many of us spend as little time preparing for dying as we do for living, which I think is yet another reason why so many of us live such unabundant and death-like existences.

Death brings us closer to life

Yes, my friend, whatever we repress we draw closer to us, which is why preparing ourselves for death has to be an integral part of making our daily life our sacred practice. I have now come to realize – you could say with my full heart as opposed to merely with my thinking mind – that we actually cannot face life properly if we don't face death, and that choosing to do so makes us more real.

It certainly did this for me. My experiences in confronting my possible demise woke me up in a whole new way and I definitely think I am more genuine than I was then. When death looks us directly in the eye and then decides to move its glance away and give us another chance, we naturally become so much more grateful for what we still have rather than upset about what we think we haven't.

We also come to see that many of the "things" we give so much importance to actually count for very little. What I particularly learned was something I have been teaching for a long time, but certainly needed a reminder of, namely, that *really the most important things in life are how much we choose to live it in a loving way, and how much we are loved*. When people go through actual near-death experiences, which I'll talk about a bit later, and get to encounter their spirit guides, they are never asked questions like "How successful have you been?" but always "How much have you loved?"

For me, three weeks in hospital was an excellent free seminar on how to be grateful for the miracle of life. It also reminded me how full of *real magic* – not the hocus-pocus conjurer stuff – life is, and that, for all people's critique of modern medicine, there's a hell of a lot we can be very grateful to it for. If this had happened to me 30 years ago, I would have died; back then they didn't have the medical advances that exist today.

I now understand why those mediaeval alchemists liked to keep skulls on their desks. It wasn't to be macabre. It was to remind them that life and death are inextricably intertwined, that death is always looking over our shoulder – actually cells of ours are dying every moment – and that we cannot properly understand one without also understanding the other. What is actually much more macabre is the way so many people, so often, choose to have nothing to do with death until it is too late.

For rajassic man, death is all too often regarded as something "bad" or negative – a failure – and therefore to be put out of mind, which of course is why old age is viewed so negatively and there exists such an obsession with "looking young". In tribal cultures, things are viewed very differently. Here death is very much included as an integral part of life, and the old are revered as wise ancestors and often play a leading role in community rituals to help people die.

No story around death/rebirth

What the old story also never does is equate death with the idea of rebirth or consider the fact that all the great world religions have particular teachings on reincarnation and the incurring of karma, revolving around the idea that our current existences just *might* reflect aspects of previous lives, and that the way we choose to live our lives today just *might* affect any future life we are born into.

From the perspective of the materialist rajassic/tamassic mindset, the idea of past lives or of our possible rebirth is regarded as just as nonsensical as the existence of a "higher power". Therefore, the notions that some of us might be "paying" today for our "misdeeds" in other past lives – or that if we are cruel and judgemental towards others in this life, it just might affect what kind of future life we will have, or that if we live decently in this life, we will accumulate good karma for our next life – are regarded as utter bunkum! In his book *The Denial of Death*, Ernest Becker reminds us how man's desire to be a hero – to do something "great" for the world or to leave some monument of himself behind – is actually predicated upon his fear of death.

As I also mentioned in the chapter on the Shadow, this heroic impulse lies behind much of the evil that gets done in the world. The paradox is that the more we try to avoid and repress death, the closer we draw it to ourselves.

Lack of education around death

The problem, then, with the dualistic, split-off modern society that we live in is that few of us are educated around this important topic. So far as I know, there are no school or university courses on it and many people feel their young children should always be kept away or "protected" from this embarrassing and horrible eventuality!

Apart from in hospices, we are also not very good at caring for the dying. Many of us shrink away in fear or embarrassment in order to be not reminded that we too will someday be no more. I always think it is so weird how, in modern hospitals, doctors try to keep people with very little "quality of life" left alive at all costs – filled up with drugs and attached to machines and cut off from their loved ones and a loving environment – while on the other hand, we have few qualms about polluting our planet and turning it into a killing field.

The old story, then, has virtually no wisdom to offer us in this arena other than the idea that death *is* the final end. Within that mindset, as I suggested earlier, who we are is simply our "ego" us; nothing exists beyond ego and when we die, that's it. That's why death is so scary. We cannot properly face it, then, unless we start looking at it from a broader and more imaginative perspective.

Fear of psychological death

Our fear of actual death also impacts upon our reluctance to "die to" our old ways of looking at, or operating in, the world – even if we recognize the limitations of these ways. In other words, it lies behind our fear of change. However, if we look more closely at the way our actual lives unfurl, we see that they basically consist of a series of deaths and rebirths that are continually ongoing. 'As we enter childhood, we are called to surrender or die to babyhood; as we approach adolescence, we are called to die to our childhood; and as we enter adulthood (which rajassic man sees as being the end of the road), we need to let go our clinging to adolescence.

I think our fear of death lies behind why we often transit these various stages so unevenly, often hanging on to fragments of our past and refusing to let them go, this being the reason why so many of us so-called "adults" still have so many childish traits. Rajassic man also has little idea that there may well be *a further death* to be considered in this life, or rather, a *series* of further deaths and rebirths, and that becoming an "adult" is in no way the end of the line but merely signifies that we have reached a certain age. In the chapter on levels, you saw that realities existing beyond worlds three, four and five exist: the true name of the game being continually to be able to die to and give birth to aspects of our selfhood at increasingly higher levels of consciousness.

However, unless we are willing to confront the reality of our actual physical death – consciously open up to the realization that one day, we, as we know ourselves as a body, will be no more – we will always have problems with and resistance towards these psychological deaths. The prophet Muhammad understood this only too well. He once remarked what a tragedy it was that so many people died physically without ever, while still being alive, considering the importance of dying to, and giving birth to, selves other than their egoic one.

The Buddha's teachings on death

We can learn a great deal about how to approach our physical death from the Buddha, who divided life into four basic realities: life, death and dying, afterlife and rebirth. Only too aware of the importance of death, he provided teachings for his students to help them not only live well but also die well.

One of the things he counselled them to reflect on was the fact that since all of us are always dying, we need to see life as being an ongoing dance between birth and death. He suggested we should not fear death, as it is not the end, but merely a transition into a new phase of being, and how well we live in our current life will determine the kind of life we will have in the future when we are reborn. This is why he stressed the importance of treating our fellow human beings with kindness, love and respect and resisting negative thoughts and actions, as this will help guarantee that in our next life, we will not be plagued with bad karma.

If, via meditation, we can truly enter into our deeper mind – the one behind our restless, chaotic ego mind – and come to realize who we *really* are, that is, experience that what is truest about us is that the *real us* has never been born and has never died and therefore that at the deepest level we are all timeless, our fear of death will go. Further, we will come to see death as it essentially is, namely, a transition into a new phase of being, our new incarnation being determined by many factors including, as we just saw, how we will have lived in this life. For the Buddha, what is crucial is to wake up and know who we truly are, which comes out of our working both at having a good life – that is, a life where we do good – and a good death.

Jesus' teachings on death

Jesus' teachings were not dissimilar. He stressed the need for us to "live each day as it were our last", that is to be mindful to complete things and not have loose ends of any kind obstructing our capacity to move forward.

This means we are called to think continually of what is required for us to live a more integrated, balanced and holistic life, one where we can a) think calmly and clearly, b) be aware of the need to work at purifying ourselves and transmuting negative thoughts, letting go of regrets and resentments and c) most important, work at forgiving ourselves for "bad things" we feel we may have done, forgiving others for bad things we feel they have done to us and forgiving God for not always making the way easy for us! We don't want to die feeling angry with anyone, especially with God, as this will stop grace coming to us. We have explored all these issues in earlier chapters.

It is also useful to live in a space of asking ourselves what death means to us, how we would feel and operate if we knew we only had a week left to live and how best to find a way of saying goodbye to people, situations and possessions we have become overly attached to, as the more attached we are, the harder it is to let go. To enter new domains fully, we need to learn to free ourselves of all inclinations to hold on to our past. This may require quite a lot of inner work on our part.

Five stages of dying

Dying brings out all sorts of repressed emotions, such as guilt, sadness and jealousy. The psychiatrist Elisabeth Kübler-Ross, whose life's work was in helping people to die, delineated five stages people often go through when they hear the news:

1) Denial: this can't be happening to *me*.
2) Anger: Goddammit, why *me*?
3) Bargaining: if I'm good, maybe I'll be spared.
4) Depression: there's no hope, all is black.
5) (eventually) Acceptance: OK, this is what is happening.
   I will go with the flow!

Some people also feel angry towards those still "lucky enough to be living", and one must take this projection on, however unfair one may find it. The point is that people who are dying need to feel heard and accepted and respected for where they are at, not judged.

The need for open-heartedness

When people are dying, it is important we do not flood them with our beliefs or try to preach to them. Dying people want to be heard – they want our love and closeness, not our instruction – and the more we can hold them inside our hearts, give them our unconditional love, visualize them being connected to the larger heart of life (again see the chapter on the heart), the better.

Ram Dass, a spiritual teacher who has meant much to me in my life, and who has worked with many dying people, once told me that a compassionate presence was the most important thing. "Just take the person into your heart and listen to them. Often there is nothing you can say, but your presence will bring great comfort if they feel you can see their pain and grief." However tempting it may sometimes be, we should not try to "rescue" someone who is dying, in other words fill them with untruths like "I am sure you will recover", when we both know they won't, as this fills the space between us with inauthenticity when what they need more than ever, as their end approaches, is truth.

Again remembering the chapter on the different levels, it is also important that we meet the dying person at the level they are at; not too elevated and not too low. Some people might be open to us talking to them about great beings of light that exist on higher planes of consciousness, but some might not, and we should not try to expect dying people to punch above their weight! Sometimes it is helpful to ask them to go over their lives and, as it were, take an inventory of their life experiences, something that in near-death experiences often occurs naturally. I recently worked with a dying woman who particularly needed help in the area of forgiveness. "I don't want to die still hating my ex-husband," she told me.

The gift of relating in this way to someone who is dying – and I stress again that our greatest "weapon" is an open and compassionate heart – is not only that it helps them, but that it also assists us in accumulating our own "good karma" and, as I said earlier, to come closer to the reality of the fact that we too, one day, will die. If this brings fear and terror up for us, we should allow it and work with it and not block it off – with some dying people we can even share it – for if we shut down, then the authenticity of the dialogue between us, which is so important for them, closes off.

If we are a close friend or relative of the person dying, we might also need to give them our permission to pass on, in order that the dying person doesn't feel guilty in abandoning their loved one. I say this as it sometimes happens that a person does not "move on" after their death but remains attached as a spirit to the one who is still alive, whom they feel their death is letting down. I came across a story about a batman in the First World War who was killed in front of the colonel he was serving. He felt so guilty about no longer being able to protect and serve his master that his spirit "stayed around" and attached itself to the colonel, to the great detriment of both parties. I refer you to my book *Awakening the Universal Heart* if you wish to learn more about spirit attachments.

Specifically preparing for our actual death

If we feel that our own death is beckoning, we need to work to prepare ourselves wisely and not necessarily try to fight or resist it. Too much of the old story around death is framed around the notion of combat. Just as we talk about fighting crime and drugs and cancer, so we are told to do the same thing with death, and most of the time it is not helpful. Yes, we can use our approaching demise as an opportunity perhaps to work on our courage, but not on our combative skills.

If we feel we are uninformed about death and what happens when we die, there is a huge amount of literature on the subject that we can connect with. Here, it is of great help if we meditate and make efforts to calm ourselves and, either with wise friends or with professional counsellors, discuss whatever fears and concerns we may have, so we can expunge them from our system.

Dying peacefully is very important and a large part of this comes through our concretely resolving things inside us that may still be conflicted. So, for example, if we can't forgive ourselves for something we did many years ago, or if there are people we still hold grudges against, we should work on these issues. Also, have we made sure that our wills are clear and fair, so that conflict won't erupt after we are no more?

As we contemplate our death, a lot of grief may come up. We may feel our lives are not finished, perhaps that we haven't done enough or been that hero we so wanted to be. We may feel too young to die or sad at leaving those we love, and we must experience all these things and not repress how we feel, as this is a key part of the completion process. Those who love us may also feel grief and it may be helpful for both parties to share their emotions.

Grieving must never be suppressed and generally it needs to be gradual. When my darling mother died, I was at the other end of the world, and as she wanted neither a funeral nor a memorial service – the purpose of both being to say goodbye and to allow for people's grief to emerge – I found later that I had suppressed a lot of my sorrow.

Interestingly, what helped me enormously was the rising tide of mourning following Princess Diana's demise, which happened only a few months after. I suspect I was not the only one to ride on that powerful outpouring of love and find that the many tears I shed were not only for the princess.

The significance of temporary death experiences

I can't discuss a more soulful way of relating to death and dying without saying a few words about near-death experiences (NDEs), which have existed since time immemorial (even the Venerable Bede wrote about them) and have taken place in every culture. Actually, I feel this name is wrong, as we do actually physically die before we are "called back". Perhaps the term "temporary death experience" (TDE) might be more accurate.

In a nutshell, what happens is that our hearts stop and we technically "die" for a short time. However, we continue to have many poignant and moving experiences. Often they revolve around going through a dark tunnel and then coming out into the light, whereupon we meet those we have been close to in this life who have passed on and with whom we can find ourselves having strong telepathic communications. A being of light often appears, who can be a religious figure associated with our culture – Buddhists may encounter the Buddha, Christians may see Jesus – and we experience much love and compassion emanating from them. Then, "hey presto", we learn that the time is not right for us to depart this mortal coil, and we wake up back in our bodies in "this reality".

While every NDE or TDE is different, and a few can be scary and painful, on the whole they are very positive and help those who go through them to "awaken" to the realization that higher states of aware-ness exist, that there really *is* such a thing as God or Higher Power. Many emerge from them no longer having a fear of dying and with a whole new understanding of the world of soul.

Consciousness exists beyond the brain

Some years ago, the neurosurgeon Dr Eben Alexander wrote a book entitled *Proof of Heaven*, based on his having contacted meningitis that put him into a coma for a week, thus rendering him to all intents and purposes brain dead. However, during his temporary brain death he had some extraordinary encounters with some very loving beings, which he wrote about in great detail as soon as he woke up, completely transformed and able to recall all his experiences. In Dr. Alexander's words:

> What I had experienced was more real than the house I sat in, more real
> than the logs burning in the fireplace. Yet there was no room for that
> reality in the medically trained scientific worldview that I had spent years
> acquiring…How was I going to create room for both realities to exist? To
> experience thinking outside the brain is to enter a world of instantaneous
> connections that makes ordinary thinking (that is, those aspects limited
> by the physical brain and the speed of light) seem like some hopelessly

sleepy and plodding event…What I had experienced is the true spiritual self that all of us are destined someday to recover…We should do everything in our power to get in touch with this miraculous aspect of ourselves – to cultivate it and bring it to light…[32]

Those last words are exactly what the Buddha said, and we hear them also from every authentic spiritual teacher.

Put simply, we are all called to wake up now, and the more we can realize, to quote neurophysiologist and philosopher Sir John Eccles, that "we are spiritual beings with souls existing in a spiritual world, as well as material beings with bodies and brains existing in a material world", the more we can start to transcend our fear of death, and if we happen to sense it beckoning us, to perhaps open up to welcome it in a positive way as a transition to the next stage.

Should we not be graced with a "free seminar" on the subject, such as a TDE of our own, the best way to prepare for death is to work at realizing that higher states of consciousness do exist and that we can invoke them or pull them down into us, that there really *is* such a thing as soul, and that the true soul self, as opposed to the egoic one, really *is* timeless. And one of the best ways to realize all these things is to do regular meditation. The more we expand into this knowing *now*, while we are still alive, the easier it is to let go of, or rather die to, our fixed, "flat earth" experiences of a limited, three-dimensional space–time world primarily composed of scarcity, suffering, separation and fear.

The more we are able to experience life's intrinsic, soulful aliveness, the easier it also is to confront and work with both our literal and our psychological deaths. It is much, much harder to face death if, to all intents and purposes, we've never yet become properly alive!

My own perceptions

My own recent confrontation with death has been very important for me because I now see so clearly how, if we are truly to start living more soulfully, we really have to be willing to die over and over again, and in all sorts of different ways, to our old identifications with the rajassic, ego-imbued stories.

I don't have any grand illusions. I don't think when I pass over that I will go into some glorious heaven. I believe we all go into a place with much the same consciousness that we primarily inhabit at the moment before we die, and realizing this, I can also say that I feel inspired to "up" my meditation and accelerate my consciousness work.

I am certainly "over" the illusion that I ought to have been a great hero and left great things for posterity. That is all about our egos talking, and as we've already seen, terrible things really do get done in the name of heroism. In the great scheme of things, apart from a few great world souls whose consciousness has changed the world, none of us are *that* important.

I view death simply as a key transition point in a vast ongoing cosmic journey where we are continually dying and being reborn, a journey that takes us through many different experiences and incarnations and leads us en route through many different gateways.

EXERCISES

- How ready are you to confront the fact that one day you will die?
- Are you more a death accepter or more a death avoider? If the latter, what do you think you specifically do to avoid thinking about death?
- Are you willing to start preparing for the eventuality of your death along the lines suggested in this chapter?
- How good are you at psychological death, that is, dying to or letting go of old habits and patterns? Or are you a bit of a stick-in-the-mud? Do you fear change? If so, how can you concretely address this?
- What qualities that we have already looked at could be harnessed to help you evolve a more mature approach to the eventuality of your physical death?
- What practically do you need to do right now to prepare for whenever your death will come along? Make a will? Talk to those you love? Deepen your meditation? In other words, what do you think is most "unfinished" in your life and what is most needed to effect completion?
- Have you ever been closely connected with death in any way? If so, make notes on it and what you have learned from it.
- Have you ever helped other people through their death? If so, what was it like and what have you gained?
- If you had to die tomorrow, what would you spend your time doing today?

◼ AFFIRMATIONS

I choose to live my current life abundantly so I can prepare myself for when I die.

I choose to approach my own death courageously and with love in my heart.

I choose to work at completing everything I need to, so that when it is my time to die, I may do so in the knowledge that I am fully ready.

CHAPTER 21

The Peekaboo God

I was a hidden treasure and I loved to be known,
so I created the world that I might be known.
— IBN ARABI

The Great Conundrum

As I made clear particularly in the chapter on the different worlds of consciousness, one way to view life is to regard it as a "game" that we all "play" at different levels, depending upon how awake or conscious we are or how connected or disconnected we are to the worlds of soul. We have also seen that people have more or less soul, or virtually none at all if this dimension of themselves remains deeply concealed.

However, this brings up a very important question. If who we all are is a soul – if soul-ness is our core, our true birthright – then why does it seem to be so hard for us to remember this? Why does this knowledge have to be hidden, which in turn makes it so difficult for us naturally to bring love and compassion into the way we live our daily lives?

In other words, why do we all seem to forget who we *really* are and instead believe who we are is our separative egoic self, which, as we are finding out, is *not* who we are, the result of all this muddle being that we then have to *work* at "outing" ourselves - at *becoming* who we really are?

It is all so complicated. Why can't we just be who we are without having to work at becoming it? And in particular, why do we all get so caught up in all our delusions about ourselves, the result being that it is so easy for our good intentions to get sabotaged? In particular, why do we all get so attached to false images about ourselves, so manacled into our old rajassic and tamassic stories around separation and suffering, with many of us never ever managing to slip free of those chains?

One can certainly understand why ideas around our "deserving to be punished" or of man being a "wretched sinner fallen from grace", as advocated by certain crucifixion-fixated Christians, have a following. It really does seem as if we are being punished for not being "good enough"! Is this true? Are we really wretched sinners after all?

I don't think so.

A sleep and a forgetting

But these are nonetheless very important questions to ask, and Wordsworth also asks them. In his "Intimations of Immortality", he wonders why it is that in order for us to develop, we human beings seem to need to move further and further away from that soulfulness that we were so close to when we first entered the world as a newborn.

> *Whither is fled the visionary gleam?*
> *Where is it now, the glory and the dream?*

His answer to his own question is:

> *Our birth is but a sleep and a forgetting:*
> *The Soul that rises with us, our Life's star,*
> *Hath had elsewhere its setting…*
> *…But trailing clouds of glory do we come*
> *From God, who is our home:*
> *Heaven lies about us in our infancy!*
> *Shades of the prison-house begin to close*
> *Upon the growing Boy,*
> *But he beholds the light, and whence it flows,*
> *He sees it in his joy…*
> *At length the Man perceives it die away,*
> *And fade into the light of common day.* [33]

The incarnational wound

What Wordsworth seems to me to be referring to is what I call the "soul wound" or "incarnational wound" that afflicts not just some of us, but all of us. He is suggesting that when we first come into the world, we all still exude the warm soulful/womb-like connection with divine beingness that is the core of who we are, but then we start to *grow away* or *distance* ourselves from that "heaven" or womb-like unity that was "about us in our infancy".

What occurs, Wordsworth suggests, is that in that process "shades of the prison-house" – that is, the conditioning of society, the rajassic/

tamassic stories – begin to close around us and gradually to snuff out our soul memories. This is particularly the case if our parents or care-givers are themselves not yet connected to their own soul nature and therefore are unable to "reflect" or "mirror" anything soulful back to us and consequently can do nothing to help keep alive the rapidly vanishing memories of our belongingness to all of life.

My way of understanding this, therefore, is as follows: our journeying through life – the process of our growing up and, in Jungian terms, our needing to individuate and become our own person – has to include a separation from, or a letting go of, our mother, with whom initially we are bonded so close with that we don't know that we are not her.

In other words, growing up requires that we all have to go through an ego-growing stage, and for this we have to separate from our womb-like bliss and enter the "old-story" worlds of separation.

However, this is not to be seen as a "fall" or a "punishment" because we are "bad" or "sinful". It is needed because it sets up the necessary conditions for the adventure of our potentially becoming a real human being.

Put simply, the process of our "growing up" (expanding) seems to require that we all have to start off by gradually distancing ourselves (shrinking) from that unitive awareness or from "God who is our home". Our growing away from and gradually feeling more disconnected from the light that was around us as a tiny baby, then, is not a sign of something necessarily having "gone wrong" but, rather, is an integral part of our evolutionary process.

A hide and seek divinity

There is therefore a good reason for this seeming "fall from grace", which in truth is not a fall at all. It is rather the case that grace or soul needs to hide from us; or, more accurately, hide *inside* us, to see if one day, after we've completed our "being a separate self" journey, we might then be moved to go looking for it.

As I see it, God or our Creator or the Universe or the Cosmos or Higher Power or the Universal Intelligence or the Force – whatever we want to call it – is wanting to *test* us all and to that end, the process of hiding inside us is intentional: that is, is all part of the game that it needs to "set up" for this very purpose. In other words, soul or divine consciousness *purposely* hides inside us, and we *intentionally* have to forget our sacred origins – forget we are a soul – in order to "set up" the necessary conditions to see if one day, after we will have individuated and found our personal identities, we are then going to be moved to commit to explore further stages of our evolutionary unfolding and go looking for who we *really* are and thus come to the realization that not only are we in truth a soul, but an ever-evolving or growing soul.

Like a game of "catch me if you can"!

Basically, then, soul or the divine is engaged in playing an intentional game of hide-and-seek with us that goes like this: "I, soul, will purposely hide myself inside you to see if you'll get so fed up with your life without me that you'll be motivated to come looking for me!"

"Peekaboo!"

"Find me if you can!"

But – and this is important – soul will sprinkle a few clues around that may lead us gradually to deduce that the separate self we have come to believe is who we are, may actually not be who we are, and this will therefore get us asking many new questions. I mean, if you and I *already* knew who we were – already knew that we were one with our Creator, one with God, one with the abundance of all life – then there would be no game; there'd be no need for us to look for gateways to move through to get there. We'd start out our journey having already arrived at our destination! How can we "out" ourselves from the closet if we are already out? How can we be moved to seek something if that something is right there in the open and not hidden?

So the idea about soul needing to be hidden inside us, or it being something that we are not initially "awake to", is very significant. And life is all about challenges and how well we respond to them. We saw this in the chapter on the Shadow, where I talked about why evil exists and where I suggested that if life was always easy, and there were no wars, no extractivists, no Brexits to be confronted, no glamorous or seductive forces to pull us away, no *wetiko* viruses to endarken us, there would be no real game to life. All these obstacles somehow serve to spice things up, make the sacred game more meaningful. *That's* why you and I *need* to come into the world asleep to who we really are!

Waking up or blocking off

The fact of our seeming to go through further "falls" – subsequently becoming entangled or lost in all the many soulless dramas going on all around us, which we all seem to do – is not, I repeat, because we are "weak, fallen, miserable sinners" in need of extra punishment! It is intentional. We have to separate from our oceanic, womb-like pre-personalness in order to enter the world and become a person, and we also have to go through further stages of becoming utterly unaware of or asleep to our own core divinity or to the possibility that there may exist higher dimensions to our humanity.

Certainly, in my own life, it has been during those times when I've felt most lost or most confused or most up against it or most uncertain as to where my life was going that I've done most soul searching!

The big problem, however, is that so many of us get trapped in our separative self egoic identities. We remain there and we don't wake up, we don't "out" the true us and thus never discover an "us" existing beyond our separate self us. We don't respond to the game of peekaboo!

In other words, despite all kinds of warning signals – crises out in the world, the realization that we are destroying our environment, our own personal unhappiness and so on – many of us never wake up. We get so firmly embedded in the quagmire of the system that we truly believe it is all there is and that nothing exists beyond what our three-dimensional space/time reality tells us exists.

In a word, we don't feel the least bit inclined to change anything.

We prefer staying asleep.

∾

This is where soul may enter the equation again, in the form of dangling certain intimations of itself before us.

I spoke about this earlier when I suggested that sometimes "visitations" from higher states of consciousness take place out of the blue, reminding us that there may be something more to life, something more mysterious and more beautiful than our mundane existences normally reveal to us. However, we sometimes at this point block off, hunker down even more. Soul light may shine abundantly around us and grace may do its best to display itself to us in all its glory, but we remain immune, closed off, and carry on with our old rajassic/tamassic pursuits. Our old "comfort zones" entrap us – hold us hostage.

But sometimes we *do* take in the messages that these intimations of soulfulness are trying to give us, and thus feel moved to make some radical shifts in our lives and work on ourselves to wake up.

Encouraging soul to stay with us

However, as we saw earlier, even if we *do* receive these powerful messages of ensoulment, and even if we *do* allow them to start opening us up and we begin to work to change things, this does not necessarily guarantee that soul will remain with us. It is very possible that we fall asleep again. Many of us do so!

In other words, the soul dimension of ourselves that has begun opening up can easily close down again if it is not properly maintained and exercised, in much the same way that we can lose muscle power if we stop exercising our bodies, or mental power if we don't continue applying our minds. Therefore, if we wish for soul to remain with us, we need always to be working at invoking it, engaging in and relating to our world in ways that bring it into greater prominence.

This is why regular prayer and meditation, visiting those areas of life where soul presence is deeply concentrated – that is, doing our best to have close encounters with the soulful forces, however or wherever we encounter them – and generally trying to live all areas of our daily lives as a sacred practice, is so very important.

I repeat again: the fact that you and I may get spiritually derailed at different times in our lives and start losing touch again with our sacred origins, does not necessarily mean that something has gone wrong. The peekaboo game simply continues. From this perspective, losing our way or getting distracted may be a very key part of our life journeying. It may even motivate us to put yet more effort into our search and as a result, attain a higher level of soulfulness!

The hidden treasure and the sacred game

One of the clearest pronouncements on understanding the purpose behind our lives lies in a simple statement spoken by the great twelfth-century Sufi mystic Ibn Arabi. Speaking as if on behalf of God and referring to God as a treasure, he intimates why God created the world: "I was a hidden treasure and I loved to be known, so I created the world that I might be known."

Treasure-ness or Godness or soulness, then, is *intentionally* hidden, but the Divine loves to be known, loves its presence to be outed – desires that it be brought out of hiding or realized. This is the whole purpose behind the creation of the world. *The reason, therefore, why you and I were created, why we have all come into being, is because as we embark on the journey of discovering who we really are – as we gradually become more fully human - we become the forms through which the divine can potentially be known. To be fully human then, is to be divine.*

In other words, whichever god or divine force created you and me – saw to it that the divine spark was implanted into us – did so in the hope that through our waking up and realizing more and more of our inherent soulfulness, a whole new space would open up inside us for our creator to inhabit or discover itself through and thus celebrate!

So when you or I are sitting on a rock feeling joy, or when we are behaving lovingly or altruistically, it is the divine celebrating its joy and love and altruism through us. The divine celebrated the courageous side of itself in Erin Brockovich and in Harry, whom we encountered in Chapter Fifteen, when he hurled himself in that beautiful selfless act onto the railway lines to save that little girl's life.

The game, then, is this: will the divine spark or the God consciousness implanted inside each of us get ignited – in which case the God presence or the divinity inside us will rejoice – or will it just remain as potential and never explode into flame?

What enables the divinity inside all of us to come out of hiding and celebrate (and perhaps in the process even discover *new* dimensions of itself) is through us doing the work to have our lives be our sacred practice, through choosing to live with heart and taking a stand for a better world by working as conscious ensoulers of our society. So when I talk about feeling that Higher Power is with me when I am teaching my retreats, another way to say this would be that in a tiny way, through the work I do to try to help others, I am creating an opening in myself for God to reveal itself and thus celebrate a little bit of itself through me!

Whenever you and I quieten down through our meditation and discover a deep, beautiful space inside our hearts that is full of joy, or when we find peace inside us, or when we help a friend in need, or when we take stands against the oppressive forces, or when we dare to express our truth or find ways to bring light into dark spaces, or when we confront danger with love, or when we give of our limited resources to help someone in trouble, or when we try to assist other people to grow, or feel moved to work towards ending conflict on the planet, or find ways of expressing our divinity through song, art or the written word, what we are in effect doing is being a space to allow the divine treasure that is hidden inside us to be outed and celebrated.

I am now going to conclude this chapter with a beautiful Gnostic tale entitled "The Hymn of the Pearl", written in either the first or second century and retold often, in which our divinity or treasure-hood is represented by a pearl.

"The Hymn of the Pearl" and the Return Journey

When I was a little child and dwelt in the kingdom of my father's house in great wealth and splendour, my parents sent me on a journey. (The journey of incarnating into the world.) But first they took off from me the robe of glory which they made for me and made a covenant with me which they wrote inside my heart so I wouldn't forget it.

"We want you to travel to Egypt and bring back the pearl which lies in the middle of the sea which is encircled and protected by the snorting monster (i.e., discover your soulfulness in the middle of soullessness), and when you will have done so and come back, you can again put on your robe of glory."

I left on my journey and went straight to the serpent and settled down close to him until he went to sleep and then I could take the pearl from him. I dressed myself in the clothes of those around me in case they recognized who I was and what my mission was, fearing they might arouse the serpent against me.

But instead they mixed me a certain drink and gave me some meat and it made me fall asleep to my mission. (The old soulless stories exist to condition us and make us forget who we truly are.) I forgot that I was a king's son and that I had come to take the pearl (i.e., find soul in the midst of soullessness).

My parents noted what had happened and they were sad and wrote a letter to me asking me to rise out of my sleep and remember who I was, remember that I was a king's son and to remember the pearl that I came to get and remember the robe of glory that I used to wear. (We experience "divine discontent" and sense something is amiss with our lives.)

An eagle (symbol of soul and grace) brought the letter to me and I read it and woke up out of my sleep and I remembered who I really was, namely the son of a king and what my mission really was, i.e., to retrieve the pearl. (Find soul out in the world.) So I set out and began to enchant the snorting serpent and charmed it to sleep by chanting the names of my father and mother. (When we do spiritual practices and meditations, the forces of soullessness begin to evaporate.)

And I seized the pearl (I started to wake up to who I *really* was) and went home to my parents, casting off the filthy garments I had put on. (I let go all my beliefs in and attachments to the old rajassic and tamassic stories.) The letter that had awakened me served as a light to guide me back home. (When soul awakens inside us, so too does our inner guidance.) As I drew near, my parents sent out my robe of glory and I put it on. (I became a "space" for God to celebrate itself through me.) When I arrived, I bowed my head and adored the splendour of my father who had sent it me and whose commands I had fulfilled. (I woke up to realize who I truly was.) [34]

This story, which exists in various forms in different spiritual traditions, is often called the "return journey" because the more we begin outing our deeper soul self, the more we understand that we are actually not going to some "foreign place" – interestingly, things only seem that way when we are asleep to who we are! – but are actually returning to that undifferentiated oneness from which we originated – that is, to our source. Only now we are experiencing being "home" at a higher twist of the evolutionary spiral.

The challenge is out there for all of us. Will you and I remain asleep and continue to live our old-story existences where the divinity within us continues to slumber, or will we choose to work at awakening and thus start celebrating who we truly are and in so doing we truly are and in so doing become a space for the healing of our society?

EXERCISES

- What thoughts does this chapter bring up for you? Does what I say about the peekaboo God, and the whole idea of the divine being hidden inside you, make sense?
- Have you ever experienced sacred overtures, i.e., the equivalent of the eagle, being made towards you? If so, what form or forms have they taken, and how have you responded?
- If they came to you right now, how would you respond?
- Does "The Hymn of the Pearl" resonate with you?
- Do you feel that through reading this book and working with the exercises, your life is gradually turning into being your sacred practice? If so, what are you specifically doing to make it this way? How are you starting to express your pearl-hood or your Treasure-ness? Is it in your singing, in your kindness, in your working as a

scientist, in your being a loving friend, in the love you show your partner, in being a compassionate social worker or an activist for some important cause you believe in? List all the ways you feel you are allowing your deeper soul self out of your closet.

■ Do you also feel you are sufficiently feeding your soul in the way you are living? In other words, are you allowing enough play, joy, creativity, meditation, time with friends and so on into your life? If not, in what area or areas could your soul do with more feeding? Are you willing to devote time and energy to this?

▮ EXERCISE on deepening your soul life

■ Close your eyes and go inside and connect to your heart.
■ Put lungs inside it and breathe in and out. And be aware that this is where your soul speaks to you.
■ What is it saying right now about ways that you can deepen your soul life?
■ Do you need to pray or meditate more?
■ Do you need to take more time to be by yourself?
■ Do you need more balance and less stress in your life?
■ Do you need to spend more time being out in nature?
■ Do you need to find a spiritual master?
■ Do you need to find a new job?
■ Do you feel drawn to take up a spiritual practice, like, say, yoga or tai chi?
■ Do you feel moved to take up a particular path? For example, are you drawn to Buddhism or Sufism or to go and work with a particular shaman?
■ Do you need to put more effort into being of service?

Write down what you see as being your next step in your soul journeying. If it includes finding new ways to be of service to the planet, hopefully the next chapter will offer some useful pointers.

CHAPTER 22

World Service as a Gateway to Soul

Service is of many kinds, and he who wisely renders it,
who seeks to find his particular sphere, and who,
finding it, gives effort for the benefit of the whole, is the
one whose own development proceeds steadily.
— DJWAL KHUL

You gotta serve somebody.
— BOB DYLAN

What is Service Work?

FOR ME, BEING OF SERVICE means working on behalf of and thus taking a stand for a cause or causes that we believe in and which are dear to our hearts, and where we feel we can make some kind of positive contribution towards a healthier world. The more we allow ourselves to become a space for the Treasure that we are to "come out of hiding", and consequently for the Force to be strongly with us, the more powerful and effective our service will be. This is why working at building up our own soul power is so important.

The would-be server, then, sees what is wrong with our planet and wants positive changes to take place and is willing to put their full heart and soul – even, in some cases, their lives – on the line to help these changes come about.

Service work can take a multitude of different forms and can occur at different levels, depending on how mature and committed we are, where our passions lie and what particular skills or gifts we can bring to the table. If we are a lawyer, we may choose to work in the area of human rights; if a doctor, for an organization like Médecins Sans Frontières, or conversely, we might do something entirely different from our current careers like my friend who did fund-raising for particular charities. Being of service can include going on protest marches, helping victims of abuse or giving lectures around the world on the importance of using solar and wind energy. Whatever one commits to, what is significant is that one is working for a cause that is much bigger than just one's own little self.

Server as activist

Another word to describe those brave men and women who dedicate a part – or in some cases all of their lives – to being of service is the one we have used before in this book: "activist". As we have already seen, sometimes being an activist can be very dangerous: when women in ultra-conservative countries such as Sudan or Saudi Arabia go on marches to protest against the abuse of women's rights, they are risking their lives, as is the dissident who single-handedly takes on a corrupt regime or the whistleblowing journalist seeking to expose corruption in high places.

Confronting the dark face of the old story or exposing the *wetiko* virus for what it is is never easy, as evil hates being exposed and, as we have seen, will often fight back using a lot of underhanded tactics. The power of one person to make a difference, however, can be summed up in the example of the teenager Greta Thunberg, who as I mentioned earlier, has dedicated her life to travelling the world lecturing on climate change. Her commitment is awesome and world leaders really listen to her. This is the power of passion and I have no doubt that the Force is strongly behind her, as it is behind all people who are dedicated to trying to do good in the world (but who are not self-righteous "do-gooders", as this courageous young woman certainly isn't).

So never think that "little me" is helpless to effect change. People who make the most difference in the world are often unable to see the consequences of their work, as not only do changes often take longer to happen than we think, but they often occur very differently to the way we might expect them to.

Being of service or being an activist of one form or another has become very fashionable among many celebrities, which is a good thing as their fame and fortune can add a powerful impetus to the causes they are supporting. Also, despite the negative press often given to wealthy people, many are philanthropically minded and in no way are the greedy monsters they are often made out to be.

That said, we don't need to be a famous film star or a member of royalty to play our little role in helping make the world a better place. If our planet is currently making many positive shifts in the right direction, it is largely because of the incredible efforts behind the lines being put in by very ordinary yet very soulful and dedicated men and women from all countries and from all walks of life. In the words of the campaigning environmentalist Bill McKibben: "The movers and shakers on our planet aren't the billionaires and the generals. They are the incredible people around the world filled with love for their neighbour and for the earth, who are resisting, remaking, restoring, renewing, revitalizing."

Serving the planet

In the old countercultural days, the activist movement always used to be split between those who opposed the suits and went on demonstrations, those who retired to ashrams to be "spiritual" and meditate, those who stood for "alternative energy" (as wind, solar and wave power used to be referred to in those days) and those who worked on healing their psyches. Never the twain (or the four) seemed to meet.

Not so today. Today, huge shifts have occurred. There is far greater integration – far more people exist at, and work out of, Spiral Dynamics' levels six, seven and eight – perhaps, as I suggested earlier, because the world situation is much more precarious than it was then, and so more people have chosen to join the ranks of activist/change agent. Today, you can be a political activist *and* go on demonstrations *and* also be an environmentalist *and* be consciously on a spiritual path, as well as wearing a suit!

The soul power of the millennials

When I wrote that last sentence, I was thinking about the millennials, and I need to say a few words about them, as I regard their presence as being of huge importance. Firstly, they do not carry the same kind of mental and emotional baggage that many of us who are older, do, and secondly, they are much more programmed to understand the increasingly technologized culture, which we now all live in. Indeed, for many of the younger ones, it is the only reality they have ever known.

The vast majority of millennials I know, I experience to be very positive in their outlook. Just recently a good friend in his twenties told me that he felt the world can get better not least because he feels much less susceptible than us "oldies" to having the wool pulled over his eyes. "We millenials have the information as to how bad a state the world is in", he told me, "so we know where our work lies!"

In my experience, millenials living in countries governed by totalitarian regimes tend to have few illusions as to the corruption all around them and therefore the kind of challenges they face and the best strategies to use to address them. They are also terrific communicators and have the tools and know-how to be in close touch with their counterparts no matter where on the planet they live. Spared the kind of entanglement in the system that besets so many of us, I find most millenials to be staunch realists (none of that "hippy-dippyness" that existed in my youth), very driven, sincere and many of them much more invested in having their lives "make a difference" as opposed to trying to clamour to the top of some dubious financial ladder! I think this is fantastic which is why so many younger people today have Higher Power working on their behalf, often without knowing it. Yes, my friend, I believe the best change agents in the world today are the millennials.

I can't help feeling a wee bit sad, though, that it is the young people of today who are called to do a lot of cleaning up of the messes that my generation not only failed to do, but in many instances, conspired to create!

The need for dissolving antipathies

One thing in particular that I think the "difference maker" needs to address is the hostility and fear that so often exists between people who see the world through different glasses. For example, disdain towards those on the opposing end of the political spectrum from oneself, reflects both self-righteousness and a lack of soul.

If we happen to be someone who hates the rich and sees all wealthy capitalists as "evil", we are simply introducing a further negative ingredient into the fray, which, as we've already seen, is a) eminently old-story and b) changes nothing other than keeping the other side even more entrenched in their old tracks. Agreed, certain billionaires of gangster and oligarchic origins I would no more like to have dinner with than they would with me. But I do not hate them or want the worst for them. As we saw earlier on, divine consciousness resides within all of us and the *wetiko* virus just has the effect of covering it up even more strongly.

I stress once more that what is important is that we come to find love and compassion in our hearts and learn to "feel ourselves" inside the beingness of those who see the world very differently to ourselves. From this place we can come to realize why certain people are, say, very materialistic and narrow-minded, why they are still moved to hang on to old colonial mindsets and prejudices and privileges that continue promoting injustice; or why people are fundamentalist in the religious sense.

Holding on to old mindsets and stories essentially comes from fear, and, as we saw earlier, there is always a strong resistance to change in those whose lives are inherently soulless. As we now know, if we try to punch rigidity in the face and play the "blame game" with it, it does not melt, but only grows stronger. What enables it to soften are the weapons of soul, truth, heart and love, espousing principles of justice and integrity, and taking stands for what is decent, good, whole and soulful. This is much more powerful than being *against* what is bad and confused and soulless. It is an idea summed up by a sentence from the famous prayer: "Where there is darkness, may I bring light." The activist is a light-bringer and in some circles is even known as a "light worker".

Inner activism

I remind you again that we can – and we do – make a huge difference, not only in what we do, but also in being who we are. To give one little example, if we are committed to relating to our fellow human beings and treating them in a respectful and friendly way, we are doing an awesome amount to advance the cause of a sacred culture in the world.

As discussed earlier, small acts of kindness are in fact big acts and they affect our collective consciousness. So anytime we assist someone who needs help, or we reveal the way forward to a person who is stuck, or we make something beautiful that used to be ugly, we are doing mighty service work. Those artists and musicians and poets and film-makers and writers and designers who seek to bring beauty and truth and joy into the world through their creativity are all doing mighty work.

My wife is someone who does mighty work all the time and being in her presence has done a lot to make me a better human being. She is my great teacher. I have seen her sprint to the flower shop to get there in time to buy a bouquet for a friend who she thinks needs cheering up. Two days ago, she spent a whole day in town to help a friend who was very low in confidence buy a dress to wear at her son's wedding. She is always there to help and give advice to her friends and many people gravitate around her for her wisdom and light which she emanates very strongly. Some people are natural servers and my wife is one of them. Her goodness flows out of her quite effortlessly.

A few months ago she was out walking and came across two tiny kittens, perhaps a week old, dying of starvation in the street. She gave up what she was doing that day to bring them home and today they are thriving, full of life and are a core part of our family. The old-story mindset might see these actions as being of small significance. (Remember how in rajassic lingo, everything has to be *big* to be given any significance.) Just flowers. Just a dress. Just two cats. Huh!

I call this mighty work and big work because it is work done directly from the heart, and this is what the rajassic/tamassic person utterly misses out on. In the words of the Buddhist mystic Shantideva:

> *All the joy the world contains*
> *Has come through wishing happiness for others;*
> *All the misery the world contains*
> *Has come through wanting pleasure for ourselves alone.*

Finding our correct service path

Each of us has a very different service path to tread and very different gifts to offer, and what is important is that we discover our own specific way or ways to be of service. We mustn't either feel we have to do everything – and so continually berate ourselves for not doing enough – or, conversely, feel we should wait until we become a saint before we lift a finger. Rather, we need to serve both at the level and in the way we are best able to right now, and we should not try to do tasks that we are unfit for.

So if, like me, you aren't a good organizer, then don't elect to organize a demonstration. If going on demonstrations isn't your thing, then don't go on them. Or if you don't feel strongly enough about animal rights – you love whales and elephants but actually you're more interested in human rights – then by all means, if you wish, send a donation to those organizations, but don't feel you have to connect more deeply with them. Others will. The world server is part of a self-organizing, interconnected network that is much bigger and much wiser than any of us as individuals can ever understand. The Force operates in mysterious ways and is at work even as I write these words.

Often, the causes that most touch us connect to areas where we have experienced some kind of wounding or suffering in our own lives. Possibly a reason why I am particularly concerned with expanding soul awareness is because the world of my dear parents was one of such monumental unawareness in this area, and I suffered because of it.

We must also not forget that we are living in changing times. I stress once more that the era of "individual-itis" – of people trying to do it all on their own – is coming to an end, and often the best way to be of service is to work in collaboration with other people. Also, in this way, wheels don't have to get reinvented.

Nine ways to be of service
I see there being nine prime ways that we can be of service.

The radiator
Radiator servers make a difference by radiating healing, loving and transforming energy out into the world. Their activism occurs through the quality of their being; their good vibrations help lift the vibrations of the environment around them. They bring calmness and light into the darkness, and in our fragmented and fast-moving culture, this work is of the very greatest importance. They are the mystics and healers and peacemakers.

The initiator
These people are the movers and shakers, the initiators of new projects to bring benefit into the world. They are always out there in the thick of it, often fighting to bring change into corporate, scientific and political structures. They have visions of how a new world might look and they are committed to trying to bring it into expression.

The infiltrator
Infiltrators are the transformational equivalents of the "double agent"! They bravely work their way into old-story organizations and subtly try to introduce new ways of looking at the world from within – hopefully without rocking the boat too strongly.

The proclaimer
Proclaimer activists heal through the power of the spoken word, like Barack Obama, who won his elections all those years ago because when he spoke, he made people believe that with him in the White House, all would be possible. Their role is to inspire us to think and act in new ways.

The innovator

Like a Jung or an Einstein, innovator servers bring something entirely new to the kitchen table. They inspire us to open up to whole new ways of thinking and acting and seeing the world.

The investigator

The role of the investigator activist is to investigate the Shadow side of life, to bring what is dark or hidden to the surface so that it may be seen for what it is and thus become "disinfected" by the light. This can be a dangerous path to follow as many kinds of regressive forces hate being "outed" and will often fight back strongly and do their best to destroy those trying to expose them.

The educator

Educator servers take it upon themselves to make people aware that it is possible to see the world in a whole new way, to let them know that many new paradigms are emerging, that there is much knowledge to be gained from looking inside ourselves and that we all contain much inner wisdom, if we only know how to locate it.

One important source of education comes to us via movies, and my hope is that more film-makers today realize the enormous potential they have to effect positive transformations. Some years ago there was a truly wonderful movie called *Avatar*, about a planet occupied by a very noble and courageous race who lived in total harmony with their environment; consequently, the Force was never not with them. However, because their planet had great mineral riches, a group of tamassically-minded extractivists from our planet landed on it with the intention of destroying its inhabitants so they might take over its wealth. Despite the invading forces possessing all the hot new technical weaponry of destruction and the inhabitants having nothing more than bows and arrows, because in their utter soullessness the invaders lacked any kind of connection with "soul force", the movie ended with the triumph of the brave-hearted ones.

I believe films can be very prophetic and why this movie touched me so much is because, as you will see in the epilogue, I believe the power of those willing to take stands for truth, love and integrity is far, far greater and far exceeds that of those who wish to destroy soul in the interest of growing materially richer. Yes, on the outside it looks as if things are the other way around; but, as the main character in the film tells us, "so much of what we believe is true is false, and so much of what we think is false is real".

The protestor

Going out into the streets as an expression of the stand one takes on a particular issue is a powerful act, especially if many people do so. Here, we remember that "people power" brought down the Iron Curtain and, in the early 2000s, in the Middle East, it also downed a bevy of singularly unpleasant dictators. More recently, we have the demonstrations in Hong Kong around issues of judicial independence and broader questions of democracy, starting in June 2019 and at time of writing, still ongoing. This strategy is a very powerful way of letting the powers that be and the world as a whole know about those issues which one feels strongly about.

The agitator

The job of the agitator server is not to make people feel calmer and more at ease. That is the radiator's role. Rather, the agitator does their best to shake us all up out of our complacency, so we may reach into our pockets more generously or generally do more to help a new culture come into expression. Their gift to us is to light rockets under our backsides in order to wake us up into action – to force us to realize that if we want our planet to survive, we are all called to be change agents and we should not leave the business of change up to others.

EXERCISE

Which of these paths of service particularly resonate with you? Maybe you are primarily on one or even on two paths but also have secondary tentacles lying in one or two or even three of the others.

Make notes for yourself and maybe ask yourself if you a) are on the right path or paths and b) are putting all your heart and soul into your work and if perhaps there is more you might like to do or are able to do. Again, no self-criticism. Just self-observation.

Write some guidelines to yourself.

Seven things we can do *right now*

Here are some things you can embark on right now, while contemplating which of these groups you belong in.

1. Spend five minutes sending good, positive healing energy to some area of the planet you feel needs it, for example, people in Yemen or Syria, or people who have lost family and livelihood as a result of some terrible tragedy or who are victims of a natural disaster.
2. Do one (or more) "random acts of kindness" a day. For example, put a pound in a parking meter near yours that you see is going to expire, or mow the lawn of the elderly person who lives next door.
3. Think of a friend who is in need, see if there is something you can do to support them and go and do it.
4. Tithe 5 percent (or more) of your earnings to a cause or causes of your choice.
5. Meditate on peace; try to treat everyone you encounter in a friendly, empowering and peaceful way.
6. If you perceive any area of "wrong" in the field in which you work – dishonesty, injustice, etc. – be willing to take some kind of stand to help rectify the situation.
7. Think of a quality of heart you feel you have more need of – love, courage, wisdom, etc. Visualize that quality operating inside your heart, and then feel how your life might change if you were to operate more out of that place. Lastly, contemplate what would be required to have more of that quality available to you every day and how it might radically change your life.

EXERCISE

- What most upsets or agitates you about the state of the world? Write about it and also explore if your area or areas of where you feel moved to serve, in any way addresses these issues. Make notes.
- How much of your time and energy do you feel willing to commit to service? A little? Quite a bit? A lot? Make notes on your response.
- Does some part of you resist being of service? (Remember: our separate ego self hates the idea and the system only wants us to serve *it*!) So if there is resistance – and there probably will be – get it out into the open and own it and write about it. Don't deny it.
- If you wish to be of more service in the world, what changes might this require in the way you a) see the world, and b) live? Make notes.

- What does the prospect of making these changes bring up for you?
- Write a list of guidelines to yourself as to how you might increase or fine-tune your activist stance.
- Write down an appropriate service plan of action that is possible for you to engage in over the next year. N.B. Not too much (or you won't do it).

Be very honest with yourself. Service must not be about sacrificing yourself, like, say, running yourself ragged to save the whales. You serve best out of feeling abundant, not deprived. Remember: not doing anything to help the world, or just living a self-centred, "me only" life is the *real* sacrifice, as it keeps us rooted in our separate self identities, depriving us of ways that our souls can grow and consequently denying us the ability to feel genuinely good about ourselves.

There needs to be a balance between what we give out and what we let in, so that our souls are continually being fed and so we are replenishing the energy that we are giving out to the cause or causes that we've undertaken to address.

Epilogue

For me, becoming isn't about arriving somewhere
or achieving a certain aim. I see it instead
as forward motion, a means of evolving, a way
to reach continuously forward toward a better self.
The journey doesn't end.
— MICHELLE OBAMA

Remembering

WE NOW ARE DRAWING to a close and I hope, my dear friend, that you feel you have ventured through some significant gateways. I hope too that you have worked at the exercises and will continue to persevere with them and go on asking yourself questions about the directions in which you wish your life to go.

I say this as the inner work is always going on and no one else can do it for us. It just changes as we change and as different kinds of gateways appear. Also, the more we practise it, the more skilled we become and the more our work becomes a natural part of our everyday lives.

Perhaps, to start out, every morning when you get up, you can *remember* to set your inner computer to the program of *choosing* to have everything about your day be lived as your sacred practice. If you start off with intentionally "logging on" to this vision, you will find that after a while, it will increasingly become second nature and will happen spontaneously. You'll naturally ensoul your friendships; you'll naturally bring soul into a walk in the countryside or being at your office.

But to start with, you need to *remember* to do this ensouling work: that is, remember to be more friendly, more generous, to respect people who see the world differently to yourself, just as you also need to remember to cut down on your consuming and to recycle your waste, eat more healthily and choose activities that are nutritious for your soul, etc. The more this new pattern becomes established inside you, or the more a new way of looking at the world takes root, the more powerfully the helping Force will be with you, and it won't abandon you unless you abandon yourself.

Remember, too, that it is not enough simply to say "no" to the old story unless at the same time you say a big "yes" to a new, more soulful one. Indeed, the more total your shift is – that is, the more your soulfulness not only embraces how you feel and think and what your core values are, but also incorporates how you live and work and relate to things like money, other people and our planet as a whole – the harder it is to slip back.

An aristocracy of soul

Coming into our own as human beings in this way, or choosing to allow ourselves to be a space for the treasure hidden inside us to be known or outed, is not only to connect with our own deeper creativity, but also to become, in my lingo, an *aristocrat of soul*. And an aristocrat of soul has nothing to do with family background or class or physical heritage. It is about our inner, not our outer, royalty. Some of the poorest, least-known people on the planet are shining aristocrats of soul.

An aristocrat of soul, then, is someone who is seeking to become ever more conscious of their essential inner royalty or soul nature (remember "The Hymn of the Pearl"?) and so behaves with a genuine nobility of spirit. They are true gentle men and gentle women. Aristocrats of soul are honourable men and women; they are honest; they behave graciously to others, especially to those less fortunate than themselves; they are kind; they share their resources; they open their hearts to the world. With genuine humility, they hold their heads up high and they never compromise their truth or give their power away. And all of us essentially have this person inside us. The question is: how fully will we allow this part of ourselves out of the closet?

The choice is always ours...

What kind of future lies in front of us?

In this context, it is important too that we ask ourselves what kind of world lies in front of us. And certainly, in recent years there have been many significant advances in many areas. Particularly since around the early 2000s we have seen big leaps forward in genetics, technology, artificial intelligence, science and medicine. As I write, the Green Party, who represent the values of Don Beck's world six, or the domain of the Sensitive Self, have been doing quite well. This is encouraging.

I am sure in another 10 to 15 years our smartphones will have become even smarter; they'll tell us our moods and read our energy and tell us what acupuncture points we need to press and what music we need to listen to and what films we should watch to rebalance ourselves. I am sure they will also be able to answer all our metaphysical enquiries, tell us what food we need to eat and even signal for our kitchen to start preparing it.

Many today wax lyrical about how in however many years from now, many of our current killer diseases will have been eliminated; we'll be able to have our aggressions genetically removed and ensure that our children are born without the possibility of ever getting cancer or dementia. And perhaps with the addition of the odd cyber-organ or two, we'll be able to live to well over a hundred years in pretty good health.

Technology and soul

At one level, all this sounds exciting. There are, however, a few questions to ask ourselves. Firstly, will these advances necessarily make us better human beings? Will our living for longer mean we will grow wiser? Will our becoming genetically enhanced result in our also becoming more soulfully enhanced? Will our biological accoutrements and increased cognitive intelligence make us more ethically mature, more able to treat our fellow human beings with love, tenderness and respect, which for me are the truly important things?

Here, I am not so sure, for the simple reason that spiritual attributes need to be acquired through inner work. They can't just be "pumped" into us, not least because they already exist inside us.

I also suspect that these advancements will be more for those able to pay for them and so we risk having yet another divide: the vast majority of us versus a small over-class of super-intelligent beings, where there is no guarantee of their being less rajassic and less susceptible to the pull of the *wetiko* virus!

I may be wrong. I would like to hope so. But these are key issues for, as we all know, all advances in science can be used both for good and for ill.

Positive futuristic scenario

Specifically regarding our future, I always observe that there seem to be two completely contradictory stories available to us. On the one hand, we have our "positivists", who believe that regardless of the huge problems we face today, the progress we have already been making in so many areas will continue. In a word, we *will* "make it".

We *will* manage to heal our environment and global warming will not have the terrifying consequences that many expect. We *will* create new institutions and new technologies that will work for the good of mankind, and the growth of artificial intelligence will actually be a very great bonus as it will help to continue to expand us in the fields of medicine and science, as well as liberate millions of people from dull and soulless work. We will also find ways to reduce war and to integrate the have-nots into the bosom of a society that will be much healthier and more caring than the society of today. Technological advances *will* assist spiritual advances. New technologies of sun, wave and wind will increasingly replace those of oil and coal, and people will learn new techniques so as gradually to liberate themselves from the tentacles of despair and alienation that are so endemic in today's soulless society.

In Bob Marley's words: "Every little thing's gonna be all right!"

Doomster scenario

At the other end of the spectrum, we have our "doomsters", who believe that we've already gone beyond the point of no return and that whatever we do now – even if there were a greater willingness on more people's part to do many of the things needed – it is too late. Thus, there is little chance of the human race surviving to the end of this century.

Fake news will increase. Increasing numbers of authoritarian demagogues will come into positions of power and will use political violence to intimidate, emotional violence to undermine and physical violence to terrorize, and the equality gap will begin again to broaden, with the rich continuing to get richer and the poor poorer. It'll be much worse than a Brave New World!

Either global warming will "get us" – our planet will become too hot for crops to survive, or melting icebergs producing tidal waves will sweep over all the large cities in the world – or we'll have a terrible pandemic that will wipe out millions – perhaps an artificially manipulated version of an existing virus that we'll have no resistance to – or a nuclear world war will break out. Even if we survive these catastrophes, artificial intelligence will destroy us. Robots, as they increasingly become smarter than us, will grow fed up with us and will take us over, and the human race will end.

We'll also not manage to get over our addiction to oil, and drama, sacrifice, separation and suffering will get the better of us. On top of all this there is the understanding that crises can happen very suddenly and unexpectedly and that we are very near the tipping point. Put simply, society will break down more and more and it is highly likely that it could happen very abruptly. In the words of my old friend Brugh Joy:

> For me, the cataclysmic prophecies that are rife in current literature foreshadow a revolution of the most outstanding proportions…I sense the approach of a psychological earthquake the magnitude of which has not been experienced in the human awareness for millennia and may not have been experienced in the human awareness ever before…[35]

Positivity or doom

Perhaps it is appropriate that we have both futures dangled before us, for if we only had the positive one, we could all just sit back, sing along with old Bob and, knowing every little thing's gonna be all right, do nothing to bring that all rightness about. Conversely, if we knew that only disaster lay ahead, we might just give up the ghost. Thus having both viewpoints serves to give us hope as well as make us realize that we've got to keep on our toes and that we need to make big shifts and do so pretty quickly!

I believe that many possible futures lie ahead of us – and this applies as much to us as individuals as societally – and that figuratively speaking, we all carry the world in our hands: that is, we determine our own future soul destinies much more than we may think. I believe, therefore, that what will transpire in, say, 50 years from now depends a great deal on how imaginative and resourceful we are today, how effective we are in opening to "higher power" or the "helping forces", or how much we still choose to persevere with our old "business as usual" approaches. The big question is: will enough of us show sufficient capacity to think outside of our old boxes and have the chutzpah to aim for the radical changes I am suggesting are required?

Despite the reservations I voiced concerning the consequences of some of our technological advances, I am very positive. I think there *are* enough of us and collectively we *do* possess the chutzpah. I also think that as increasing numbers of us start emerging from our closets and begin accessing a more unitive awareness – which I see happening more and more, as well as more and more powerfully – we are, species-wise, starting to find ourselves having access to whole new resources and thus the Force is able to work with increasing numbers of us. The result is that profound positive changes are starting to take place in the fabric of our society;

changes that, interestingly, many of us change-makers responsible for making them happen are often insufficiently aware of, a) because many of them are not yet very visible, and b) because they do not often get reported on. I quote you Jim Garrison's words again: "Things are getting better and better and worse and worse, faster and faster!" I personally think much more force is with the first part of his statement, and feeling deeply into the heart of this new pathogen which, just as I was about to hand in this manuscript, has suddenly exploded into all our lives, in no way inclines me to wish to change my point of view.

Coronavirus: agent of destruction or harbinger of soul?

I think this is very definitely the "psychological earthquake" which Brugh Joy spoke about, a) because it embraces all of us and there is no escaping its tentacles whoever we are and wherever we live on the planet, and b) because we are being hit simultaneously at all levels. Not only is our physical, emotional, social, and financial survival at stake, but so too are many of our institutions that some of us have become so embedded into.

As I write, a week into the emergence of the Coronavirus, I am seeing that everything that I lumped under the heading of the "old story" or the rajassic reality is beginning to crumble more quickly, and I think one can probably safely say that the world as we used to know it will never be the same, and that the death knells of neoliberalism and economic globalization have most probably been sounded.

For those who espouse rajassic and tamassic worldviews, this is undoubtedly an unmitigated disaster and some may well try to rebuild the old structures. However, I believe the rules of the game have radically changed and I do not think this will work any more.

If this virus is hitting those of us in the wealthier nations hard, what might be the repercussions if it spreads in the poorer nations, which, by the time this book sees the light of day, may have occurred. What will happen to the millions on our planet who constitute the "under-classes"? What if this virus spreads in refugee camps, in places like the Gaza strip, Yemen, the South African townships? Will their poverty and suffering and unemployment get worse?

This thought is a depressing one, which is why all effort needs to be made to ensure the most vulnerable on our planet are adequately cared for, for if not, the virus may well reverberate back to us having powerfully mutated, wreaking even greater havoc.

Rudolph Steiner described a virus as "the excretion of toxic cells" and we don't need to use too much imagination to realize that this hasn't emerged out of nowhere, but is our own human toxicity (described in chapters 2, 3 and 4) come back to wham us in the face. What many of us are particularly having to confront is the sum total of our many negative beliefs, values and behaviours. Yes, my dear friend, you and I and the whole human race, each of us in our different ways, are together journeying into the heart of our personal and our human-collective Shadow sides. Many of us are facing many "inconvenient truths" we'd prefer not to look at. And this involves some suffering.

The soul consequences of the Coronavirus

But please remember two key things that I said earlier on: firstly, *that dawn emerges when night is at its darkest,* and secondly, *that soul is to be found in the deepest heart of our darkness!*

My strong hunch is that underneath this seeming curse, lies – if we evolve a long-term perspective – a very profound blessing, and that a story or a "world of consciousness" that I have been arguing needs to die, is actually doing so much more quickly, and is therefore quietly creating a space for something new to be born that very much needs to be born. Basically, this pandemic has actually come to save us from ourselves!

Seeming to be only an agent of death, I see the pandemic as one of resurrection, as its very power is serving to make us question much of our old, limited, blinkered thinking and curb many of our old behaviours. By causing us to think more expansively and with more heart, it is helping our deeper humanity to awaken.

Up until now, as a species, we have been both unable and unwilling to deal creatively with most of the truly serious crises on our planet. This is mainly because we haven't tried hard enough as these crises haven't so far impinged sufficiently upon our own comforts. (Why, I ask, aren't we acting in a similar way in the face of the millions who die of starvation or the nuclear threat?)

From now on, we will no longer have an excuse. The situation is being taken out of our hands. Global warming, inequality, poverty, etc., will no longer be ignored as we increasingly come to understand the interconnections between all our world crises.

Indeed, the insights that we are receiving regarding how best to handle this particular virus, will help us deal more appropriately with our other crises. What nations are particularly learning is that no solutions will be forthcoming unless they all club together in a cooperative way and show a willingness to share their resources. Put simply, humanity has been given a strong wake-up call. There is a teaching element to this virus. It says to us: "Re-organize yourselves. Evolve. Spend money where it is *really* needed. Take the blinkers off your eyes. Start thinking long-term and in the light of larger wholes. Give birth to your latent wisdom, and compassion, and your deeper human potential, and if you don't and don't use your latent human virtues and strengths for a higher good, you will perish. Quite a simple message.

And, my friend, this emergence of compassion and wisdom and heart and soul is exactly what I see taking place the world over. Yes, there is fear and uncertainty in the air. Yes, people have lost their loved ones and their livelihoods. But many are not being pulled down by this. Rather, they are being pulled up! The thing about huge shocks is that if they don't kill us (which they certainly can), they can help us grow more fully human. What happens when we are forced to face a crisis of a calibre that we cannot run away from or pretend is not happening, is that our masks fall off and we start to get real, to ask ourselves what is really important and what isn't.

Some fear, not without reason, that what is happening will encourage more nationalism and protectionism and that there will be a desire to build more walls in an "every country for itself"-mindset. There is also a concern that those governments forced to adopt emergency measures, will hang on to them afterwards, and that they might then be "weaponized" to serve political ends. Others are scared that the technologies of surveillance that have been used will increase.

While in no way groundless, I don't share these concerns because I see soul power as their antidote growing in strength all the time. I see increasing numbers of us the world over, learning to empower ourselves in whole new ways and thus becoming increasingly aware of the lies and fake news spouted at us by politicians of low consciousness. I feel that in the future, we will ask for honesty and integrity from those who govern us and we simply won't elect people whose intention it is to hoodwink. I also believe many wealthy people will start opening up their resources to improve the lot of the have-nots.

Yes, my friend, my heart is full of hope. But I do feel, as I suggested earlier, that things may need to get worse before they get better – perhaps the planet will need to hit a rock-bottom place – and that nothing will happen overnight. *As such, while fierce and seemingly unforgiving, this "tough-love" Coronavirus is perhaps the greatest "soul teacher" we could ever have.*

Breaking on through

To quote a line from a song by the Doors, I believe that though it may not seem like it at present as all we are aware of is what is collapsing, we are in effect in the process of quietly "breaking on through to the other side". Indeed, my sense is that over the next half-century, we may well start seeing two key changes. The first is that a lot of what seems to exist at the very peripheries of our society will start moving very powerfully into the centre. And by this I mean the kind of thinking that I am advocating in this book. The second is that many of the dramatic theatrics that are currently occupying centre stage on our planet and that are all reflective of old-storyhood will start crumbling away and moving out into the invisibility of the fringes. In a word, a radical role reversal.

Let me put it like this. As human consciousness collectively expands, as the heart of humanity begins increasingly to open, as activists of every shape and inclination escalate their increasingly soul-infused work in their respective fields that makes a difference and as soul force grows bigger, the effects will slowly start to be felt in more and more areas of life. Thus, I predict that within a half-century, we will be witnessing a radical turn-around taking the form of rajassically- and tamassically-centred people having less and less of a say in how our world is run, as well as their stances on life no longer being seen as normal.

So, for example, people whose values dictate that one needs to be more interested in whether one's real estate has gone up in value than in the health and well-being of those living around one, will start being regarded as weird and abnormal! In a word, a greater emergence of planet-centric consciousness.

Similarly, as increasing numbers of people awaken out of their closets and evolve into their higher-order reality selves, it will increasingly be seen both as normal and natural to want to open your heart to your fellow human beings and to nature, as well as to delight in sharing your resources with those who have less than you. What I see is a new world gradually arising where more and more people start to operate at levels six, seven and eight, and a few even at nine.

Also remember this: the more evolved and whole we are, the more soul we have, the more capable we are of a) letting our past go and b) going with the flow. Put simply, the more mature we become, the more the Force will be with us to guide us if necessary, whereas the more we continue to remain in our old clenched and rigidified stances, the harder these shifts will be to navigate.

New order

So OK, what might our new society look like? I repeat: my prediction then is that, within about half a century from now, the polarities will have very radically shifted, and what today is central in our society – rajassic/tamassic man and the stories and values he abides by – will start moving out to the peripheries of society, while what used to be peripheral, namely heart-centred, soul-filled man, will start moving into the centre and playing an enhanced role in determining world affairs.

However, simply because there will be a lot more good eggs around in positions of authority on the planet doesn't mean that there won't still be some bad eggs around creating a nuisance and continuing to challenge us. Evil, in its various forms, will still hang around. Remember the Shadow and Peekaboo chapters, which speak about our needing the dark side if we are to continue to evolve.

So we'll still have our challenges. Only I suspect they will be different from the ones we face today. Yes, there will probably still be some dishonest and greedy public figures, and some corporations may still continue to worship the god of greed. But I think we'll see a lot less of them.

The turning point

I suspect, therefore, that not only might we be much closer to that enigmatic "turning point" which Fritjof Capra described in his seminal book of that title written so many years ago, but that we may have already turned the corner.

And what this means is that *as a species, not only is our time not up, but we are moving into a whole new phase of our collective evolutionary journey. Not only are we going to make it but we will be converging to a whole new level – to a whole new era of harmony and synthesis. So let us open to our future with joy in our hearts and let us imagine our future coming back to us in space and time and enfolding us tenderly in its arms as it gently draws us all up towards it.*

Positive Future Scenario

I want, therefore, to conclude this book with pointing you more concretely in this direction, because, as I said earlier, the more we all work at visualizing a positive future, the more likely it is that we will materialize it for ourselves.

Many of the future scenarios I am about to present you with are my own. Some are taken from Charles Eisenstein's talks (I see him as one of the brightest visionaries on the planet) and some are gathered from other people's ideas that have resonated with me and which I just jotted down in my journal. Sadly, as I have omitted to note down where precisely my sources are from, I hope that if any of you reading this see your own wise words being repeated verbatim, you will be big-hearted enough to forgive me for failing to credit you and instead be happy that your visions are making a difference and are again being used for a sacred purpose here.

Please read the following statements in a prayerful manner, holding in your heart that every intention you speak, will come to fruition. Maybe you can read this list to yourself a few times a week and share this prayer with others.

Prayer for the Creation of a New, Soul-Filled Society

I pray that:

- A consciousness of fullness of being or abundance permeates the thinking of more people in more countries, and the mindset of scarcity, suffering and separation continues to fall away.
- More and more we come to respect our fellow human beings and acknowledge everyone's human rights irrespective of class, colour, religion, gender, sexual orientation or nationality.
- Increasing numbers of people open their hearts more to the spirit of joy and play and create more celebration in their lives.
- We start seeing conflicts more and more in terms of new creative opportunities being offered us.
- We are more willing to take risks in the interest of innovation and not be downhearted if things don't always work out the way we'd like.

- Visionaries or activists for a better world are honoured and not treated as crackpots, but as people displaying true brilliance – for example, farmers who transform deserts to grow food, or mediators who rebuild war-torn societies – and so are properly acknowledged for the enormous contributions they are making.
- Personal achievement is no longer measured in money or power, and being wealthy is no longer defined by what we own, but in the quality of our lives – how connected we are to our creativity, how much we are loved and able to love, how healthy we are, how much we are able to live with kindness and heart.
- Economic collapse, nuclear war, terrorism, famine and ecological collapse are no longer fears on the horizon.
- We create a participatory society, where all people have a voice in the decisions that affect their life and future.
- There is less speed and stress and more depth and quiet.
- The self-centred nation state, utterly disconnected from its soul and therefore its true *raison d'être* in the world community, gives way to a transnational system where individual nations, beginning to connect to their higher purposes, explore the interface between honouring what serves them as individual nations and what also serves the larger world community.
- Poverty is eliminated and everyone's right to food, housing, education and socially remunerative work is recognized and respected.
- A new level of the meaning of democracy comes into being, where all people have a voice.
- There is no longer one law for the rich and another for the poor, but justice for all prevails in a world where the rights that need to apply to all human beings are extended to animals and to our planet as a whole.
- There is more peace and less war. Where war still exists, may techniques of conflict resolution be used instead of brute force.
- Resources are available freely to enable people in pain or suffering to be helped to heal their wounds or traumas and that are encouraged to grow and develop their humanity.
- A new model of what it means to be human emerges so that we no longer deify people who are glamorous, or who have fame, power, notoriety or wealth. Instead we come to see that our real heroes or

aristocrats of soul – the real "great and the good" of the planet – may be those who live unselfishly, humbly, wisely, kindly, simply and unpretentiously and it is these people's lives that we should be moved to emulate.

- The very rich realize that the way to be happy is to share much more of their fortunes with the very poor, and to do so in imaginative and creative ways that enable the latter to feel empowered and more able to lift themselves up by their own bootstraps.
- Nations that have huge debts as a result of exploitation that goes back for centuries are released from their obligations as the wealthy nations open their eyes to see the huge damage that has been done in the name of advancement.
- All corporations embrace a mindset of "giving to" as opposed to "taking from" and put the well-being of people and planet before profit.
- The large fossil fuel corporations give up their old "extractivist" mindsets, come to see the futility of making large profits by increasing global warming and so threatening the survival of all life on earth, and understand that it is eminently possible right now to shift to wind, wave and solar power.
- Those people in the world who are most resistant and hostile to change are given opportunities to see the light and realize the damage they do by opposing the natural flow of evolutionary advancement.
- Increasing numbers of us are moved to explore our dark or Shadow sides, so that instead of projecting our negativity or destructiveness onto other people, we instead own it and work it through inside ourselves.
- More people move away from embracing institutional and superficial religions, together with all their prejudices, and start embracing a spirituality predicated on recognizing that we are all united, all equal in the mind of God, and that there exists a divinity that is not only beyond us and greater than us, but also lives inside each of us.
- Increasing numbers of us are moved to live lives that are less artificial and less determined by outer circumstances, and which emanate more from our inner being.

- We realize that we can be happy with less and that if we bring more quality into our lives, quantity will become less important.
- More people come to realize that they are stewards to help earth's delicate ecosystems recover.
- Politicians learn to be braver and stronger and refuse to be "bought" by the large corporations, and all forms of government based on repression vanish from the face of the Earth. No longer will psychopathic tyrants or autocratic families using their countries as their own private bank be tolerated.
- More people of the world learn to mobilize together and join forces to work to create the world they want.
- We find new and creative ways to diminish the power of evil.
- All forms of violence and oppression towards minority groups of any kind cease.
- Women receive more respect in those areas of the world where this is not the case and increasingly come into positions of leadership.
- A new, higher-order value system comes into being whereby honesty triumphs over corruption, kindness over indifference and generosity over greed.
- Those who take stands for a new and more harmonious planet are both respected for the work they do and recognized as representing a new emerging spirit of leadership that is not about control and domination but about empowering and ensouling.
- Our education system is more imaginative so that children learn life skills relative to a new emerging culture and are helped to value being creative, as opposed to primarily having to struggle to pass exams in order to slot more easily into a dysfunctional system.
- The economic system is radically reformed of its corruption, and bankers attend courses where they are taught how to operate with honesty and integrity.
- Money will be used in a new way, spent only on things that make for a better world. The global economy will be transformed in such a way that the wealthy don't just grow wealthier, but money is distributed equally so that no one is marginalized and the less well-developed economies can be assisted by the more well-developed ones.

- Technology is increasingly seen as a tool to ensure well-being and a greater quality of life.
- Education should not be to help people be better adjusted to enter a deviant society, but to see the deviancy and prepare them to bring a better world into being.
- Religions are stripped of more and more of their institutionalisms and dogmas that have been such a source of violence in the past, so that their deeper spirituality is allowed to emerge, whereby people may feel invigorated and inspired by a connection with a spirit and soul that feels real and alive.
- The desacralized, de-animated, soulless vision of nature as inanimate – a vision leading us to feel we can use or abuse nature as we wish, which has become the foundation of modern science, our economic system and the whole mechanistic worldview – falls away, leading to a vision where we see nature as alive.
- As a balance against the "cyberfication" of life, we focus on connecting with what is real, purifying everything about the way we eat and think and relate and work and generally live our lives.
- The media, which so strongly affects how we see the world and at present primarily deals with money, houses, celebrities and crises, and delights in finding fault, undergoes a strong level shift.
- Psychotherapy undergoes a strong shift so that it is not primarily about fixing wounded egos and helping people feel better, but also focuses on helping people evolve and become better human beings who realize that one of the best ways to heal themselves is to grow in their capacity to become activists for a healthier world.
- Support is withdrawn more and more from the entity we call "the system", thus allowing it to evolve and transform into something that supports the emergence of a sustainable and harmonious world.
- People recognize that mind and analysis are only one half of the equation and that the domain of the heart is equally important and central to the development of an abundant mindset.
- More films are made that inspire us and fewer that simply glorify violence and triviality.

- Society is happier and more balanced, and people think more in terms of what will serve the larger community and not simply enhance their own personal lives. As a result there will be less resentment and hatred, less crime, less drug addiction, fewer gangs, fewer murders and more people policing their own local communities.
- We choose to move more slowly, think more deeply, love more fully and let our culture grow peacefully and organically. It is normal to love our neighbours as ourselves.
- More people allow themselves to be "fed" from higher sources of inspiration and to see the value of choosing to have their daily lives become their sacred practice.

Maybe you can hold groups in your own house; gather friends around to share the contents of this book. There is plenty of material here to enable you to become an activist of soul. Bless you.

Notes

1. Joseph Campbell and Bill Moyers, *The Power of Myth* (New York: Doubleday, 1988).

2. Theodore Zeldin, *The Hidden Pleasures of Life: A New Way of Remembering the Past and Imagining the Future* (London: MacLehose Press, 2015).

3. Erich Fromm, *The Art of Being* (London: Constable, 1993). Copyright © Erich Fromm, 1993, *The Art of Being*. Continuum Publishing, used by permission of Bloomsbury Publishing Plc.

4. Charles Eisenstein, *The More Beautiful World Our Hearts Know Is Possible* (Berkeley: North Atlantic, 2013).

5. Helena Norberg-Hodge and Steven Gorelick, "Globalization and the American Dream", *Common Dreams*, 9 June 2016, https://www.commondreams.org/views/2016/06/09/globalization-and -american-dream (accessed 6 August 2019).

6. Hannah Arendt, *The Origins of Totalitarianism* (New York: Harcourt, Brace, 1951).

7. Satish Kumar, *Spiritual Compass: The Three Qualities of Life* (Totnes: Green Books, 2007).

8. Serge Beddington Behrens, *Awakening the Universal Heart: A Guide for Spiritual Activists* (London: Umbria Press, 2013).

9. Naomi Klein, *This Changes Everything: Capitalism vs the Climate* (New York: Simon & Schuster, 2014).

10. Scilla Elworthy, *Pioneering the Possible: Awakened Leadership for a World That Works* (Berkeley: North Atlantic, 2014).

11. Patrick Hosking, "The 'yes' men at HSBC mislay their moral compass", *The Times*, 26 November 2014.

12. Andrew Harvey, *Radical Passion: Sacred Love and Wisdom in Action* (Berkeley: North Atlantic, 2012).

13. Thomas Moore, *Care of the Soul: A Guide for Cultivating Depth and Sacredness in Everyday Life* (New York: HarperCollins, 1992).

14. HRH The Prince of Wales, *Harmony: A New Way of Looking at Our World* (London: Blue Door, 2010).

15. Seyyed Hossein Nasr, *Knowledge and the Sacred* (Edinburgh: Edinburgh University Press, 1981). Used by permission of Suny Press.

16. Matthew Fox, *Original Blessing: A Primer in Creation Spirituality* (Santa Fe: Bear, 1983).

17. Sri Aurobindo, *The Life Divine* (Twin Lakes, WI: Lotus Press, 1990).

18. Christopher Fry, *A Sleep of Prisoners* (London: Oxford University Press, 1951). Used by permission of Dramatists Play Service, Inc.

19. Stanislav Grof, *Beyond the Brain: Birth, Death, and Transcendence in Psychotherapy* (Albany: State University of New York Press, 1985).

20. Mohamed ElBaradei, *The Age of Deception: Nuclear Diplomacy in Treacherous Times* (London: Bloomsbury, 2011).

21. Robert A. Johnson, *Inner Work: Using Dreams and Active Imagination for Personal Growth* (San Francisco: Harper & Row, 1986).

22. Roger Woolger, *Other Lives, Other Selves: A Jungian Psychotherapist Discovers Past Lives* (New York: Doubleday, 1987).

23. Chris Bache, *Dark Night, Early Dawn: Steps to a Deep Ecology of Mind* (Albany: State University of New York Press, 2000). Used by permission of Suny Press.

24. Pitirim A. Sorokin, *The Ways and Power of Love: Types, Factors, and Techniques of Moral Transformation* (Boston, MA: Beacon Press, 1954). Copyright © 1954 Pitirim A. Sorokin, renewed 1982 by Peter P. and Sergei P. Sorokin. Originally printed 1954 by Beacon Press. Paperback edition published in 2002 by Templeton Press (W Conshocken PA).

25. William Blake, Letter to Dr. John Trusler, 23. August 1799. The William Blake Archive, http://www.blakearchive.org/copy/letters?descId=lt23aug1799.1.ltr.01

26. Aung San Suu Kyi, *Freedom from Fear and Other Writings* (London: Viking, 1991).

27. William Blake, "Auguries of Innocence", *The Pickering Manuscript* (composed c. 1807). The William Blake Archive, http://www.blakearchive.org/copy/bb126.1?descId=bb126.1.ms.13

28. Matthew Fox, *The Coming of the Cosmic Christ: The Healing of Mother Earth and the Birth of a Global Renaissance* (San Francisco: Harper & Row, 1988).

29. E. F. Schumacher, *Good Work* (London: Jonathan Cape, 1979).

30. Tarthang Tulku, *Skillful Means* (Berkeley: Dharma Publishing, 1978). Copyright © 1978 Dharma Publishing. Quoted by permission Dharma Publishing. dharmapublishing.com

31. Gail McGovern, "Lead from the Heart", *Harvard Business Review*, March 2014.

32. Eben Alexander, *Proof of Heaven: A Neurosurgeon's Journey into the Afterlife* (London: Piatkus, 2012).

33. William Wordsworth, "Ode: Intimations of Immortality from Recollections of Early Childhood", in *The Collected Poems of William Wordsworth* (Wordsworth Poetry Library), rev. ed. edition (Ware, Hertfordshire, UK: Wordsworth Editions Ltd., 1998).

34. "The Hymn of the Pearl" – author unknown. Reprinted by arrangement with Shambhala Publications Inc., Boulder, CO. www.shambhala.com

35. W. Brugh Joy, *Avalanche: Heretical Reflections on the Dark and the Light* (New York: Ballantine, 1980).

The author appreciates the wisdom of fellow writers and speakers and has undertaken every effort to credit quoted material appropriately. Thank you for granting permission to use your words.

Exercise Overview

Index

Acknowledgements

I AM VERY GRATEFUL to the thinking of Scilla Elworthy and Satish Kumar; I have learned much from their views of the world, from which I have also had their permission to quote. I am also grateful to Charles Eisenstein and Naomi Klein, whom I have also quoted from quite extensively, and whose ideas have also inspired me.

I am also grateful to my friend Anne Baring, whose great book *The Dream of the Cosmos: a Quest for the Soul* touched me very deeply, and for the many people who have worked with me over the years and from whom I have learned so much about what it means to be human.

I also want to thank my wonderful editor, Jacqui Lewis, who at all times has handled me with so much patience, graciousness and wisdom. And I would like to acknowledge my darling wife for tolerating long absences of my disappearing into my office; and my friend Ian Smith for reading an early draft of this book and allowing me to realize that what I say may well be seen as "preachy" to those who are not interested in changing themselves and the world.

But I do not apologize. We all are as we are and the archetype that I have always most resonated with is that of the priest. But not of the churchy variety. I prefer to see wildernesses and oceans as my temples.

About the Author

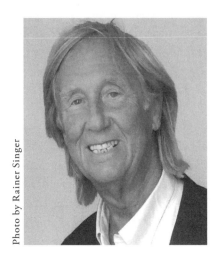

Photo by Rainer Singer

Serge Obolensky Beddington-Behrens, M.A. (Oxon.), Ph.D., K.O.M.L., is an Oxford-educated transpersonal psychotherapist, shaman, activist, and spiritual educator. In 2000, he was awarded an Italian knighthood for services to humanity. For forty years he has conducted spiritual retreats all over the world. In the 1980s, he cofounded the Institute for the Study of Conscious Evolution in San Francisco. The author of *Awakening the Universal Heart: A Guide for Spiritual Activists*, he divides his time between London and Mallorca.

If you wish to be informed of courses that Serge teaches on the subject of this book or if you wish to attend one of his personalized retreats or work with him in some way, please contact him on *infosergebb@gmail.com*.

For more information see his website: **www.spiritual-activism.com**

FINDHORN PRESS

Life-Changing Books

Learn more about us and our books at
www.findhornpress.com

For information on the Findhorn Foundation:
www.findhorn.org

Also of Interest from Findhorn Press

Out of Your Comfort Zone
by Emma Mardlin, Ph.D.

OFFERING A STEP-BY-STEP GUIDE to confronting and transforming fear,
Emma Mardlin explains how to create an unstoppable mindset with a custom-
izable approach that incorporates psychological, emotional, and physical techniques to release fear, limitations, and anxiety for good. She also offers a test to
measure your comfort zone and the "baby steps" methods to develop confidence.

Whether you experience irrational fear, have a phobia that plagues you, look
back on a lifetime of anxiety and limitations, or suffer from nerves and a lack of
confidence, this guide provides a full range of comprehensive resources and tools
to help you fully transform your fears, discover your true ambitions, and achieve
everything you can in life.

978-1-62055-824-9